The Moiseyev
Dance Company
Tours America

A Volume in the Series

CULTURE AND POLITICS IN THE COLD WAR AND BEYOND

Edited by
Edwin A. Martini and Scott Laderman

The Moiseyev Dance Company Tours America

"WHOLESOME" COMFORT DURING A COLD WAR

VICTORIA HALLINAN

University of Massachusetts Press

AMHERST AND BOSTON

ISBN 978-1-62534-751-0 (paper); 752-7 (hardcover)

Designed by Sally Nichols
Set in Minion Pro by Westchester Publishing Services
Printed and bound by Books International, Inc.

Cover design by adam b. bohannon
Cover photo by Yevgeny Umnov, *Russian Suite*, Moscow 1966,
from Anna Ilupina and Yelena Lutskaya, *Moiseyev's Dance Company*, trans.
Olga Shartse (Moscow: Progress Publishers, 1966).

Library of Congress Cataloging-in-Publication Data
Names: Hallinan, Victoria, 1985– author.
Title: The Moiseyev Dance Company tours America : "wholesome" comfort
during a Cold War / Victoria Hallinan.
Description: Amherst : University of Massachusetts Press, 2023. | Series:
Culture and politics in the Cold War and beyond | Includes
bibliographical references and index.
Identifiers: LCCN 2023013412 (print) | LCCN 2023013413 (ebook) | ISBN
9781625347510 (paperback) | ISBN 9781625347527 (hardcover) | ISBN
9781685750350 (ebook)
Subjects: LCSH: Gosudarstvennyĭ ansambl' narodnogo tant͡sa So͡iuza
SSR—History. | Moiseev, Igorʹ, 1906–2007. | Folk dancing, Russian. |
Folk dancing, East European. | Cultural diplomacy—United
States—History—20th century. | Cultural diplomacy—Soviet
Union—History. | United States—Relations—Soviet
Union. | Soviet Union—Relations—United States.
Classification: LCC GV1786.G6 H35 2023 (print) | LCC GV1786.G6 (ebook) |
DDC 793.3/10947—dc23/eng/20230627
LC record available at https://lccn.loc.gov/2023013412
LC ebook record available at https://lccn.loc.gov/2023013413

British Library Cataloguing-in-Publication Data
A catalog record for this book is available from the British Library.

For Dean and Judy Jones

Contents

PART THREE

Figures and Tables

Acknowledgments

Without the aid and encouragement of many individuals and institutions this project would not have been possible. My research experience benefited enormously from the help of enthusiastic librarians and archivists over the years. The Library of Congress and Performing Arts Division of the New York Public Library in particular laid the foundation for much of my research and the librarians at both institutions were always interested and essential to the research process. My international research, focused largely at the Russian State Archive of Literature and Art, proved an incredibly rich experience in terms of information gathered and the memorable personal experiences of Moscow itself.

This project began during my graduate studies at Northeastern University, and my advisors in that time period were many, including: Elizabeth Wood, Lynn Garafola, Jeffrey Burds, and Ilham Khuri-Makdisi. These advisors acted as invaluable sources of inspiration, support, and patience. Laura Frader served as mentor and advocate from the moment I came to Northeastern, and her guidance in teaching and how it can inform and be informed by research interests augmented my early teaching endeavors. Harlow Robinson always knew the right words of encouragement or thoughtfully worded criticism which ensured this project continued to move forward but with the right measure of work, consideration, and depth. As a fellow proponent of cultural history, he considered my topic worthwhile but also emphasized that a cultural history case study needs to be properly grounded in order to enhance my own understanding and that of my audience.

Throughout my academic career my friends and family have always been there with physical, emotional, and spiritual support. My parents, Eric and Rebecca, and my siblings, Kara, Rick, Dean, and my cousin Maggie, always had faith in my pursuit of a career in academia. Along the way they have been joined by Mel Lum, Liza Sabine, Alexis Sabine, Tim and Linda Hallinan, Mike and Kim van der Sleesen, and Katy and Nick Coughlin, and I cannot stress enough how this expansive web of family and friends serve as models for me in my professional and personal life.

I am thoroughly indebted to Stacy Fahrenthold and Ross Newton for our "writing parties," which kept the writing process moving forward and during which I often got the best advice and ideas to continue this book writing journey. As this project continued, my Poorvu peers provided essential support and care and this would not have moved forward without Beth Luoma, Kim Kuzina, and Melissa Scheve.

I want to humbly thank the Women's Faculty Forum at Yale, who awarded me a seed grant for this publication, and to share my everlasting gratitude to Matt Becker and the editing team at UMass Press for their kind patience and expertise to move this publication forward.

And finally, my husband Sean and my children, Tessa and Erin, have been the cornerstone of my confidence and persistence in this endeavor. Little did Sean know that our first meeting in college would lead not only to marriage, but to life as a coeditor, personal and academic counselor, and sounding board. He has witnessed the more mundane part of writing this manuscript, and throughout this process he and the girls helped me maintain my sense of humor, stamina, and sanity.

I dedicate this manuscript in memory of my departed and missed grandparents, Dean and Judy Jones. They, and my grandparents Eric and Anne Waxman, offered me constant encouragement but also ensured that I maintained a realistic perspective and did not take myself too seriously—these are vital qualities to adopt in academia and in life.

The Moiseyev
Dance Company
Tours America

INTRODUCTION

> We know there are some members of our State Department who feel
> that the President's Fund for Cultural Exchange is a gesture, nice, but
> unimportant. . . . We think they are wrong. It is extremely clear that
> a large part of the American public is enjoying, and being affected
> by, Russian propaganda currently here in the form of the Moiseyev
> Dance Company. . . . If there must be a cold war, we think that the
> best possible weapons are those of the arts.
>
> —Lydia Joel, *Dance Magazine*, June 1958

In April of 1958, the State Academic Ensemble of Folk Dances of the Peoples of the USSR, more commonly known as the Moiseyev Dance Company, arrived in the United States.[1] Their repertoire included dances from Soviet controlled or influenced territories such as Uzbekistan, Crimea, and Poland. Each dance represented these cultures with colorful costumes and acrobatic dance moves. Most importantly, the dancers as a unit represented these cultures as incredibly happy to be part of the Soviet Union and fully accepted by this Cold War superpower. In addition to a nationally broadcast television appearance on the *Ed Sullivan Show*, the Moiseyev Company performed in multiple cities including New York, Detroit, Chicago, Los Angeles, San Francisco, Cleveland, Washington, Boston, and Philadelphia, and correspondingly directly reached over forty million people in North America. The tour marked the first official Soviet cultural representative sent to the United States as part of the recently signed Lacy-Zarubin Agreement, which inaugurated official, direct cultural exchange between the two superpowers.[2] Accordingly, Americans attached huge significance to the troupe and its 1958 tour with corresponding press coverage and personal documentation reflecting this interest.

The Moiseyev Company fascinated American audiences and let Americans draw direct comparisons between their culture and that of the Soviet Union. Americans found evidence for these comparisons in the ensemble's dances and dancers, even though these by no means represented stereotypical folk dance or stereotypical Soviet citizens. The Moiseyev Company insisted that their dances were authentic representations of national folk dances and that each dance did, in fact, depict the nature and character of a specific nationality. This rhetoric is problematic considering how much the dance itself, its costumes, and its performers differed from the original dance—yet the rhetoric employed allowed Americans to view the dances as reflecting everyday life in the Soviet Union. The Soviet dancers represented the first Soviet people most Americans had ever seen and were thus thought to represent the Soviet Union overall. Americans, furthermore, learned much about the dancers offstage, which again Americans used as a basis of comparison between American and Soviet ways of life.

The company evoked a range of responses, including protest, admiration, and fear of American cultural inferiority. Newspapers and magazines across the country widely discussed how the group influenced political relations, representing a variety of viewpoints.[3] One critic held that the enthusiastic welcome given by Americans demonstrated that cultural performance constituted a non-political space in which mutual respect between the two superpowers could be achieved; art could transcend the current Cold War political tensions.[4] Other critics and political commentators, like *Dance Magazine* editor Lydia Joel, felt that the troupe offered only pure propaganda, and possibly even dangerous propaganda at that. In press coverage and in individuals' personal reception of the dancers, Americans expressed attitudes toward the Soviet Union but also attitudes toward American and Soviet identity, gender, race, and ethnicity. Americans looked to the company and its dancers to provide answers about what Soviet life was like. They drew comparisons between "American" and "Soviet" habits and institutions, from shopping and eating to ideas about relationships and life goals.

Though reception included both positive and negative viewpoints, the majority of the response to the dancers reflected an understanding of America's Cold War enemy as surprisingly human. Americans felt the Moiseyev tours revealed Soviet citizens to be likeable, genuine people who were quite similar to Americans in terms of values and dreams. On a personal level, many Americans revealed their amended views of the Cold War narrative of superpower enmity through their reaction to the Moiseyev, which demonstrates the complicated nature of American society during the Cold War period. Far from furthering the distance between American and Soviet people by accentuating differences when viewed up close, the tour instead engendered empathy toward the peoples of the Soviet Union and a sense of easing of tensions during this part of the Cold War. The reaction to the Moiseyev did not typically increase fears of the spread of a communist contagion, nor did it further the rhetoric that Soviets and Americans could not live peacefully together.

The Cold War Narrative

As the Cold War moves further away from the realm of the contemporary, it becomes simplified into a narrative of democracy versus communism, comprising only major political events and larger-than-life figures. This simplification neglects how much of the actual direct confrontations between the United States and Soviet Union took place in the cultural arena rather than a traditional battlefield. Instances of cultural confrontations are where we can understand the Cold War as an experience of individuals rather than major figures taking part in political events. Indeed, cultural confrontations like cultural exchanges became opportunities for individuals to negotiate the black and white narrative of the United States versus the USSR as they permitted individuals to actually see their Cold War enemy in person and to decide if these two systems were, in fact, incompatible.

Cold War scholarship, such as Odd Arne Westad's explorations of Cold War interventions and grueling proxy wars, increasingly focuses on this narrative of incompatibility as propaganda. Political leaders used the narrative to rationalize actions which were, in reality, based more on individual figures' goals than genuine threats. Additionally, gender, cultural, and American studies scholars expand beyond a Cold War history limited to politics and major historical figures to view the conflict through lenses of culture, race, and gender to complicate the propaganda narrative both superpowers espoused.[5]

Cultural exchange in particular is an intersectional opportunity for scholars to understand the Cold War as an individual's experience that responded to, shaped, and sometimes defied the Cold War narrative. Such exchanges were moments when American or Soviet audiences had to directly face their Cold War enemy "Other" and either fit that "Other" within the Cold War narrative or complicate the narrative with their own understanding. This trend in scholarship to unpack the Cold War narrative of incompatibility frequently portrays only one side of the conflict, for example by scrutinizing US actions without exploring the Soviet Union's parallel efforts to create their own Cold War narrative and disseminate it. Indeed, it can be argued that Cold War cultural exchange "enabled novel types of interaction" in addition to a strong support of cultural production.[6]

Without examining cultural exchange further, including analyzing both superpowers' perspectives, we fail to appreciate how the Cold War project drove both superpowers' use of culture to display their political system as the Cold War "victor" on the international stage. Indeed, this lack of understanding continues to fuel the US–Russia relationship we see today and the continuity of the narrative of incompatibility still employed.

There have been multiple recent books addressing the usage of cultural representatives in Cold War diplomacy, though usually explored solely from either an American or Soviet perspective. Danielle Fosler-Lussier in *Music in America's Cold War Diplomacy*, Lisa Davenport in *Jazz Diplomacy*, and Penny Von Eschen in *Satchmo Blows Up the World* discuss musicians that the United States sent abroad as cultural representatives during the Cold War. These scholars utilize these examples of cultural exchange to show how exchange influenced race relations and domestic events as part of defining American versus Soviet identity. These scholars (among others) have laid the groundwork for how examples of Cold War cultural exchange can be effectively used to discuss larger issues in this time period, including the agency of cultural exchange representatives and how, who, and what was selected for exchange reflects ideas around culture, race, gender, and other elements of identity. In the following chapters, I take up the other side of the story by examining cultural representatives the Soviet Union sent to the United States and its impact on notions of American and Soviet identity.

The American reaction to the Moiseyev Company complicates the Cold War narrative of unremitting conflict between the United States and the USSR and establishes that this narrative was more complex, as historians in this area contend. More specifically Americans—even if they held certain beliefs about the incompatibility of American and Soviet ideals—felt the Moiseyev tours revealed Soviet citizens to be likeable, genuine people who were actually quite similar to Americans in terms of their desires and interactions with others. On a personal level, Americans showed their amended views of the Cold War narrative through their reaction to the Moiseyev, which demonstrates the complex nature of American society during the Cold War period.

Other scholars laid the path of examining this particular form of cultural exchange. For instance, in *Dance for Export: Cultural Diplomacy and the Cold War*, Naima Prevots offers a perspective on the American side of the use of dance in the Cold War. In addressing the Moiseyev Dance Company and its impact, particularly on its first tour to the United States in 1958, she argues that the company proved able to win over even those critics and Americans who were not enthusiastic about this step toward greater cultural exchange. Authors such as Prevots discuss the positive reception of the group among American audiences and point to how these audiences celebrated the company's dancers. However, Prevots does not address the impact of the multicultural message on American perceptions. While many Americans certainly came to see the Moiseyev dancers, the question remains whether they left with a differentiated view of the Soviet peoples as a result of the performance.

Additionally, Anthony Shay recently published *The Igor Moiseyev Company: Dancing Diplomats*, which treated the Moiseyev in a full-length work. Shay shares his own personal experience with the dance troupe and fleshes out the significance of the creativity behind the choreography and storytelling of the repertoire as part of arguing the Moiseyev-influenced dance spectacle for decades to come, including future dance groups like Riverdance. My own treatment of the subject comes at it from an historical perspective to highlight this moment of cultural exchange as an important juncture of political, racial, and gender issues in America and how it changed or reinforced American ideas about the Cold War and American and Soviet people.

Scholars agree that Americans were extremely impressed by the troupe and its performances and were incredibly eager to learn more about the dancers. I argue that the appeal of the Moiseyev can be traced to its own origins and how the company reflected American notions of ideal, simplistic, multicultural, and heteronormative values. The impetus behind the group was to depict a positive picture of a unified Soviet Union through the use of stylized folk dances from multiple cultures living within Soviet borders.[7] Including dances from the Ukraine, Azerbaijan, Kazakhstan, Mongolia, and other territories, as well as those from Soviet bloc countries like Poland and Hungary, the group's repertoire and skill of execution presented its audience with an image of precisely coordinated dances in a variety of steps, colors and rhythms. This image could be interpreted as representing a correspondingly unified *esprit* among the different peoples living under direct and indirect Soviet control, which was one of the main points of the Soviet Union's own corresponding Cold War narrative.

Igor Moiseyev, the founder, choreographer and artistic director of the troupe, explained that "The Soviet Union is a multi-national country, extremely rich in folklore. . . . The folk art of the many ethnic groups of the Soviet Union is our richest source; it unfolds before us the most diverse aspects of people, who differ so greatly in their character, temperament, customs, cultural development, methods of expression."[8] Moiseyev aimed to share the folk dances of these different peoples (albeit in a synthesized or condensed version) to demonstrate how peoples in the Soviet Union lived and expressed themselves, but always in an affirmative way that did not criticize the Soviet regime and often contradicted the reality of life in the Soviet Union.

The 1958 tour of the Moiseyev Dance Company in the United States functions as a window into the American mind and as a gauge of Soviet and American Cold War relations. After the signing of the Lacy-Zarubin Agreement (1958) and the beginning of more friendly relations between the Soviet Union and United States, this initiation of cultural exchanges marks a moment in which culture is privileged as one arena in which the United States and Soviet Union could engage and compete. The Moiseyev expressed both a national and multiethnic identity which the American audience noted and compared with its own corresponding identity.

By probing both the Soviet and American goals for and reactions to this first official exchange moment, I give attention to both sides of the Cold War narrative rather than only one superpower's perspective. I determine that rather than reinforcing the narrative of incompatibility, the Moiseyev tour afforded an opportunity for those who experienced the Cold War on a daily basis to negotiate the narrative. In order to unpack the 1958 visit as well as later visits by the Moiseyev troupe, I utilize an intersectional approach of gender, racial, and national identity lenses put forth by recent Cold War scholarship, applying them to both American and Soviet sides. I emphasize the positive American reception to this Soviet propaganda tool in the form of the Moiseyev while highlighting the hypocrisy of the multicultural message the Soviet Union wished to impart. Furthermore, positive American reception was tied to the comforting depiction Soviet dancers conveyed of multiple races dancing together in harmony and clear, traditional gender roles.

I argue that although this reception occurred through the filter of simplified racial and ethnic tolerance and acceptable heteronormative values, it encouraged a view of universal humanity. This overwhelmingly positive reception complicated the Cold War narrative of incompatibility while also glossing over the fact that the troupe was itself a carefully crafted Soviet propagandistic tool intended to show multicultural solidarity in a nation which sometimes targeted its own people. Accordingly, highlighting this moment of positive Cold War engagement also means understanding *why* Americans felt they could relate to their enemy on display, namely because the dances focused on heteronormative, "wholesome" relationships in the form of middlebrow entertainment. It is through examining this particular moment of Cold War engagement that I show how the Cold War was a lived experience by individuals and that we see its continued impact today in contemporary Russo-American relations.

Elements of the American Cold War Narrative

The Cold War narrative, posited by scholars like Anders Stephanson as an entirely American project, influenced how Americans described and received the Moiseyev. The first few years after World War II in particular created the discourse utilized by the US government and, in this case, personal and critical accounts of the Moiseyev. Here, three examples are given of what formed the basis of this Cold War narrative and how Americans viewed and spoke about themselves in comparison with the Soviet Union. In his "Iron Curtain Speech," Winston Churchill in some ways set the tone for the American view of the Soviet Union and the spread of communism. Churchill contrasted life in the United States and United Kingdom with life in the Soviet Union. In the United States and United Kingdom, citizens enjoyed individual rights and freedoms while in the Soviet Union and communist countries, these rights were absent or limited. Communist regimes were police states in which the government interfered in people's lives. Churchill furthermore pointed to the international goals of communism, a view he supported by noting how "from Stettin in the Baltic to Trieste in the Adriatic, an iron curtain has descended across the continent." Eastern and Central Europe fell under the spreading communist yoke and this was not the end of communism's spread; Churchill claimed fifth columnists were present in other countries attempting to undermine established governments and win more states over to the communist side.[9] Churchill depicted a world divided between communism and democracy and that these two systems represented opposites. This view of the nations as a dichotomy, enemy spies among us, and ongoing communist spread, would pervade the narratives the US and USSR adopted during the Cold War.

George F. Kennan's eight-thousand-word "Long Telegram" also described the Soviet Union and United States as adversaries and that the systems could not cooperate diplomatically in the future. Kennan believed that Russia's historic fear of invasion affected the style of rule in the pre and post-revolutionary period. Marxism flourished in Russia because of Russia's fear of invasion and lack of friendly neighbors which played into Marxism "viewed *the* economic conflicts of society as insoluble by peaceful means." Because of Russia's long-established fear of invasion and the impact of Marxism, the Soviet regime employed a strict view of the "outside world as evil, hostile and menacing." The non-communist world was "diseased" and eventually would lead to communist revolutions like Russia's own and international communism. Kennan echoed Churchill's view of a divided world in which the two superpowers could not cooperate because the Soviet Union would not allow democracy to stand. In order to ensure its own stability, the Soviet Union would feel it necessary to support the international spread of communism to replace capitalistic democracies.[10] Correspondingly, the United States would craft a narrative of needing to stop the spread of communism through a variety of actions, including cultural exchange, to support non-communist regimes. The opportunity to show the superiority of democracies, such as through cultural exchange, became part of American foreign policy.

President Harry Truman added to this narrative in which the Soviet Union represented tyranny and repression, while the United States represented freedom and tolerance. Truman reinforced his concept of freedom and how it contrasted with the style of rule and life in communist countries with the Truman Doctrine. In his speech to Congress on March 12, 1947, Truman claimed it was necessary for the United States to "help free peoples to maintain their free institutions and their national integrity against aggressive movements that seek to impose upon them totalitarian regimes."[11] He believed that each nation had to choose between communism, based on "the will of a minority forcibly imposed upon the majority. It relies upon terror and oppression, a controlled press and radio, fixed elections, and the suppression of personal freedoms," and democracy, based on "the will of the majority, and is distinguished by free institutions, representative government, free elections, guarantees of individual liberty, freedom of speech and religion, and freedom from political oppression."[12] As a model of democracy, Truman said the United States had to act on behalf of those fighting communism, such as providing support to struggles against communism in Greece and Turkey. Truman's words lent urgency to the Cold War narrative by focusing on the idea of ongoing struggles between communism and democracy across the globe and America's role as model and champion of democracy.

Though the death of Stalin marked a movement toward closer relations and openness between the two superpowers, the above notions remained present in American views of the Soviet Union and communism in general, including the ideas that the Soviet Union wanted to conquer the world, the authoritarian and repressive nature of Soviet rule, and the need for the United States to demonstrate its superiority in respect for individual freedoms and standard of living. This narrative furthermore emphasized the urgency of the situation and the need for constant effort and vigilance.

While the narrative remained in place, a possible relaxing of tension became noticeable after Stalin's death. Journalist Peter Edson noted the change in atmosphere: "Russia's apparent desire for greater cultural exchanges with the West, the receptions given to [American] pianist Van Cliburn and the Moiseyev dancers, the friendlier . . . new Russian ambassador to Washington, Mikhail Menshikov all are cited as evidence of this new trend [of openness and exchange]." Edson expressed doubt about whether Khrushchev's regime marked a break with past Soviet repression, citing the execution of the Hungarian liberal leader Nagy after the 1956 Hungarian Revolution and the continued tensions between the Soviet government and Tito in Yugoslavia. The Soviet Union's alleged willingness to cooperate with the United States "will mask completely the real Communist intent to gain world domination by complete ruthlessness, as revealed in the other news emanating from Moscow."[13] Even with an apparent change in the political atmosphere and American–Soviet relations, this did not immediately expel the Cold War American narrative of an ever-spreading international communism bent on world domination.

The new trend in exchange and openness furthermore afforded President Eisenhower an opportunity to get in touch with the Soviet people. Journalist Drew Pearson argued: "in dealing with an autocracy, the only safeguard you have as a check on its rulers is friendship of its people." In a democracy like the United States, the president needed popular and institutional support to take major actions like declare war, while in the Soviet Union. by contrast, leadership changed without elections or foreknowledge and permission for major actions was not necessary. Accordingly, Pearson believed, it was important to get the Soviet people on America's side and the first step toward that goal was getting the Soviet people to like President Eisenhower. The exchange agreements and other recent actions leading to greater exposure to the West in the Soviet Union was already bringing down the Iron Curtain as Soviet people saw the wonders of the Western lifestyle. In comparison to the "blunt, brutal aloofness of Stalin's day . . . the change is nothing less than a political miracle" and could be directly compared to the opening of Japan by Admiral Perry in 1835.[14] The Cold War narrative looked to incorporate cultural exchange as an effective way to demonstrate American superiority and grow American power and, in Pearson's depiction, drew on a longer-term American strategy of cultural diplomacy that had already proven effective in places like Japan in the past.

As historian Clare Croft and others point out, we need to consider the Cold War narrative carefully; the expression of it created a myth of "consensus culture" that this book and other historical works look to poke holes into to better understand the actual experience of Americans during the Cold War. Indeed, the Cold War narrative, and corresponding myth of consensus, proved an effective Cold War weapon against the Soviet Union and others as well as a way to distract Americans domestically from the upheaval of post–World War II society.[15]

Soviet Interest in Cultural Exchange

Culture played a central role in the Soviet government, both in terms of its internal endeavors to support its political system and its external ones. The Soviet government prioritized cultural expression as "an essential tool" in the creation of the new system's society which in turn could also be used to "mold the world views of those who consumed it, at home and abroad."[16]

The Soviet Union included art, with an emphasis on accessible art, as a way to support the understanding of and conversion to the Soviet system.[17]

As is explored further in chapters 2 and 3, for the Soviet Union, cultural diplomacy was directly linked and even inextricable from its political goals.[18] Between 1955 and 1973, the Soviet Union sent two thousand artists to its Cold War American enemy, evidence of the importance the Soviet government attributed to culture as a Cold War weapon.[19] There were multiple reasons why the Soviet Union chose to take part in cultural exchange, including the broad goal of improving the image of the USSR and communism aboard.

The Soviet Union saw exchange as an effective tool, both proactively and reactively, in this broad goal of supporting a positive image internationally. For instance, in 1962, when an American spy plane was shot down and the pilot captured by the Soviets, cultural exchange formed part of the Soviets' response to the incident. Based on a perceived need to show Soviet strength and calm amid a tense moment, the Soviet Union decided to send pianist Sviatoslav Richter to the United States. Indeed, scholar Meri Elisabet Heerla argues that this decision was part of displaying Soviet cultural prestige and to soothe the difficult situation.[20]

One emphasis to highlight is that the Soviet approach to cultural exchange gave careful attention to cultural production, not just its dissemination, which will be discussed further when considering Soviet cultural exchange aims in greater depth. The Soviet Union aimed to demonstrate that cultural products created under their system were not only superior, but "the best continuation of shared Western traditions."[21] It was imperative to demonstrate that the Soviet regime and communism supported vibrant cultural production.

Earlier Cold War Cultural Exchange

While the State Academic Folk Dance Ensemble of the USSR was the first representation most Americans saw or heard about as part of Cold War cultural exchange, there were earlier efforts made. On the American side, earlier exchange initiatives relied more heavily on non-governmental entities and individuals to facilitate exchange.[22] The US government expressed a desire for formal exchange with the Soviet Union prior to the 1957 agreement, even suggesting an exchange program with the Soviet Union during

World War II that met rejection, but this desire went unfulfilled. The State Department suggested an exchange of artists, exhibitions, and students again in October 1945, including an American tour of the Red Army Chorus, but once more, the Soviet regime did not agree. On the Soviet side, cultural diplomacy and exchange similarly had a longer history though its cultural exchange operations would be run directly by the government from the start. After Stalin's death in 1953, the Soviet regime's view of cultural exchange between the United States and Soviet Union directly shifted. Accordingly, when the American opera *Porgy and Bess* toured Europe in 1955, it received an invitation to perform in Moscow and Leningrad, this was followed by a tour of the Boston Symphony Orchestra in 1956. On its part, the Soviet government sent pianist Emil Gilels and then violinist David Oistrakh to the United States in 1955.[23] Further details of earlier exchange and as official, direct exchange between the superpowers will be fleshed out in the upcoming chapters here.

In addition to cultural performance exchange, more general exchange of ideas occurred after the death of Stalin. For instance, Soviet agricultural officials came to the United States and toured the Midwest in order to learn about American agriculture and American officials did vice versa. While these earlier exchange initiatives met acceptance if not enthusiasm, the Lacy-Zarubin Agreement, which foregrounded the Moiseyev Dance Company's 1958 tour, established direct, official exchange between the USSR and the United States, including cultural, educational, and other kinds of exchange. The agreement, signed on January 27, 1958, cemented a new view of how the Soviet Union and United States would interact during the Cold War and identified exchange as a way to further Soviet-American relations. The agreement itself called for an exchange of five hundred people, but by 1959, "as many as 1700 individuals have already participated in the program and negotiations for its extension for an additional two years are to be opened shortly."[24] Once initiated, intergovernmental exchange took off and became a regular part of Cold War relations for the duration of the Soviet Union's existence. Indeed, how well exchanges went and how willing the two governments were to carry out a particular instance of exchange "served as a barometer of U.S.-Soviet relations." Thus, exchange flourished when relations between the two superpowers were good, while during the tense moments, such as the Vietnam War and the Soviet invasion of Afghanistan, exchange correspondingly suffered.[25]

Overview

Chapter 1 describes the origins of the State Academic Ensemble of Folk Dance and its formation after a festival of folk arts in 1936 in the Soviet Union. The initial goals for the ensemble, both on the part of the government and on the part of Igor Moiseyev, are important to consider, particularly as the overall Soviet policy regarding nationalities changed in the late 1930s into the 1940s. Chapter 2 picks up on how these goals changed as time went on and the company became more popular; soon the Moiseyev would be a tool of cultural diplomacy not just within the Soviet Union, but also outside its borders. The initial purpose of the group and the new goals it acquired as part of international cultural exchanges influenced how the group presented itself when visiting the United States and how Americans perceived it.

Chapter 3 addresses the process of opening cultural exchanges between the Soviet Union and the United States and examines why the Moiseyev became the first group to visit the United States. It highlights the expectations on the part of the American government and American people for cultural exchange generally and what they hoped to experience as a result of the tour.

The more nuanced aspects of American perception are the basis of Chapters 4 and 5 in which I categorize the kinds of reception on the part of the American audience in the 1958, 1965, and 1970 tours. While by and large the American reception was positive, here it is useful to break down the reception to highlight *why* Americans loved the Moiseyev. Chapter 4 does this work with the political framing and Cold War narrative vocabulary in mind while Chapter 5 delves more deeply into how the dancers came to be seen as human beings similar to Americans in a variety of ways.

Chapters 6 and 7 apply the lenses of gender and ethnicity/race, respectively, to American reactions and how these reactions are tied up with the politics of the Cold War and with American fears of cultural inferiority. Americans held certain preconceived notions of gender and gender roles in the Soviet Union, usually emphasizing the Soviet ideal of gender equality. Many Americans were surprised to find that the Moiseyev dances displayed traditional gender roles and heteronormative relationships. Even in observing the dancers offstage, Americans concluded that Soviet men and women had similar goals and desires in life to their American counterparts, despite the fact that they lived under a communist regime. In the context of American fears and anxiety about emasculation and women leaving traditional gender roles, Americans found the Moiseyev's depiction of gender comforting, which contributed to the troupe's success.

Similarly, the Moiseyev's multicultural message and alleged appreciation for people of all backgrounds provided reassurance in the context of the civil rights struggle and the racial violence that accompanied it in 1950s America. The Moiseyev presented an idealized vision of all peoples living harmoniously together, which Americans, as part of the Cold War narrative, supposedly supported. Accordingly, Americans were extremely receptive to this simplified vision of freedom and cooperation among people, as it seemed more attractive than the reality of America's contemporary racial issues.

PART
ONE

CHAPTER 1

Creation of the State Academic Folk Dance Ensemble of the USSR

Moiseyev was staying in a village near Kishinev one summer. He went to the village club in the evening and asked the girls he met there to show him some new dances. Laughing, they invited him to join them, to which he readily agreed. Taking off their boots, they did a dance for him which consisted of one single movement; they simply tapped their bare feet, now slowly and wistfully, now fast and merrily, changing the beat and rhythm all the time. Moiseyev repeated it after them. He made up the dance later. A suite, not just a dance. And all the inspiration he had was a single movement—the barefoot aping of some Moldavian peasant girls.

—Anna Ilupina and Yelena Lutskaya, *Moiseyev's Dance Company*

According to contemporary histories, press coverage, and Igor Moiseyev himself, the company's choreographic process required close observation and study of a nation and its folk dances before creating a dance that would represent that nation. As described above in one of the Soviet-produced materials supporting the dance company, Moiseyev could allegedly soak in the dances he observed and understand the spirit and identity of the culture on display before then taking it and transforming it into something even better—"A suite, not just a dance"—which remained authentic to the source material—"the barefoot aping of some Moldavian peasant girls"—while refining it for a more global audience. Using this technique, Moiseyev developed the repertoire of the State Academic Folk Dance Ensemble of the USSR. The ensemble claimed it could represent the spirit of the peoples of the Soviet Union through dance. Contemporary histories of the Moiseyev and news articles published both in the Soviet Union and United States claimed that the intrepid choreographer Igor Moiseyev carefully crafted the dances to represent the different peoples both fairly and faithfully. Moiseyev traveled throughout the Soviet Union to observe, learn, and then distill the dances he saw so that they best represented the spirit of the people (and so that they were entertaining for a variety of audiences). At the same time, the Moiseyev dance repertoire represented a carefully crafted tool of Soviet propaganda that served to "fight" the Cold War culturally by utilizing an idealized positive view of how the Soviet regime treated the different ethnicities and nationalities living within its borders.

The fact that the ensemble represented a fabricated view of ethnicities and nationalities in the Soviet Union can be traced to the process that folk dances underwent to become part of the ensemble's repertoire. Igor Moiseyev desired to display the spirit of the people, but this did not mean creating an exact replica of a particular folk or national dance. Instead, after gathering information about the dance and the people it represented, Moiseyev made the executive decisions to tweak and improve the dance for the purposes of the State Academic Folk Dance Ensemble's performances to make the dances accessible to a contemporary global audience and entertaining. Moiseyev began his study of folk dance prior to the group's formation in 1937, but with the official support of the Soviet regime, the repertoire expanded to include a greater number of dances and of dancers for the company.

The Moiseyev Dance Company reflected the larger Soviet view of "guiding" national identities of peoples living within the Soviet Union to support the regime's power and positive image of a multicultural entity. This entailed simplification and mythologization of the origins of the dance troupe and the choreographic process employed to study and distill "authentic" folk dances. This façade would support the groups' efficacy as a propaganda tool in culture exchange in the United States and elsewhere.

The Moiseyev's 1958 US tour complicated the Cold War narrative because it presented (albeit in a highly stylized version) the American Cold War ideal of specifically American-made freedom and respect for the various people in a large, multiethnic populace which contrasted with a view of their Cold War enemy as oppressing peoples living within Soviet borders. The Moiseyev utilized a multicultural message that had great appeal to the American audience. This multicultural message imparted by the Moiseyev originated in the nationalities policy of *korenizatsiia* under Stalin in the 1930s, which celebrated and encouraged the cultural expression of the many peoples of the Soviet Union. However, once this policy shifted and different ethnic and national groups became targets of Stalinist purges and resettlement, the ensemble survived the shift in nationalities policy (and survived past the eventual fall of the Soviet Union). The ensemble's survival, especially during the latter part of Stalin's regime and then after his death, was based on Stalin's own personal admiration for the troupe, the ensemble's popularity within the Soviet Union, and its usefulness as a diplomatic tool for the newly formed communist governments in the Soviet Bloc and (after Stalin's death) in Western Europe and beyond.

The Moiseyev became a tool of international diplomacy gradually, mirroring Soviet recognition of and admiration for the ensemble, as well as Soviet interest in cultural exchange within the Soviet Bloc and throughout the rest of the world. Soon after its formation, the Soviet government used the ensemble to demonstrate support for the nations and cultures living within its borders, and to this end the ensemble performed not just in Moscow and St. Petersburg but also throughout the Soviet Union. The tours met with huge success, and the group increased in popularity. Indeed, it was a visible presence during World War II, giving wartime performances to improve morale. The goal of representing Soviet nationalities and tolerance in a positive light became international as the ensemble extended its terrain to countries in the Soviet Bloc (and incorporating dances in its repertoire to represent these countries). Once more, audiences received the ensemble with enthusiasm and delight. Noting this popularity and the positive image the ensemble reinforced, the Soviet government sent the ensemble to the West following Stalin's death during a relaxation of tension between the Soviet Union and Western. Based on wildly enthusiastic Western European reception and press coverage, the ensemble became an internationally known group with a prestigious reputation. Convinced of the group's ability to present a positive picture of the USSR, the Soviet government extended the Moiseyev's tours around the globe and encouraged written and visual coverage of the ensemble.

As the ensemble began to tour Europe in the mid and late 1950s and to the United States in 1958, the Soviet Union published histories of the company to accompany the dancers. These histories painted the dancers and international reception as wholly positive and no doubt took artistic license in its depictions to enhance and even fabricate evidence of the Moiseyev troupe's impact when it toured abroad. Within these histories there are no doubt exaggerations and event fabrications in order to serve the

Soviet propaganda purposes of cultural diplomacy. International press coverage (and the histories themselves frequently being translated into other languages) drew on these histories and accordingly, they simply became part of the Moiseyev's domestic and international propaganda message. Given the way they came to be used locally and how they lauded the Moiseyev's efforts abroad, and the positive influence the Moiseyev had on peoples living in communist and democratic states, they served to further support Soviet goals for cultural diplomacy. For instance, the 1966 *Moiseyev's Dance Company* opened with, "We meant to begin with the words: 'Meet Igor Moiseyev.' But surely it is not possible that you have not heard about Moiseyev and his folk dance company, for by now, this group of 110 dancers has toured most countries of the world." The book fed into the mythologization of the troupe's success and impact. Such histories served as another way to influence the image of the Soviet Union abroad, for the benefit of both those who could and could not see the dancers in person, since the book endeavored to "recapture the delight of watching a Moiseyev show" by relating the history and reception of the Moiseyev and with images of the dances.[1] While these histories are used extensively throughout this book, they are used with full recognition of their original intent and corresponding problematic nature; rather than drawing on them as purely factual accounts, they serve as a further artifact of the Soviet propaganda efforts to be analyzed and to give a sense of what Americans may have seen or heard about the Moiseyev Dance Company.

In *The Folk Dance Company of the USSR: Igor Moiseyev, Art Director*, written by Mikhail Chudnovsky and published in English in 1959, the author recounts the company's successful trip to Lebanon and how the local press recognized the diversity of the repertoire in performing dances beyond Russia. The account presents a perfect opportunity to demonstrate how such histories fed into the propaganda efforts. For instance, this account works hard to emphasize how the Moiseyev achieved its goal of demonstrating the USSR's appreciation of the cultures living within its borders with the added framing of how the company functioned within and was influenced by its Cold War context. Thus, the Moiseyev's (and Chudnovsky's) propagandistic message not only celebrated multiculturalism but also insisted upon the supremacy of the Soviet regime and its peoples as demonstrated through dance. As Chudnovsky retold the alleged overwhelming success of the Lebanon trip in his history of the company, he accordingly also adds commentary from a local newspaper:

> While the Soviet Union has given us the possibility of seeing its friendly art which helps to bring the nationalities closer together ... the Americans send us warships. What different aims the two missions pursue is clear.[2]

Chudnovsky notes the company's political impact: demonstrating how different cultures within the Soviet Union all live peacefully together and produce works of art, like the Moiseyev's dances, brings Lebanese citizens closer to the peoples of the Soviet Union. This contrasts strongly with the alleged message of the Americans, as represented by weaponry and warships. Given the overwhelmingly positive depictions in such histories and the propagandistic goal underlying them, it is again important to treat them with skepticism in terms of their accuracy and rather than use them as entirely reliable, to instead view them in terms of how the Soviet Union chose to depict itself and its cultural diplomacy efforts. These histories utilized the Moiseyev's success as a launching pad to exhibit the Soviet Union's superior culture and superior tolerance of different nationalities. The regime intended this pointed propagandistic message to contrast with American racism and the allegedly crude and materialistic nature of American culture.

The Issue of Nationalism and Nationalities Policy in the Soviet Union

The State Academic Folk Ensemble of the USSR formed and gained early support in large part because of the contemporary view of nationalities living in the Soviet Union. This view (and the Moiseyev's goals) changed over time, and it is helpful to touch on the origins of the nationalities policy as this was crucial to the development of the dance troupe. The Bolsheviks' view of nationalism grew out of their ideas about the relationship between capitalism and imperialism. Before the 1917 Revolution, Lenin spoke out against the negative aspects of Western European imperialism and identified this as the highest stage in the development of capitalism. He argued for self-determination and an end to imperialism's abuses.

However, even at this earlier stage, the tension existed between Bolshevik support for nationalism and the fear of losing centralized control.

While drawing on nationalist feelings had aided the Bolshevik's revolution-ary movement, the question was how to now rule this large, multinational, multiethnic empire once in power. Georgii Piatakov and Nikolai Bukharin argued for a universalist view, claiming that the revolution would make nationalism no longer necessary. Self-determination would, in fact, encour-age counterrevolution. Lenin felt that though nationalism could be a ral-lying cry for counterrevolutionaries, its benefits of dispelling the notion of Russia as oppressor and helping to gain the trust of different national groups outweighed this drawback. Accordingly, Lenin, along with Stalin, continued to advocate for nationalism and self-determination.

Lenin believed that nationalism created a forum for peoples' complaints against the empire and unified them to fight again imperialistic domina-tion.[3] This was especially important given Russia's multiple nationalisms, nationalities which Lenin identified as potential tools in the uprising against the Tsarist regime. Encouraging other nationalisms living within the Russian empire also involved criticizing specifically "Russian" nationalism. Lenin saw "Russian" nationalism as chauvinistic and imperialistic; like the bourgeoisie, it, too, needed to be destroyed. In the years leading up to and immediately following the Bolshevik Revolution, Stalin supported Lenin's ideas regarding nationalism, and his *Marxism and the National Question* (1913) would be used by the Bolsheviks to develop their initial nationalism policy by the Bolsheviks once they were in power. Stalin explained that "a nation is a historically constituted, stable community of people, formed on the basis of a common language, territory, psychological make-up mani-fested in a common culture."[4]

Lenin and Stalin's early support for nationalism was translated into the policy of korenizatsiia, or indigenization. This policy not only encour-aged nationalistic expression and pride in national identity but aided the development or creation of a "nation" defined through language and cul-ture. Korenizatsiia meant promoting local elites to higher local government positions, standardizing notation and alphabets of languages, and aiding cultural production which reflected national identity.[5]

The problems with the nationalities policy began to emerge in the late 1920s and early 1930s with purges of some local elites and concern about the loyalty of ethnic groups who lived along the Soviet borders with the West. Ukraine in particular became an area of tension and then change in the nationalities policy. At first the Soviet regime had supported Ukrainian culture and history, especially the use of the Ukrainian language on street signs, stamps, newspapers, and in other public ways. Resistance to collectivization in the late 1920s and the low yield of grain caused the regime to change its stance on Ukraine. In 1932, the Soviet regime promulgated a series of anti-Ukrainization decrees that found that the nationalities policy had not only failed to be correctly implemented in Ukraine but had also created resistance. Supposedly, traitors had found their way into positions of power and had been able to sabotage grain requisition.[6]

As examined by historian Jeffrey Burds, the shift in nationalities policy entailed a reframing of who was the enemy and would entail a change in the policing and persecution of certain peoples by the government as well as what the government supported in terms of cultural expression. Burds traces how in the 1930s, rather than targeting class-based enemies such as the *kulaks* or the bourgeoisie, the regime viewed an "enemy of the people" to be ethnically based. The Soviet secret police, the Peoples Commissariat for Internal Affairs (NKVD), usually carried out the actions reflected the change in those targeted by the Soviet regime. This change can be seen in a series of NKVD Resolutions addressing German espionage and sabotage. In a resolution from July 25, 1937, the regime warned of informers living in the country's German communities. Another resolution, from August 9, added Polish subjects as possible informers as well. This was further expanded to include other nationalities, such as the Chinese, Greeks, and Estonians.[7]

Stalin's December 1935 speech addressing the "Friendship of the Peoples" underlined this shift in policy with a new definition of nationalism, which claimed that the various peoples of the USSR now completely trusted each other and shared strong bonds of friendship. Rather than identifying Russian culture and identity with imperialism as they once had, the different peoples of the Soviet Union could now trust and admire all things Russian. Indeed, rather than encouraging the development of culture and identity of different nationalisms, the Russian identity and Russian people would be put first, particularly because of their role in the Revolution. As part of this changed definition and policy—and further influenced by reports of German preparations for aggression—Stalin stepped up greater persecution of ethnic minorities in late 1940. Burds in particular explains how this affected peoples from the borderlands who worried Stalin's secret police, the Peoples Commissariat for Internal Affairs (NKVD),[8] would turn against the Soviet Union because of religious belief. As a result, 657 Chechen and

Ingush nationalist guerrillas were killed, 2,762 captured, and 1,113 surrendered in the NKVD action of 1940–1944.[9]

In order to deal with potential traitors before war was declared with Germany, and after the Red Army regained control over the Ukraine and Caucasus, Stalin promulgated a series of resolutions directing the forced resettlement of certain national groups. This was carried out by Lavrentiy Beria, the head of the NKVD. In a resolution dated September 22, 1941, Stalin ordered the resettlement of over 100,000 Germans living in the Ukraine to Kazakhstan.[10] Stalin feared that certain nationalities' loyalties did not lie with the USSR; these nationalities would take any opportunity to betray the USSR and free themselves from Soviet control. These kinds of fears contrasted strongly with the earlier policy of korenizatsiia, which celebrated national and cultural differences rather than viewing these differences as potential dangers.

The targeting of national minorities included those who the Moiseyev depicted on stage. For instance, a similar decree to the 1941 German resettlement stated:

> During the Patriotic War many Crimean Tatars betrayed the Motherland, deserted Red Army units that defended the Crimea, and sided with the enemy, joining volunteer army units formed by the Germans to fight against the Red Army. As members of German punitive detachments during the occupation of the Crimea by German fascist troops, the Crimean Tatars particularly were noted for their savage reprisals against Soviet partisans, and also helped the German invaders to organize the violent roundup of Soviet citizens for German enslavement and the mass extermination of the Soviet people.

Based on these crimes, Stalin ordered the resettlement of all Tatars to Uzbekistan to be carried out by the NKVD.[11] Even as this persecution occurred, the Moiseyev dancers performed *The Dance of the Tatars from Kazan*. With smiling faces, the dancers utilized humor and acrobatics to depict two young women playing a trick on two young men, an image of stark contrast to the reality of the Tatars' situation.

Additionally, in the Crimea, Stalin ordered the resettlement of "German collaborators" among the Bulgarians, Greeks, and Armenians living there, totaling 37,000. In July of 1944, Beria reported on the resettlement process, noting that the NKVD had resettled a total of 255,009 people, including Tatars, Bulgarians, Greeks, Armenians, Germans, and other foreigners.[12]

FIGURE 1. Dance of the Kazan Tatars performed by Sergei Tsvetkov and Mikhail Alexandrov. Source: M. Chudnovsky, *The Folk Dance Company of the USSR: Igor Moiseyev, Art Director* (Moscow: Foreign Languages Publishing House, 1959), 53.

Though the view of different nationalities had clearly changed, the Moiseyev continued to dance using different nationalities as inspiration; the Moiseyev did not change its goals or repertoire to reflect contemporary policy. Despite the dramatic shift in the view of nationalities and their role in the Soviet Union, the Moiseyev survived because of its established popularity and recognition across the USSR, especially as it toured during World War II to increase morale.

In the post-Stalin period, the emphasis on the "guided" development of different peoples to catch up with Russia diminished. Stalin claimed that the peoples who made up the Soviet Union could pass through historical phases in an accelerated manner aided by the state. But Khrushchev saw the changes as more gradual and put the end date at 1980. Khrushchev's attempts to move away from Stalin allowed ethnographers in the new 1959 Census to declare that the previous census's list of nationalities did not correctly represent all the nationalities within the Soviet Union. Thus, the 1959 census allowed ethnographers to put nationalities back on the list. However, ethnographers still felt the need to show the progress of the goal of socialist universalism, and thus in 1970 and 1979, there were fewer nationalities on the list, but this was achieved by not including "foreign" nationalities like the Italians and French. Leonid Brezhnev, General Secretary from 1964–1982, in turn, saw no end in sight for the achievement of universalism, but believed that "the Soviet Union would remain at its current stage of 'developed socialism' for quite some time." Post-Stalinist leaders did not see the state-sponsored acceleration of nationalism leading to internationalism as a goal for their particular time period but rather as a more general future goal. Under General Secretary Mikhail Gorbachev's policy *glasnost*, establishing greater transparency by the government in the mid-1980s, the forced deportation of populations like the Crimean Tatars could be discussed in public. Gorbachev chose not to continue earlier rhetoric about the goal of socialist universalism and instead focused on providing national rights to the different peoples of the Soviet Union. Thus the 1989 census actually increased the number of recognized nationalities.[13]

The Implementation of the Nationalities Policy in Cultural Expression

The cultural policy enacted in the 1920s mirrored that of the nationalities policy outlined above. With regard to music as one area of a nation's culture, the policy consisted mainly of "the idea that each nation had its own music that would be systematically collected, studied and used as a basis for composition," and that the music of different nations should be celebrated and disseminated as part of this policy. Paralleling the general nationalities policy, Moscow believed that promoting national music idioms was a stepping stone toward an eventual all-encompassing musical institution promoting a universal view of music in which there would be no distinction between nationalities. For instance, in Armenia, this cultural policy meant institutionalizing folk orchestras and selecting the best known Armenian folk instrumentalists to be a part of these orchestras. This often involved combining folk instruments that previously had not been played together and bringing together many more instruments than was typical in traditional folk ensembles. Finally, a conductor became a part of folk orchestras, which was a completely new addition.[14] This change in the composition of folk ensembles and the institutionalization of folk orchestras in turn led to an emphasis on musicians learning notation and writing music down so that by the 1950s, all members of folk orchestras could read musical notation.

Michael Rouland examines Kazakh music as another example of how this policy played out, but links the way the Soviet regime carried out the policy with its larger goal of modernizing Kazakhstan. Kazakh music—culturally preeminent because a print culture formed in Kazakhstan only in the late nineteenth century—was a way to spread the idea of a Kazakh nation. Thus, as Kazakhstan became an autonomous republic in 1920, its government also set up a Commission for the Collection of Kazakh Songs. Alexander Zataevich, a Russian composer, was asked to collect and classify folk songs, which in turn were published as *A Thousand Songs of the Kazakh People* (1925). However, at the same time Zataevich "corrected" some of the music he put into the collection in order to make it understandable according to standard Western musical notation. Thus, as in Armenia, folk music became "national" music in part by standardization and served the overall Soviet regime's purpose of moving towards nationalism along the path to universalism.[15]

In addition to these efforts within nations like Armenia and Kazakhstan, the Soviet government hosted the All-Union Folk Festival in November 1936 in Moscow. *Pravda* published information about the upcoming festival, including the purposes behind it. The Union Committee for the Arts organized the festival, and *Pravda* noted that "The upcoming festival should show you the richness and variety of folk dances in the Union," and identify folk dances that should be examined more closely. Identifying folk dances would serve to help Soviet ballet; *Pravda* claimed that Soviet ballet had not achieved the same development and success as other fields of Soviet art and folk dance was a potential source for aiding Soviet ballet's development. Folk dance represented the Soviet Union's diversity and utilized modern themes which better represented the Soviet way of life.[16] The festival received positive feedback from the Soviet press as the dancers fascinated "the viewer [with] exceptional charm [and] . . . special melodious movements." The festival included dances from Armenia, Kazakhstan, and the Crimean Tatars (among others), and each dance demonstrated the traits of its corresponding nationality. For instance, the Kazakh dance showed the "amazing complex of extraordinary culture, rich people's fantasy, fine art [and] humor." The press noted that it was impossible to list and discuss all of the amazing dances on display in the festival but that the festival certainly suggested the way to enhance Soviet ballet as it currently stood. The folk dance should be used as a "lesson," and subsequent development of Soviet ballet should use the folk dance as its inspiration.[17] Later articles and histories tied the festival directly to the creation of the State Academic Folk Dance Ensemble of the USSR.

The origin story of the Moiseyev Dance Company became both simplified and mythologized as the Moiseyev became better known in the Soviet Union and internationally. All versions of the story agreed on a few major factors leading to the group's formation. First, the group formed after the 1936 All Soviet Union Folk Festival in Moscow featuring folk dances from a variety of Soviet peoples. Moiseyev himself, with the encouragement of the Festival Government Committee, served as choreographer for the festival. According to the overly exuberant Soviet histories of the Moiseyev company, the festival appeared to educate the Soviet public, but also Igor Moiseyev himself: "During this festival Moiseyev was able to see a diversity of folk dances, varying from nationality to nationality, in all their dazzling brilliance of colour and costume. And it made him feel all the more convinced that he must henceforth concentrate on folk dancing."[18]

Moiseyev allegedly came up with the idea of the State Academic Ensemble of Folk Dances of the USSR during this festival and he chose the first members of the ensemble from the performers there.[19] Though newspaper articles usually lauded the festival's achievement of an impressive display of diverse folk dances, in his memoirs published in 1996, Moiseyev noted many difficulties with its execution: "We had to teach the basics of folk dance performers, including movements that are not known to classical ballet, [and] the ability to transform into a national style. . . . Each style—Slavic, Oriental, Caucasian—has different coordination systems, traditions, rhythms. Dance is a language. If you want to be understood in France, it is necessary to learn French."[20] In utilizing these memoirs, it should be noted that, given their publication after the fall of the Soviet Union, Moiseyev's recollections should be carefully evaluated since they might not entirely reflect his thoughts and actions at the time. Publishing them after the fall of the Soviet Union and the end of the Cold War may mean they reflect a desire to distance Moiseyev's active participation in the Soviet regime's propaganda and cultural initiatives. Accordingly, like the official Soviet histories of the troupe, when the memoirs are used throughout this book,

Moiseyev's claims with regard to how he viewed the Soviet regime and, in particular, Stalin's patronage, are viewed with careful scrutiny.

Igor Moiseyev—An Idealized Version of His Life and Work

Moiseyev's own personal story and how he moved from classical ballet to folk dance formed a major part of the ensemble's origin story. Accordingly, it is worth including his biography, as well as the depiction of his role in the development of Soviet folk dance. Igor Aleksandrovich Moiseyev was born on January 21, 1906, in Kiev. His father was a lawyer and his mother a costume designer. Igor spent part of his childhood in Paris, where his mother's brother worked as an architect. In Paris, Igor was exposed to ballet from a young age. Contemporary Soviet histories note the early visibility of Igor Moiseyev's talent. For instance, Mikhail Chudnovsky's history of the ensemble, *Dancing to Fame*, noted that Igor had a friend who was considered a good dancer in Paris but simply "by imitating her Igor soon mastered her 'technique' and performed on the points with great effect."[21] As histories of the established ensemble reflected back on the origins of the troupe, they claimed that Igor's talent was undeniable and that he himself could easily learn the classical ballet form celebrated in French culture. This early, allegedly self-evident talent would form the basis of the folk dance ensemble and its mythology.

After returning to the Ukraine for a year when he was seven, Igor's family moved to Moscow where he attended school. Igor was a good student, and enjoyed drawing, poetry, and sports. However, "his natural gifts made him realize that dancing was his true calling."[22] He began to study at the studio of Vera Mosolova and was eventually admitted to the Bolshoi Theatre school. Moiseyev showed not just natural gifts but also a willingness to work hard and a desire to know as much about dance as possible. He hungrily absorbed any material he could find about the "art of the dance," going beyond what dancers traditionally studied as part of their education.

As a result of this independent study, "Moiseyev became deeply interested in that vast but little known field of choreography—the folk dance, whose great resources have hardly been tapped by the professional dancer."[23] Moiseyev did not pursue this interest right after graduating from the Bolshoi school, instead joining the Bolshoi Ballet company.

Igor desired to expand his talents beyond performance and began to choreograph his own dances. It was through early works, such as *The Three Fat Men* and *The Football Player*, that contemporary histories pointed to "signs of a search for new means of expression."[24] Igor felt that the Bolshoi suffered from "stagnation" and suggested trying new approaches, including the staging of folk dances. However, the Bolshoi rejected folk dance as beneath their traditional repertoire.[25] After the folk ensemble became so well-known and became a tool of cultural diplomacy, Soviet histories claimed that Igor Moiseyev was not satisfied with pre-revolutionary ballet forms and felt the need for an art form that would better express emotions and contemporary life.

Moiseyev began to use his summers to travel to different regions of the Soviet Union, including the Ukraine, Belorussia, Tajikistan, the banks of the Volga and throughout the Urals. The narrative of his travels included an emphasis on his determination; Moiseyev did whatever it took to reach the "remotest villages," including riding horseback or walking, in order to learn about folk dance and the lives of Soviet peoples.[26] During his visits he would observe the "character, ways of living and customs of the people, and above all to learn as much as possible of the various dance heritages of the nationalities inhabiting his vast homeland."[27] He felt that in order to learn a nation or culture's dance, more was necessary than knowing the steps, melodies, and rhythms. Early on, Moiseyev identified national character and way of life as vitally important to understanding cultural expressions such as folk dance. This enhanced his knowledge of folk dance but, more importantly, served as inspiration for his choreographic endeavors. As Moiseyev put it, "Folk art showed me my vocation."[28] In describing the origins of the State Academic Folk Ensemble of the USSR himself, Moiseyev played into the mythologized version of events that contemporary Soviet histories espoused.

In his memoirs, Moiseyev recalled a visit to a village in Belarus. He noticed young girls walking along, singing about potatoes and asking for good weather for the potato crop. The Belarusian name for potato, "bulb," along with the rhythm of the polka formed the crux of the song. In Moiseyev's hands, he molded the original source material into his own version, *Bulba*, which would be widely performed by the State Academic Folk Dance Ensemble of the USSR as one of their signature dances. He claimed that he drew on the authentic source; Byelorussians themselves recognized the Moiseyev *Bulba* version of the dance as reflecting the long history of the "bulb" dance in their culture and validated his use of and changes to the original dance. This, according to Moiseyev "is the highest form of recognition."[29] He, and Soviet propaganda, emphasized the way the Moiseyev dance troupe's repertoire represented authentic, if elevated, versions of national folk dances.

Moiseyev explained his choice specifically of folk dance as undergirding the dance troupe's repertoire in his memoirs, noting that folk dance expressed the "national soul" and was an "inexhaustible treasury of many priceless gems." He particularly stressed the emotional expressiveness of folk dance, in contrast to the "rational" nature of classical ballet. Classical ballet was the dance of fantasy, otherworldly, while folk dance belonged to the "earth."[30] In his explanation of his inspiration and choreographic approach, Moiseyev carefully framed the Moiseyev dance troupe as broadly accessible and as truly reflecting the citizens of the Soviet Union, making it a clear appropriate choice for continued Soviet support in its domestic and international performances.

Formation of the Ensemble

Soviet histories of the ensemble varied in detailing how the idea of the ensemble, inspired by the 1936 festival, led to the creation of the State Academic Folk Dance Ensemble of the USSR. Most simply noted that the festival inspired Igor Moiseyev, who in turn discussed the possibility of the ensemble with the Soviet government, received permission, and continued apace with its formation. Such histories depicted the formation of the ensemble as a linear progression from original idea that, coupled with official support, led logically to the ensemble's creation: "It could not have been otherwise, for as soon as the company was formed it received generous grants from the state, and practically unlimited freedom to experiment, seek and create."[31] With the 1936 festival behind him, when Moiseyev suggested the creation of the folk ensemble, the government readily agreed. The Soviet regime then appointed Moiseyev the artistic director of the State Academic Folk Dance Ensemble of the USSR.[32] Moiseyev allegedly easily assembled a group of dancers and began quickly choreographing the dances. Though at first the group lacked a proper performance space, this only played into the themes of the Moiseyev story: "Hard conditions could not scare them off, however, for they believed in their leader who drew them on with the dream of creating an entirely new form of dance art—the scenic folk dance."[33] Again the story around Moiseyev and the dance company continued to emphasize not only Igor Moiseyev's dogged determination but that his choreography and the dance repertoire represented something both authentic and an elevated innovation.

However, the actual circumstances and formation of the company were much more complicated. There were those who doubted and "prophesied complete failure for Igor Moiseyev." These critics thought Moiseyev was foolish for leaving the celebrated Bolshoi Ballet in order to pursue the less prestigious folk dance. But the "courageous" Igor Moiseyev carried on, and his faith in the future of folk dance was such that he remained resolute in pursuing the creation of the ensemble. Accordingly, he held the first meeting of the new company on February 10, 1937, in a house on Leontyevsky Street in Moscow. Forty-five interested people attended, with Igor Moiseyev at age thirty being the eldest.[34]

This group worked for six months to prepare its first program. The State Academic Folk Ensemble of the USSR premiered with thirty-five dancers in October of 1937, but the performance revealed the group's the lack of training at this early stage in its development. This, however, could be passed off as understandable, as the dance troupe was made up of idealistic young people who "until then they had been operating machine tools, working in offices and on farms" (though it should be noted that this is again an idealized depiction, many of the dancers who would form the regular ensemble were classically Bolshoi school–trained). Additionally, the ensemble was only able to prepare the minimum number of dances to fill a program, with the open-air premiere at the Green Theatre in Moscow included Ukrainian, Byelorussian, and Georgian Dances. These obstacles would allegedly prove inconsequential as despite the difficulty in putting together the program, the company reportedly "swept the audience off its feet. Here was something new. Here was talent in the interpretation of the folk dance."[35] Once more this mythologization of the founding of the troupe also strove to point out how fitting the troupe was as a cultural product representing the whole Soviet Union, both for its ability to entertain and specifically for its usage of Moiseyev's folk dance choreographic approach.

Judging by this first performance, histories of the Moiseyev claimed that the Moscow audience immediately recognized Igor Moiseyev's endeavors:

"He revealed to the amazed spectators a new world of thoughts, emotions and moods they never suspected existed in it." Moiseyev's revolutionary ethnographic choreographic approach proved able to entirely transport and transform its Moscow audience, setting a precedent for its propagandistic usage in the USSR and beyond. Though the ensemble needed to build up its repertoire and human faces, contemporary histories noted the great success in dealing with this problem. The ensemble soon had 143 people and a diverse dance repertoire to draw on.[36]

Contemporary historians created a linear history of the ensemble, from the initial idea for the group in the 1936 festival to the creation and first performance of the company in 1937, to a superbly trained ensemble with a wealth of dances in its repertoire and domestic and international renown. Indeed, such historians claimed that within a year-and-a-half of its founding, the ensemble was a "well-knit group" with a comprehensive repertoire and high-level performances.[37]

A letter Moiseyev cowrote on July 30, 1938, around the year-and-a-half marker, offers some insight into the reality of the group's formation and early years. In it, Moiseyev recounts the execution of the All-Union Festival of Folk Dance in 1936 and its results, which endeavored to create exposure for folk dance. Interestingly, the letter notes that "because the festival was badly organized . . . it did not create a strong following." Sadly, the festival did not document its performances: no systematic attempt was made to record the music, note the choreography, or photograph the costumes. The festival, furthermore, did not fully represent the numerous dances and peoples of the Soviet Union. For instance, Moiseyev pointed out there were no dances from Tajikistan at the festival. And, with regard to Russian folk dance, the festival actually "distorted the impression about Russian dance."[38]

Moiseyev noted that the Soviet Union should be more conscious of the value of studying folk dance, since at that time, "there's a blossoming of national arts" and of "national artistic creativity." In places like Kirgizstan and Turkmenistan, Moiseyev pointed to the new creative impetus which he felt the Soviet regime currently did not recognize. He accordingly called for a new All-Union National Dance Festival to be organized for 1939 that would actually study, record and organize the dances on display. A properly organized festival such as the one Moiseyev had in mind would accomplish certain results. These results included: "the study and recording of dance forms and themes and subject"; the "fertilization of professional choreography of folk material"; identification of dancers from amateur groups who would be suitable for further development; the recording of folk music, instruments, and costumes; and the "stimulation of further growth and blossoming of Soviet choreography by means of mutual exchange" of folk dance.[39] This goes against the narrative of the 1936 festival organically and logically leading to the creation of the State Academic Folk Dance Ensemble of the USSR. While the picture of the reality of the 1936 and 1939 festivals and their impact is incomplete, these pieces of information certainly indicate that the creation of the group was not as smooth or streamlined as depicted in the propagandistic materials the Soviet Union would later create to convey the troupe's history.

The State Academic Folk Dance Ensemble of the USSR, while it became enormously successful, did not experience an easy transition from idea to established institution. It took dogged persistence and pleading for official and popular recognition of the value of the folk dance cause. Though before, during, and after the 1936 festival (especially in light of the korenizatsiia policy) folk dance garnered some interest, this interest was yet to develop into a consistent meeting of the minds between the Soviet government and Igor Moiseyev.

Igor Moiseyev's Goals and Approach to Folk Material

Contemporary Soviet histories treated Moiseyev's approach to the original folk source material and how he changed it in a similar manner to the origin story of the ensemble. These histories simplified the process and justified the revisions Moiseyev made to the original material while still claiming the dances were "authentic" and truly represented how the Soviet regime treated ethnic and national groups living in their borders and these groups' ways of life. Writing about Moiseyev's artistic approach in this manner aided the Soviet regime's ability to use the ensemble as propaganda and a diplomatic tool. Accordingly, at the time the State Academic Folk Dance Ensemble of the USSR was founded (and later when recalling his original approach to the ensemble's formation and repertoire), Moiseyev insisted on interweaving authentic folk material with his own creative changes, molding the original folk dances:

> Folk dance needs to be carefully examined. We are not collectors of dance and [we] do not prick them like a butterfly on a pin. Based on

international experience, we strive to empower the dance, enriching it with the director's fancy [and] dance technique, through which he expresses himself more clearly. In short, we come to the folk dance as material for creation, not concealing his [the choreographer's] author-ship in each folk dance.

The final dance creation reflected national character and the inspiration of the original dance but with unashamed changes by the choreographer. These changes in fact elevated the dance while purportedly remaining authentic. Moiseyev conceived of this approach and refined it as he worked on the 1936 festival and the State Academic Folk Dance Ensemble of the USSR. After the 1936 festival, Moiseyev recalled in his memoirs how the fes-tival demonstrated "an enormous wealth of folklore" but that the folk dances were disorganized and haphazardly recorded (if at all). The question was, how to approach this source material and "how to protect a unique national character [in the dance] and at the same time make a living art of dance, not [simply] transfer [the dance] as museum exhibits?"[40] Handily enough, Moiseyev had the answer.

Moiseyev asserted that, through his study of folk dance, he learned to identify which aspects of the dance were most important. In order to accomplish this, he examined not just the dance steps themselves, but the themes, style, way of life and history of the national group.[41] Moiseyev stated his goal for the ensemble:

to create classic patterns of the folk dance, and while casting off all the artificial and alien elements, to achieve a high degree of artistry in the performance of folk dances, to develop a number of old dances, and to influence the further shaping of the folk dance.

Elevating the dance to achieve that "high degree of artistry" in reality meant making the dances more entertaining and accessible to a broad audience as well as changing the corresponding outfits to be more visually appealing. Subsequently, the ensemble worked to popularize folk dance so that more people in the Soviet Union would learn about it and appreciate it. Tour-ing the Soviet Union also enabled the Moiseyev to learn of dances from more locations throughout the Soviet Union, from cities to small villages. The ensemble desired to revitalize folk dance and use older, "undiscovered" folk dances as inspiration for the construction of new ones.[42] The ensemble privileged itself as being the proper entity to "discover" these older dances rather than the folk dance's own people and that it was only in Moiseyev's capable hands that the dances could be appropriately elevated for the dances' new audiences.

In addition to paying greater attention to the study of folk dance, Moiseyev pointed to the need for a new dance form to be created which his choreographic approach fulfilled. He wanted to mold Soviet ballet using folk material as the basis. Moiseyev acknowledged the use of folk dance in ballet prior to his own ensemble's creation, but felt that the previous approaches to folk material were quite different from his own, because they involved either simple imitation or too much change.[43] As part of justifying Moiseyev's own approach to and use of folk material, he and contemporary historians had to discredit other choreographers who had used folk dance. Thus, Moiseyev and contemporary historians claimed that after 1917, though there *was* an increased interest in using folk material, scholars and artists continued to follow the wrong approach of the past when using folklore in dance. Historian V. N. Vsevolozhsky-Gerngross of the Ethnographic Department in the Russian Museum attempted to collect folk dances and songs in Leningrad between 1929–1933. However, Vsevolozhsky-Gerngross insisted on "keeping to the originals as closely as possible," and employed nonprofessional dancers to perform his findings. This approach disappointed Moiseyev, who felt it did not allow for creativity in ballet choreography and that, while it had to the potential to produce excellent dancers of folk dance, this would not truly represent the "very nature and essence of the folk dance."[44] Audiences would not be as enthusiastic about this more academic—or reconstructionist—approach to folk dance. If Moiseyev or other Soviet artists wanted to increase interest in Soviet dance, they needed to fashion more accessible dances with wider appeal.

In discussing his creative process, Moiseyev used multiple examples to show how his method improved upon past attempts that used folk material. For instance, he noted that for the Moldavian dance *Zhok*, he went to Moldavia and studied the people—their characteristics, their way of life and their dances. The Moiseyev version of *Arkan*, a Gustul folk dance, achieves the goals outlined above: "since it conveys the national atmosphere, the characters and freedom-loving spirit of the mountaineers." And most importantly, beyond demonstrating the success of this process, the real marker of accomplishment was the audience's reaction. When Byelorussians viewed a performance of *Bulba*, they immediately knew the dance it referred to and recognized it as a Belarusian folk dance, even though it had been transformed by Moiseyev's creative process.[45]

Moiseyev continued to speak of the authenticity of his folk dance creations even while supporting the changes he made to the folk dances. An artist who studied the national character of a people and its dance "can and must apply his talent, his creative imagination to accelerate that complex process" of choreographing the dance. The artist's creativity "enriched" the dance. Moiseyev did not label himself (nor was he labeled by others in the Soviet Union) as an ethnographer; he did not think his folk dances should be exact copies of the original dance. The new dance creation needed "living qualities, the expressiveness and the character of an art created by the people and by life." Simply copying the dance, or even inserting folk dance material into classical ballet to try to create something worthwhile, would not achieve the goal of constructing a Soviet cultural product that represented the different nationalities of the Soviet Union.[46] Instead, the folk material foundation needed to take into account the context of the dance and the people who originated it; from there, the choreographer used his imagination to improve the dance and best represent the national character. Moiseyev fully acknowledged that he changed folk dances, but insisted that his changes improved them; "the final result was a choreographic work of art that, without losing its folk character was immeasurably richer, more romantic and uplifted, than the original as it is danced in everyday life."[47]

Just as folk dances reflected national character, so too should the costumes. Again, costume designers did not strive simply to reproduce the form of dress, but took the original source material and elevated it while supposedly maintaining its authenticity and ability to capture the spirit of a national or ethnic group. Once an ethnic or national outfit left "its natural surroundings" for the stage, it had to "be altered, in some cases added to, in others simplified." Costumes also had to take into account the practical needs of the dancers. For example, designers frequently chose lighter fabrics, rather than the original heavy fabrics of the original national costume, to facilitate dancers' movements. In order to ensure visibility of the costumes' characteristics, lighting, staging, and the audience's perspective were taken into account. For example, these considerations often meant the use of embroidery rather than the original use of appliqués. Finally, changes were made to ensure theatricality and visual appeal. The skirts of the "Russian Quadrille," for instance, "were made wider with gathered basques and numerous flounces to give the girls the appearance of flowers."[48] As with the dances themselves, Moiseyev portrayed these changes as enhancing and elevating the dances.

In its performances, the Moiseyev dance company seldom used scenery, but when it did, it was usually a simple backdrop. This again provided a rationale for changing the original outfits for the stage; the costumes had to provide the "decorative background." The result was "so rich in the ethnographic features stressing the character of the dance that absence of décor is in no way a handicap."[49] All together, the dance movements, music, and costumes worked together to present a proper image of the national group on stage. To accomplish this, the choreographer, composer and costume designer worked closely together in the creation of individual dances and programs.

Moiseyev's creative process was not without its critics. In his memoirs, published six decades after the first All-Union Festival of Folk Dance, Moiseyev still felt the need to defend his process against one particular ballet critic, Viktor Eving. Eving published an article in *Soviet Art* that accused the Moiseyev of not knowing folk dance well and of distorting it in creations. Moiseyev quoted his response directly: "One of the most popular dances of the inherent qualities is its vitality, cheerful enthusiasm and humor. Denying these qualities in a Russian dance is tantamount to denying them the character of the Russian people." Moiseyev pointed out that Eving accused the Moiseyev dances of caricature, particularly because of the use of humor. However, Moiseyev claimed that humor, like the other qualities of his version of the dances, once more represented the character and way of life on display. Moiseyev in turn accused Eving of taking far too narrow a view of folk dance.[50] He defended his position as arbiter of his specific new form of Soviet folk dance though certainly seemed aware of how his approach could be viewed critically.

For the most part, Soviet critics embraced Moiseyev's approach and acknowledged that the ensemble's dances represented "artistic invention" rather than ethnographic studies or fantasies. Indeed, the fact that every part of the ensemble's repertoire "bears the hallmark of Moiseyev's creative genius" did not mean any disrespect toward the original folk dances or inauthenticity in Moiseyev's own creations.[51] This lack of criticism for Moiseyev's approach no doubt reflected official policy and the Soviet regime's support of the Moiseyev Dance Company. When speaking about the company, Moiseyev and Soviet critics utilized vocabulary reflecting korenizatsiia or directly quoting the policy. For instance, the flourishing of national dance was a "result of the Lenin-Stalin national policy based on the equality of the peoples making up the Soviet Union, on their close fellowship and collaboration in economic and cultural life," asserted the critic Vladimir Potapov.[52]

Similarly, Natalia Sheremetyevskaya, a former Moiseyev dancer and chronicler of the company's history, emphasized how effectively the Moiseyev embraced the Soviet Union's many nations: "At a concert of the Folk Dance Ensemble of the USSR you sort of travel throughout this multinational country, covering thousands of kilometers from Bashkiria to Moldavia, meeting various national cultures."[53] Clearly Soviet critics and dance constituents reinforced the notion that the Moiseyev Dance Company could present the multiple ethnicities and nationalities within its borders in an accurate and accessible way as part of relaying the Soviet Union's propagandistic message that this multicultural superpower included different groups in a supportive and non-oppressive way.

Indeed, the dance company's endeavors allegedly even spread awareness of dance as an art form. Moiseyev noted the way the nationalities policy and its support of folk dance led to the dissemination of dance among peoples (such as Kazakhs, Kirghiz, and Buryats) who purportedly had not included dance among their cultural expression prior to Soviet rule. It was entirely "Thanks to the Stalinist friendship of the Soviet peoples this change was possible."[54] These kinds of statements omitted the real history of ballet in many cities prior to the establishment of official Soviet theaters in the late 1920s and 1930s and the history of folk dance in Russia generally, which will be addressed further in the following chapter. Instead, these statements reflect the Soviet regime's desire to demonstrate the benefits of the nationalities policy and how it was advancing and enlightening the different national groups living in the Soviet Union. Moiseyev embraced the nationalities policy and used it to suit his needs and to aid his troupe's success, even if this meant ignoring a nation's cultural heritage; garnering official support and ensuring the Moiseyev's survival took priority.

CHAPTER 2

Internal and External Propaganda Tool

> Almost everyone likes to watch folk dancing. It is enjoyed equally by
> the man who spends his life in building machines and the man who
> devotes his time to teaching children. Both the ordinary man and the
> artist find it refreshing. The artist is fascinated by its play of form, its
> wisdom and versatility, and can draw inspiration from it for his own
> work.
>
> —Anna Ilupina and Yelena Lutskaya, *Moiseyev's Dance Company*

Despite multiple Soviet regime changes, the Moiseyev Dance Company
proved able to survive, even beyond the fall of the Soviet Union to today.
The early part of this longevity is in large part due to the Moiseyev's ability
to be considered an answer to the search for a specifically "Soviet" dance
form and Stalin's personal interest in the group. The troupe functioned as a
domestic propaganda tool to demonstrate the appropriate "Soviet" culture
and promote the idea of a unified Soviet Union. Upon realization of the
dancers' popularity, the Soviet regime began to use if more widely as a propaganda tool in satellite nations and, as opportunities for exchange opened
up, abroad.

Igor Moiseyev's personal relationship with Stalin, particularly at the
beginning of the dance company's existence, solidified official recognition of
the group. That being said, in his memoirs (again, to be considered with care
as a source), Moiseyev described interactions with the NKVD in which
he himself feared the worst; that he was to be arrested and possibly sent to the
gulag or executed. This never happened, and although Moiseyev occasionally mentioned in passing in his memoirs the arrest of a colleague, he himself
continued to work with the Soviet regime unscathed. Moiseyev's interactions with the NKVD and other government officials revealed the Soviet
regime's increasing interest in Moiseyev and his work. This interest enabled
him to found the ensemble and survive changes in policy over the decades.

Building a Relationship with the Soviet Government

Moiseyev's relationship with the Soviet government grew and became solidified early on as he worked to create the troupe. In 1937, while still assembling the ensemble, he also organized athletic parades in Red Square. In one of these parades, Moiseyev used performers from Belarus, and the performance went so well that the group received an award. Moiseyev himself, though, did not receive an award. Instead, he was summoned to Lubyanka, the NKVD headquarters. Moiseyev noted, "I did not expect to come back." It turned out the NKVD wanted to present him with the award personally. However, Moiseyev learned he had the recently arrested President of the Committee for Physical Culture of Belarus, Kuznetsov, to thank for it. After being questioned regarding his possible connection with Kuznetsov, Moiseyev was let go. He rejoiced being let off so easily, and noted that afterward, he "vowed" never to get involved with parades again. However, "fate decreed otherwise."[1]

Before the next public parade, Komosol[2] secretary Alexander Kosarev called Moiseyev to ask him to participate once more. Kosarev assuaged Moiseyev's concerns by explaining that Stalin had enjoyed the Byelorussian group's performance so much that he had asked who directed it. Learning this was Moiseyev, he declared: "Let him do it." Moiseyev had to agree, despite his earlier vow, "How could I argue with Stalin?" Moiseyev put together the routine, "If Tomorrow, War," utilizing gymnasts with shields forming human pyramids, displays of representatives for the various military branches, racing motorcycles, and space battle scenes. While the Soviet regime labeled Kosarev an enemy of the people and arrested him, Moiseyev was able to escape the purges occurring around him and in fact grow his recognition and influence.[3]

This does not mean, however, that he did not experience his own moments of doubt about his fate, especially as he became more successful. Moiseyev still experienced the atmosphere of fear the purges engendered. As part of his parade organization duties, Moiseyev wanted to support artists and accordingly carefully selected the performers to appear in the parades. In Kislovodsk, a city in southwestern Russia where he had gone to see a young ensemble, Moiseyev received a telegram from the new Chairman of the Committee on the Arts, Mikhail Borisovich Khrapchenko (the previous chairman had been arrested), summoning him immediately to Moscow.

Moiseyev ignored the summons, sending back a telegram saying he was busy. But upon receiving a second official telegram repeating the summons, Moiseyev got on a train to Moscow.

When the train arrived in Moscow, two KGB officers asked for Moiseyev. The passengers hid, and the soldiers with whom Moiseyev had just been playing whist feigned ignorance of him. The KGB officers took his bags and escorted Moiseyev off the train. Moiseyev assumed he was being arrested. Surprisingly, the KGB officers offered to take Moiseyev home before taking him to his official destination. The officers did not ask his address; they knew it already. When Mrs. Moiseyev opened the door and saw the KGB officers, she paled and Moiseyev recalled trying to reassure her, "But how can you have peace of mind at the sight of security officers in your apartment in 1937?" The KGB officers called headquarters and, after Moiseyev spoke with a "friendly voice" on the other end of the line, was allowed to spend the night. Assuming this was his last night at home before heading to prison, Moiseyev lay awake pondering his fate.[4] The next day, he was brought to Mr. Milstein of the Transportation Department who explained that he had used Khrapchenko's name to get Moiseyev back to Moscow as quickly as possible. After the arrest of NKVD head Nikolai Yezhov, his replacement Lavrentiy Beria had rejected a planned performance for a parade the following month, and Milstein rushed to get Moiseyev to Moscow to help with the last-minute change in plans.

Moiseyev argued he could not prepare something in so little time and felt a performance would surely be a failure. Milstein did his best to be persuasive: "Dear Comrade Moiseyev, if you need one hundred assistants, you will have one hundred assistants. If you ask a hundred thousand dollars, you receive them. But to deny our organization . . ." Moiseyev agreed to think it over for the night, but decided he would not do it. Upon arriving at the Lubyanka prison the following day, however, he entered Milstein's office to find it full of people. Milstein announced "Comrades, I present to you the chief parade society." Each of the men in the crowded room, which included chief of border troops, KGB department heads, and heads of labor communes, came up to Moiseyev and told him how many athletes they could provide for the parade. Moiseyev recognized there was no escape. Milstein ordered everyone present to cooperate with Moiseyev; otherwise they would face "the laws of our secret police discipline."[5] In his recollection of the start of his closer relationship with the Soviet government, Moiseyev continued to point to his lack of enthusiasm and even his fear of personal repercussions. Through the lens of his post-Soviet memoir, it is difficult to say how accurate his representation of his fears and lack of enthusiasm are, but it is helpful in terms of understanding the events which started and then solidified his relationship with the Soviet government which would be so crucial to the continued support of the Moiseyev Dance Company.

Given the time crunch for the parade, Moiseyev arranged only two rehearsals and utilized Milstein's car and personal secretary to deal with the preparations. The government clearly wanted the performance to come off and come off well; Moiseyev recalled that if he needed anything, it "happened as if by magic." Milstein's secretary would trail behind Moiseyev throughout his day, write down everything he said, and act upon his instructions. When Moiseyev noted they needed two thousand pairs of athletic shoes, ten minutes later Milstein's secretary told him they were ordered and would soon arrive. Moiseyev met with Beria, who wanted an update on the preparations. Moiseyev noted the "sharp glance of his eyes hidden behind his glasses with square lenses, and an evil, dark, very tired sallow face." The performance, while it had moments of difficulty, proved a success.[6] Official support for Moiseyev's parade work aided his folk dance initiative and the creation of his ensemble.

As for the success of the folk ensemble itself, in his memoirs Moiseyev linked it directly to Stalin's influence. "We quickly gained recognition and for fifty-eight years did not know failure." In 1938, the ensemble received an invitation to perform at the Kremlin in light of its successful early performances and the fact that it had become a "favorite" of Stalin. At a banquet after a concert, Moiseyev recalled that he suddenly felt a hand on his shoulder and turned to find Stalin beside him. "Well, how are you?" asked Stalin. Moiseyev felt a jolt of excitement from this sudden interest on the part of Uncle Joe. Moiseyev told Stalin he was disheartened, because the ensemble did not have a proper place to rehearse (they used a stairwell). The following day, First Secretary of the Leningrad Regional Party Committee Aleksandr Shcherbakov met with Moiseyev, showed him a map of Moscow, and asked him to choose the ensemble's future headquarters. Eventually, the ensemble found a home at Tchaikovsky Concert Hall.[7]

This favor notwithstanding, in his later memoirs Moiseyev claimed he felt the need to be cautious in his dealings with Stalin. He avoided Stalin's inner circle or kept his distance from the leader. Moiseyev noted: "Stalin did not like people who were smarter than him, and to be smarter than him was not too difficult."[8] Accordingly, he cautiously accepted Stalin's favor (when he offered it) but did not try to take further advantage of it. Moiseyev demonstrated an ability to navigate and negotiate with Soviet officials that would once more support the dance troupe in establishing itself and becoming a government-sponsored propaganda tool with strong backing for decades.

Though the ensemble flourished under Stalin's patronage, Moiseyev criticized the leader later, writing in his post-Soviet memoirs: "I am convinced that Stalin distorted the nature of the Russian people, [making them] dwell forever in mistrust and fear. [Stalin] developed methods of herd mentality [and] general panic." Moiseyev furthermore noted that on tours in the eastern part of the Soviet Union and Siberia, he saw firsthand some of the camps of the gulag and even performed at some.[9] Certainly, Moiseyev did not openly express criticism of Stalin during the latter's lifetime; he allowed Stalin's personal interest to advance the ensemble's goals. It is difficult, given that Moiseyev published his memoirs after the fall of the Soviet Union and long after Stalin's death, how much these anti-Stalinist sentiments reflect Moiseyev's feelings while Stalin still lived. Of course, Moiseyev had to make compromises, even if he did not like Stalin or feel that Stalin was acting appropriately on behalf of the Soviet people. Moiseyev acknowledged Stalin's favoritism and used this to develop his ensemble. This meant cooperating with Stalin's vision of Soviet culture and the Soviet regime's use of the ensemble as propaganda that did not reflect the reality of how the Soviet regime treated nationalities after the shift away from korenizatsiia, with persecution and with placing the Russian ethnicity at the top of the nationalities hierarchy.

The Search for Soviet Dance

Functioning as an answer to what Soviet dance should look like was another factor which permitted the Moiseyev to both survive and thrive. Once the Bolshevik regime was established, artists and officials endeavored to figure out how cultural production should develop to reflect the social and political changes of the 1917 Revolution. In general, the Soviet regime promoted a proletarian culture and attempted to eradicate elements of bourgeoisie cultural expression. This initiative entailed selecting what aspects of folk and popular culture should be used in proletarian arts and which should be rejected. It was perhaps easier to choose what to reject—the elitist culture of the past and its visible icons—rather than to easily label what exactly proletarian culture looked like.[10] Cultural production in the 1920s represented a period of experimentation and one in which modernism and the avant-garde flourished.

However, in the 1930s, the Soviet cultural policy and Soviet cultural production shifted under Stalin. He took a personal hand in guiding the direction of the arts and through his changes, worked to cut off the experimentation of the 1920s in which avant-garde production thrived.[11] In its place, he promoted a view of art that should be more accessible and realist in nature, dubbed "socialist realism." Though more recent scholarship underlines that there was still negotiation with Stalin's cultural ideas and with those who helped promote them, we can speak broadly about socialist realism's call to focus on nationalism, especially nationalism in folk form, and accessibility.[12]

Beginning with the Congress of the Union of Soviet Writers in 1934, Stalin, Maxim Gorky, Nikolai Bukharin, and Andrei Zhdanov identified socialist realism as the best way for cultural expression to reflect the changes in society wrought by the Revolution. The Congress explained that socialist realism "demands from the artist a truthful, historically concrete depiction of reality in its revolutionary development. At the same time, the truthfulness and historical concreteness of the artistic depiction of reality must coexist with the goal of ideological change and education of the workers in the spirit of socialism." Socialist realism, furthermore, meant ridding Soviet art of Western influences and of "formalism," any art that was complex and difficult for the masses to understand.[13]

Defining socialist realism fully and how much it truly impacted artists' creations can prove challenging. In her examination of the process and awardees of Stalin Prizes, Maria Frolova-Walker enhances our understanding of how cultural production under socialist realism did not entail all creative works suddenly adhering strictly to the guidance provided, nor all art growing very similar. Indeed, in looking at the first Stalin Prizes in music in 1940–1941, not all awardees could be easily identified as reflecting the values of socialist realism Stalin put forth, such as Nikolai Myakovsky's *Symphony #21* and Dmitri Shostakovich's *Piano Quintet*. Instead, both with the 1941 awardees and later, variety is present rather than pure adherence to socialist realist principles. The 1948 prizes, during the height of limitations and guid-ance at its strictest, does show a growing trend in "mass and popular songs" complete with a piece specifically devoted to Stalin (Juozas Tallat-Kelpša's *Stalin Cantata*) but Frolova-Walker sees one awardee whose work could be questioned as socialist realist in nature, Kara Karayev's symphonic poem, *Leyli and Majnun*.[14]

Though clearly Stalin gave a strong sense of the kinds of values he felt Soviet artists should use as inspiration, socialist realism was not compre-hensively defined but rather, examples were put forth of what cultural products did or did not adhere to it.[15] Indeed, socialist realism needs to be viewed as an evolving concept, even in the period of the purges with its harsh crackdowns. Katerina Clark complicates the notion that social-ist realism allowed for no real compromise or leeway, specifically through her examination of the works and words of the composer Dmitri Shosta-kovich. Instead, she elucidates the debates around interpretation of social-ist realism. Indeed, Clark argues that even during the purges, members of the intelligentsia still publicly advocated for "a more expansive conception of acceptable artistic production that socialist realist doctrine and practice had as yet afforded."[16] Clark highlights the need to recognize debate and difference in opinion, and to remediate a commonly held view of the initial establishment of socialist realism in the 1930s as a time of strict limitations imposed on artists. Western historians actually overemphasize Soviet con-trol and accordingly fail to recognize the greater nuances of the time period, especially the "extent to which there were still intense debates among Soviet intellectuals about the direction their culture should take (though the parameters of the possible had narrowed)." Clark shows how Shostakovich took part in such debates, even as artists experienced the purges, including artists like Vsevolod Meyerhold.

Though Shostakovich himself would receive public official criticism in the Soviet periodical *Pravda* for his opera *Lady Macbeth of Mtsensk* and his ballet *The Limpid Stream*, he nonetheless saw opportunity to offer his perspective on Soviet art in the form of music.[17] Shostakovich's perceived ability to express his personal views on cultural production can be seen in the 1935 "Discussion about Soviet Symphonism," in which Shostakovich and others expressed different views, with Shostakovich focusing on the emotions and internal life of Soviet people as worth of expression in sym-phonic form.

For dance, the 1920s consisted of the same push for experimentation, such as the dance symphony which endeavored to interweave dance and music further. While at first the regime looked upon this kind of modernism and experimentation in dance with approval for its ability to eradicate symbols of the old Tsarist culture, once the regime became more established there was a shift in the view of dance in Soviet culture. By the late 1920s, the regime, through actions like the 1925 resolution "Concerning the Policy of the Party in the Realm of Literature," noted the need for accessibility in art. This in turn led to a strong emphasis on realism in art in the late 1920s onward.[18] Soviet choreographers had to react to socialist realism and Stalinism in culture in the same way other artists did.

Moscow's Island of Dance Company's trajectory followed the path of Soviet culture on a larger scale. The company's venue, located in Gorky Central Park of Culture and Recreation, opened in 1928 and featured many different kinds of performances. While the Island of Dance, and Gorky Park at large, featured avant-garde performance in the 1920s, this changed with the 1930s and the promulgation of socialist realism. For instance, by the mid-1930s, "all tendencies in dance except classical ballet and folk idioms were 'outside the law.'" Correspondingly, the Island of Dance featured a program of *Dance of the Soviet Peoples* in 1936, in contrast to its earlier use of experimental ballet, the company now focused on the use of folk material and mass dances.[19]

Contemporary historians of the Stalin period claimed ballet was one area in which artists struggled to represent Soviet art, despite the recent ballet past of healthy experimentation and numerous new works being created in the 1920s. Moiseyev recalled that under the Soviet regime and the guidance of the Central Committee, "there was a clear discipline: what was allowed and what is not." This, of course, elides how Soviet artists struggled to conform to the ever-changing nature of socialist realism and approved cultural expression. With the mixed messages of freedom of expression and cultural expression strictures, Soviet choreographers grappled with how to represent contemporary life in the Soviet Union through dance. Moiseyev blamed this obstacle to successful, worthy Soviet ballets on the "specific qualities of ballet art."[20]

Folk dance was a potential answer to the issue of creating specifically "Soviet" ballet, and it furthermore reflected the contemporary nationalities policy. Indeed, Gorky told Soviet writers to look to folklore as inspiration as it would better reflect contemporary life and form the basis of socialist realist expression:

> I again call your attention, comrades, to the fact that folklore, i.e. the unwritten compositions of toiling man, has created the most profound, vivid and artistically perfect types of heroes.[21]

Additionally, since the Soviet Union was a "multi-national state," its culture and therefore Soviet ballet should reflect this. Folk dance once more proved an answer with regard to appropriate depiction and could potentially increase understanding among the Soviet nationalities and aid the development of national cultures.[22]

This support of "folk" as dance source tied into the nationalities debate and the dance troupe could function as a way to support Soviet nationalities policy. For instance, Moiseyev and Soviet writers claimed Moiseyev's work enabled the development of dance in places where folk dance was either little developed or was in danger of being forgotten, such as Belarus and Middle Asia, which reflected Soviet nationalities policy as discussed above.[23] Histories asserted that the folk dances of the Caucasus and Central Asia utilized distinctive steps and roles for female and male dancers because of the region's pre-revolutionary past, during which women living in these areas experienced a "segregated life and enjoyed few rights." This reflection of the past also demonstrated the Soviet Union's positive influence—now women danced with the men just as they now experienced liberation due to Soviet rule. Discussing Soviet ballet, Yury Slonimsky pointed out that before Soviet rule, the Mongols and Kirghiz "had never danced at all owing to their nomadic way of life and to religious taboos."[24] Claiming that groups simply did not experience dance the same way (or at all) before Soviet rule and only now did so fed into the Soviet Union's narrative of being a welcoming system that not only included a variety of ethnic and national groups but also enabled them to develop further.

Even nationalities with a rich dance history did not always preserve their dances as now, condescendingly, the Moiseyev did for them. Soviet histories claimed that Armenians and Georgians, for example, were banned from professional dancing. The Moiseyev now highlighted and performed the dances of these national groups on a professional level. However, with Soviet rule, folk dance troupes and national ballet spread throughout the USSR and often utilized the Moiseyev as a model.[25] Historians claimed that national dances in the Soviet Union held "a place of special eminence" among national cultures—but sometimes needed Soviet help. Soviet choreographers worked to study and revive "long-forgotten" national dances and proved able to successfully "reclaim" them from possible extinction. Because of these endeavors, every republic held dance festivals and created their own dance ensembles, sometimes modeled after the Moiseyev.[26]

According to Moiseyev and the Soviet regime, the 1917 Revolution and Soviet rule developed folk choreography and exposed Soviet peoples to folk dance in a positive and productive way. The Soviet regime claimed it supported folk dance in a way the past imperial Russian rule had not; it gave folk dance a proper role in Soviet society and recognized folk dance as a worthy artistic expression. In its endeavor to develop Soviet art, folk dance benefited and became a more treasured part of Soviet culture. This emphasis on folk dance made sense since the "younger generation of Soviet citizens, belonging to many nationalities, has a passionate and vivid feeling for life and can love and hate; there is no doubt that it can express its dreams and delights, its love and its friendship through the language of the classical dance."[27] The new generation needed an earthy, realistic, new dance form as cultural expression and folk dance was the suitable choice and the Moiseyev provided it.

The Soviet regime's claim to have discovered and developed the role of folklore in truly emotionally expressive dance completely ignored the very real history of folk or national dance in Russian and European ballet established in the nineteenth century during the Romantic period. National dance served as part of a regular performance repertoire and formed major parts of operas and ballets themselves in Europe in the nineteenth century. Indeed, a soloist ballet dancer would also know and perform national dances regularly as part of the known dance repertoire. Artists used folk dance as an important part of the overall work, often in the form of ballet-pantomimes when national dance appeared in narrative ballet. National dance established the context and landscape of a ballet and could highlight the characteristics of a narrative ballet's characters (especially as main characters often represented a certain ethnicity or nationality). On a non-professional level, Europe experienced a "veritable national-dance craze" in the social context in the 1830s and 1840s.[28] Moiseyev (and Soviet histories of the dance troupe) claiming to create something wholly new in his folk dance ballets that stemmed specifically from Soviet identity obscured the folk dance precedents in Russia itself and across Europe.

Indeed, contemporary dance discourse in Tsarist Russia in many ways mirrored Moiseyev's justification of his choreographic approach to folk material. Writers like Carlo Blasis focused on folk dance and encouraged further study of these dances and discussed how artists could create "authentic" dances. In *Dances in General, Ballet Celebrities, and National Dances* (published in Moscow in 1864), he explained how national dance should be performed according to the original folk source:

> the musicians and choreographer must study the vast array of national music and dances and through their work must make visible those mutual relationships that exist between songs and dances.[29]

However, though study was required to best represent national dances, changes were necessary before the dance could be performed to the entertainment public. Thus, despite an expressed desire to be "authentic," choreographers of national dance by no means had to simply recreate the original folk dance on stage. Instead, like Moiseyev, choreographers needed to distill the essential aspects of a national dance and a national character.

Choreographers of the nineteenth century studied national groups as Blasis described above. For instance, Marius Petipa, in choreographing a dance for the opera *Ruslan and Ludmila*, communicated with Caucasian soldiers to learn about their folk dances before attempting to choreograph one himself.[30] Moiseyev and Soviet writers' ideas about national dance and authenticity were not new; Moiseyev did not reinvent dance in the way he claimed but instead drew on the long history of this kind of approach to folk material and its possibilities.

Labeling folk dance as the answer for the development of Soviet ballet also meant tweaking Russian/Soviet dance history to suit. This pattern of molding the Moiseyev's approach as a new, specifically "Soviet" form of dance continued in discussion of more recent dance. Though some modern choreographers like Michel Fokine and Vaslav Nijinksy utilized folk material, Soviet histories claimed that these choreographers focused too much on demonstrating the excellence of skill through performance rather than the process of creating a worthy folk dance. Their corresponding compositions allegedly did not use an effective creative process and did not properly evaluate and use folk source material. These choreographers and others contributed to an atmosphere of liberalism in art, but their artistic products did not succeed in utilizing folk dance in a successful manner. Classical ballet remained "aloof" and apart from folk dance due to a stubborn cling-ing to tradition, especially by theater management.[31]

Moiseyev did, in passing, acknowledge the influence of Fokine and others who came before him, but maintained a claim to originality in his approach to material and to his dance creations. However, Moiseyev neglected or chose to ignore the way he very much imitated the other Russian artists' ideas. Moiseyev's conception of a total work of art that carefully considered all aspects of performance to create an organic final product was nothing new; for instance, *Ballets Russes* founder Sergei Diaghilev was noted for guiding modern ballet to create a piece that was a "fusion of art, music, and dance."[32] Moiseyev claimed Fokine focused too much on dance steps and precise execution but this completely disregards Fokine's actual goals in his works. Fokine endeavored to make reforms in classical ballet (in the same way Moiseyev claimed to) and was a "champion of expressivity over pure dance."[33] Like Moiseyev, Fokine found this expressiveness in national dance. Indeed, Moiseyev's claims for his creative process ignored the fact that Moiseyev continued an established tradition of the use of national dance and the notion of national dance's expressiveness dating from the nineteenth century. This, once more, largely ignored the rich history of folklore as inspiration for Russian cultural expression.

Moiseyev's use of folk dance conveniently combined the nationalities pol-icy with socialist realism to produce a dance form that broke with Russian ballet tradition and could be described as representing contemporary Soviet life. With Moiseyev's insistence on a creatively new approach to ballet, his work represented headway in the development of Soviet art for ballet. The Moiseyev Dance Company claimed it successfully incorporated emotional expression into dance to replace the aloofness of Russian classical ballet and expanded the "language" of dance to better depict contemporary life and the changes Soviet rule wrought. While Moiseyev did not try to move entirely away from classical ballet, he recognized that art had to change as life changed. Only Moiseyev was able to "find the essential, the most vivid choreographic means and images to express the national character, the emotions and thoughts of a given nationality, and then to remould these means to attain an even greater expressiveness."[34] According to Moiseyev and his contemporaries, the State Academic Folk Dance Ensemble of the USSR represented the solution to the problem of Soviet ballet through the culmination of post-Soviet dance experimentation and previous dance traditions. As with the other elements of the mythologized founding of the dance company, Moiseyev and others carefully crafted the message of the Moiseyev's ability to answer the question of Soviet dance to allow for the troupe's continued success and government sponsorship.

Early Recognition of the Moiseyev and Tours of the USSR

The popularity in its reception lent further support to the deftly established narrative of the Moiseyev as "Soviet" dance. After "winning the hearts" of the Moscow public, the company began to tour domestically. The first stop was Leningrad, the cradle of the 1917 Revolution and a city whose population was known for its artistic taste. The Moiseyev passed the test of Leningrad "with flying colours. The house shook with applause and demands for encores. Newspaper reviewers said the company was responsible for the rebirth of folk art and hailed it as a great popularizer of that art." The continued positive reception played into the Soviet narrative and the Moiseyev's touring expanded beyond major Soviet cities. The Moiseyev encountered diverse audiences and venues on its tours, performing in factories and even outdoors for workers, farmers, medical professionals, and scientists. Staying close to the people was very important for the Moiseyev, given the source of his dance material; the dancers performed not just in large cities like Moscow and Leningrad, but also smaller cities and towns near Moscow and in the Urals.[35]

In the summer of 1938, the Moiseyev traveled to Ukraine and once more met with uproarious success. The company's tours "enabled it to keep in close touch with the tastes and desires of the ordinary people." The Moiseyev went to cities like Lvov in Ukraine and Tashkent in Uzbekistan, as well as visiting Tajikistan and Latvia, all with similar results; the press noted the success of the Moiseyev and its appeal to Soviet audiences across territories, republics, and Soviet-influenced nations. *Soviet Lithuania* touted that "the great idea of friendship among all Soviet nationalities has found artistic embodiment in the work of the company." From 1937–1940, the Moiseyev gave six hundred performances in thirty-five Soviet towns. Beyond seeing national groups in their local habitats, the Moiseyev endeavored to meet with the local dancers and dance groups as part of continuing to expand the troupe's repertoire. The meetings "proved of mutual benefit. The Moiseyev dancers broadened their knowledge of local dancing traditions while local dancers were able to see how great professional mastery and a serious approach to folk art had transformed their dances."[36] The success of the dance troupe and its propagandistic message once more guaranteed its continued government support and positive view of this valuable tool.

The Test of World War II

In his memoirs, Moiseyev recalled the suddenness of the Second World War, and the atmosphere of "vigilance, vigilance, vigilance. Endless arrests, trains with prisoners." Reinforcing its role as propagandistic tool, during the war the ensemble performed throughout the Soviet Union in order to raise morale amongst troops and civilians. They visited hospitals in the Urals and Siberia, as well as spending over four months with the Pacific Fleet.[37]

When asked later which tour left the greatest impression on him, veteran Moiseyev dancer Mikhail Tarasov spoke of the wartime tour circuit. He noted that the Soviet regime wanted to continue the ensemble's performances "at all costs." The ensemble traveled for eighteen months straight; the dancers grew closer as a result, but the touring was not easy. Though favored by the Soviet regime, during the war the dancers did not always have enough to eat. They had to wash and look after their costumes and transport all their supplies. These difficulties paled in comparison with the knowledge that almost everyone knew someone fighting at the front. Even as dancers heard of the death of a loved one, the show had to go on: "One of the dancers would get news that her husband, father or brother had been killed, and though her heart was breaking she'd do her dance just the same. . . . I'd think she'll never be able to dance. But dance she would, gulping down her tears, and she'd smile too."[38]

The Moiseyev dancers shared this resolve with their audiences; workers who were exhausted and who lacked proper clothing and nourishment "shivered but smiled. They enjoyed our dancing." Tarasov and the other dancers felt they helped soldiers, workers and ordinary people cope:

> I understood then how important it is sometimes to give a person a moment of enjoyment, a breathing spell. We knew, of course, that they were hungry and cold, and that they worked terribly long hours for the

front, for the people. They were an example to us, and we tried very hard to be worthy of them.[39]

Tarasov's reminisces underscore how Moiseyev and the dance company cultivated a role as an effective propaganda tool that could reach people even in the most challenging times.

Despite the circumstances, the ensemble celebrated its thousandth performance and fifth anniversary during the war. By this time the ensemble had increased and diversified its repertoire while maintaining close contact with the life of the different Soviet peoples, which was important to the ensemble's goal of representing "Soviet" art.[40] Igor Moiseyev solidified the ensemble's continued existence with the creation of a school for folk dance, which welcomed students from all over the Soviet Union: "These young dancers have learned to bring with them onto the stage the national atmosphere from which their dance originated."[41] The choice of words emphasized how the dance company presented a positive multicultural image of the Soviet Union which would could be effectively disseminated domestically and abroad.

Travel to Eastern Bloc Countries and Beyond

As in the United States, the Soviet Union had a longer history of cultural diplomacy and exchange. In the 1920s, the Soviet Union began to send artists abroad and multiple corresponding support organization existed it the government, including the State Committee for Cultural Ties (GKSS) and the Ministry of Culture and its later division, Goskontsert (founded in 1956).[42] After World War II, Soviet endeavors continued with the goal of showing the world Soviet cultural products which they claimed were democratized and more accessible to an international audience. Cultural representatives like the Moiseyev Dance Company traveled internally within the large Soviet empire and externally to Eastern Bloc countries and across multiple continents.[43]

Accordingly, during, and especially after, World War II, the Moiseyev traveled farther afield. The ensemble traveled to cities like Kiev, Odessa, Kemerovo, and Sverdlosk within the Soviet Union, where they met with ovations; their popularity and message clearly appealed, and the Soviet government correspondingly expanded the geographic reach of the troupe. In 1942, the ensemble traveled to the Mongolian People's Republic and gave seventy-eight performances to enthralled audiences, "to people who live amidst scenery which has retained a strange primordial fascination, who cherish dearly the legends of their ancestors." The 1945–1946 tours to Finland, Romania, Bulgaria, Czechoslovakia, Hungary, Austria, and Yugoslavia also proved very successful. In Romania, the ensemble gave twenty-seven performances to over 33,000 people and in Budapest in Hungary, one concert alone had an audience of 100,000. In Czechoslovakia, "The Soviet dancers gladly responded to the eager demands for encores, performances often lasting three and a half hours instead of the prescribed two or two and a half. The audiences were so delighted that there would be as many as eighteen or twenty curtain calls."[44] The evidence of the efficacy of the dance troupe in reaching diverse audiences and conveying its propagandistic message was clear, or certainly was in Soviet coverage of it, and Igor Moiseyev looked to continue to build on that message with each country they visited.

As they toured more and more abroad, the ensemble began to incorporate the dances of the countries visited into the repertoire. For instance, during the company's tour of Romania, the dancers undertook a close study of the Romanian people, their traditions and their art. The dancers went to performances of Romanian groups, listened to their music and watched their dances. In Hungary, they learned new dances directly from Hungarian dancers and achieved cultural exchange between the Soviet Union and Hungary.[45] This practice of adding more dances from places visited would align perfectly with the future Soviet cultural exchange policy which stated that the Soviet Union pursued cultural exchange in part due to a desire and ability to learn from other nations as a result.

By 1959, the Moiseyev's twenty-second year of existence, it had visited over four hundred Soviet towns and covered more than 160,000 kilometers in territory. Touring increased the company's international renown and "not only broadened their knowledge of the world but has deepened their understanding of art."[46] Though Stalin changed his mind about the policy of korenizatsiia (and about his support of nationalities on a more general level) in the latter half of the 1930s, the company successfully weathered the shift in policy.

Other Examples of Folk Dance Ensembles

The Moiseyev was by no means the only folk dance ensemble in the Soviet Union or the only one to visit the United States. For instance, Nikolai

Bolotov and Pavel Virsky founded the Ukrainian Folk Dance Company in 1936–1937, in the same time period as the Moiseyev, and similarly enjoyed official recognition and the position as a tool of cultural diplomacy.[47] The troupe came to the United States multiple times, in 1962, 1966, and 1972 with Sol Hurok serving as impresario.[48] The troupe made its American premiere in April of 1962, and, like the Moiseyev, toured across the country to great acclaim. The American audience enjoyed the performances so much that critic John Martin of the *New York Times* wrote "If Mr. Virsky is aiming at recruiting not only tourists but even settlers for the Ukraine, it must be noted that he is a first-rate propagandist."[49]

However, the Ukrainian Folk Dance Company never achieved the same renown and popularity as the Moiseyev did.[50] Even though their visits to the United States were successful, they were viewed with the Moiseyev in mind and the previous experience of the Moiseyev colored American reception of the Ukrainian troupe. Critics explained to Americans that the dancers performed in "the tradition of the Moiseyev company"[51] and "the [Ukrainian] company routines may be compared to the Moiseyev Company from Moscow that caused a sensation in their tour of America several years ago."[52] American audiences would be "familiar" with the Ukrainian company's style of performance because of the earlier Moiseyev experience and indeed, the company was "unequalled except by their spiritual cousins, the Moiseyev dancers." When interviewed by American reporters, like Moiseyev, Virsky tied creation and success of dance group to Revolution and Soviet regime. In his discussion, he noted, "You see, I am doing publicity for Moiseyev!"[53] Even given the familiarity Americans achieved with the Moiseyev, unlike their response to the Ukrainian Folk Dance Company, they continued to impress and wow its American audience through multiple tours across the remaining decades of the Cold War.

The Moiseyev furthermore served as a model for other Soviet national groups' own state folk dance ensembles and as a model for other state and private folk dance ensembles internationally. According to Anthony Shay, as the Moiseyev began to tour more extensively beginning in the 1950s, waves of the creation of similar groups can be identified. In particular, countries influenced by the Soviet Union during the Cold War demonstrated just how popular the Moiseyev was; for instance, by the 1980s seventeen folk ensembles had formed in Bulgaria. The waves of folk dance ensembles began in Eastern European nations in the early 1950s; with the second wave in the later part of the 1950s in other areas, like the Philippines and Mexico; and a final wave of the establishment of ensembles in the 1960s and 1970s in, for instance, Turkey and Iran. Additionally, private folk dance ensembles formed in multiple countries during this time period as well. The United States, which did not have a state sponsored folk dance ensemble, witnessed the creation of private companies instead.[54] The formation of these kinds of ensembles served as one further way the Cold War was "fought" and the Soviet Union felt it could claim victory in states which adopted the Soviet approach to folk dance.

As with the Moiseyev, the issue of authenticity became part of folk dance ensembles' rhetoric. Often these ensembles (including the Moiseyev, as discussed above) claimed to perform "authentic" dances but this did not reflect the reality of how choreographers created their repertoire. Labeling these as authentic dances that drew from contemporary ideas and sources ignored the dances' clear use of the established tradition of character or national dance. Furthermore, choreographers modified dances in many ways in order to theatricalize them and make them suitable to the audience. Many of the modifications were made with commercial and critical success in mind; even the use of a suite of dances reflected this goal: "In this manner, the choreographer can string together, with artful transitions, a series of simple dances that would be theatrically uninteresting if used alone."[55] The changes were not framed as problematic but rather reflecting Moiseyev's overall approach to folk dance choreography discussed above; that he was able to elevate folk dance while remaining authentic to the source and to representing Soviet dance.

In his discussion of state folk dance ensembles, Shay underscores the political nature of the use of folk dance. Part of forming an ensemble's repertoire involved the claims that nations and cultures were discrete; they were easily identified and dances and dance steps representative of a nation's specific character could be easily identified and culled for use in the ensemble. This furthered the idea that "these dances originate in some primordial source of the nation's purest values and that folk dances, music and costumes are timeliness and date from some prehistoric period." Such a notion already divorced the dances from the reality of a national group and its culture and aestheticized politics. Because the dances endeavored to represent the nonpolitical by the use of a "timeless" art form and apolitical plot elements, such as a peasant boy farming or a peasant couple falling in love in a very non-sensual manner, the dances "actually achieve the highly political choice of depicting and representing the nation, in its essentialist entirety, in this 'non-political,' 'innocent' cultural fashion."[56]

For the Moiseyev the ability to represent nations in this manner served very practical purposes for the Soviet regime as propaganda demonstrating the alleged celebration and support of national groups living in the Soviet Union. Shay similarly notes the contrast in dance depiction versus reality with the Ballet Folklorico de Bellas Artes from Mexico when it visited the United States in the late 1990s. The dancers performed with a similar enthusiasm and spirit to the Moiseyev yet this "gave no hint of the harsh reality of insurrection" in areas of Mexico occurring at that time.[57]

Soviet Cultural Exchange

Before the Lacy-Zarubin Agreement and even before the start of the Cold War, the Soviet Union had a history of using cultural diplomacy to further its own ends. Soviet cultural diplomacy efforts can be traced to the 1920s, with the broad goal of putting a successful, ascending Soviet system on display. As Kiril Tomoff argues, the Soviet Union can in face be viewed as a cultural empire even before the advent of the Cold War and increased commitment to cultural diplomacy. After World War I, Soviet artists worked to make art accessible, drawing on older cultural precedents familiar to Western audiences paired with socialist realism in a kind of "democratized cultural fusion." The Soviets felt the resulting cultural products struck the right balance of refinement and accessibility, avoiding the pitfalls of commercialized mass culture like Hollywood films, on the one hand, and the esoteric nature of high modernism, like musical serialism, on the other.[58]

After World War II, Soviet cultural diplomacy efforts first focused on adjacent or nearby countries, many of which would become directly or indirectly controlled by Moscow in the post–World War II era. These included countries like Poland, Hungary, and Finland—nations which the Soviet Union wanted to ensure it was on friendly terms, broadly speaking, and able to influence. Like the United States, the USSR selected who would be sent abroad with great care and attention. For instance, to be selected to tour Western democracies entailed vetting of artistic success and political adherence on previous tours.[59]

The Soviet Union utilized both cultural diplomacy and their coverage of it to support its larger international political aims broadly and to directly impact specific, more discrete, political events and opportunities. Simo Mikkonen examines how the Soviet Union used cultural diplomacy to influence elections in Finland after World War II. Mikkonen traces the ebbs and flows of Soviet cultural tours to Finland to find a pattern; before elections (from the local up to the presidential level), the USSR would send dance or other groups to Finland.[60]

Indeed, the Moiseyev toured Finland in 1945 as part of the Soviet endeavor to influence the Finnish people, as well as the larger goal of supporting a positive image of the Soviet Union abroad, both through the demonstration of a vibrant culture and the act of sending this "friendly" gift to other nations. These tours served other goals as well, for instance, the cultural diplomats could gather information about the places they toured. In Finland specifically, the Soviet Union worked to influence and engage the Finnish "cultural elite" with the aim of impressing on them the superiority of the Soviet political system as symbolized by its cultural output.[61]

The Soviet rationale for participating in cultural diplomacy included the foundational belief in the Soviet system as successful and unparalleled. They felt that in any direct cultural clashes with their American enemy, the Soviet Union was the victor, proving the efficacy and rationalization for continuing support of cultural endeavors. The positive Western press reaction to Soviet artists "presented an image of Soviet cultural development, even sophistication, to the rest of the world, scoring propaganda victories for the Soviet system."[62] A further reason to support cultural diplomacy was financial; record deals with and commissions from foreign nations and companies afforded the Soviet Union further financial recognition and legitimacy.[63] At the same time, the Soviet's robust support may have actually contributed to the eventual breakdown of the Soviet system by forcing the USSR and its artists to participate in the US–dominated global financial and cultural media systems.[64]

Even with these multiple reasons and rationales for Soviet support of cultural exchange, there is still the question of why ballet as one of the cultural representatives sent, despite the comparable larger amount of logistical challenges and financial cost. The USSR "wanted to renew their cultural image abroad" and ballet showed continuity with Tsarist Russian culture and the refinement of the Soviet Union. Using the dancers could enhance the Soviet Union's cultural reputation and corresponding view of the Soviet system.[65]

The repertoire of Soviet musical artists in their early post–World War II tours demonstrate the USSR's goals for cultural diplomacy. These repertoires included: Western classical works and Russian classical works, both of which could be easily recognized, and new works by Soviet composers. The familiar classics gave legitimacy and recognition to the virtuosity of Soviet artists and enabled them to directly complete and/or be compared to their non-Soviet counterparts in terms of the virtuosity of their performances. And the new Soviet works were a way of showing the vibrancy of Soviet culture through the ability to create art that could be appreciated across the globe, art which was neither unrefined mass culture products like Western pop music nor the esoteric modernism of the Twelve-Tone System. Rather, Soviet works were to be understood as "models that best bridged the gap between the shared classical heritage and a healthy modern culture."[66]

The Moiseyev after the Death of Stalin

After World War II, the ensemble continued to grow in renown and solidified its position as a Soviet program. With Stalin's death in 1953, the company lost his personal support, but the Moiseyev continued to thrive. Multiple factors aided the ensemble's survival. The increased interest in cultural exchange generally encouraged the Soviet regime to continue official support of the ensemble. Indeed, after Stalin's death, the USSR "revised and upgraded its cultural diplomacy machinery in order to conduct an outreach campaign on a truly global scale."[67] Even with the fading of socialist realism after Stalin's death, culture and its role as educator remained.[68]

The Soviet regime considered the ensemble an important political tool as it embraced cultural products as an effective way to present a positive image of the Soviet Union; they did not need translators and moved among nations more easily than diplomats. Folk dancing, in particular, demonstrated this facility in travel among foreign peoples of varying backgrounds; "It is enjoyed equally by the man who spends his life in building machines and the man who devotes his time to teaching children."[69]

The Moiseyev and the way the Soviet regime utilized the ensemble reflected current events. The tours to Eastern Bloc countries were formed as part of the June 1945 program "'The Dances of the Slavic Peoples,'" which the Soviet regime aimed at newly communist countries. The regime created the program as part of an endeavor in which it "extended a hand of friendship . . . to the countries that had joined the socialist camp." The Soviet-published (and thus very enthusiastic) coverage of the ensembles efforts claimed that the troupe was highly successful in this effort, relaying how allegedly everywhere the ensemble traveled in Eastern Europe, it was "welcomed with joyous smiles, open hearts and the warmest handshakes. Our dances were heaped with praises." Again, such coverage clearly had political aims behind it; this success was tied to the Soviet Union's political and military actions: "People thanked us for their liberation from fascism. Many who surrounded us had tears in their eyes."[70] The depiction of the Moiseyev Dance Company picking up where World War II left off shows how the Soviet strategy shifted to support cultural exchange endeavors post–World War II in its continued efforts to maintain and grow power in Eastern Europe and that the government chose the dance troupe as an effective way to support this strategy.

Moiseyev acknowledged the role the ensemble played as a diplomatic tool and embraced it. In an interview, he proclaimed, "I'll tell you what means more to me than all the critics' and other experts' passionate declarations of love for the Company. It's hearing someone in a foreign audience say something like this: 'I think I really know now what Soviet people are. As I watched the dancing I realized that they are a kind, strong and courageous people, with a fine sense of humour and great generosity in everything they do.'" Moiseyev claimed he had heard this kind of comment from multiple people in multiple countries, which led him to believe the work he had done in forming the group—and its continuous development—was worthwhile.[71]

In 1954, the ensemble visited mainland China, albeit with trepidation. Given China's wealth of cultural history, the ensemble was unsure if the Chinese would find the ensemble's performances entertaining. However, Chinese audiences received the Moiseyev with "great elation."[72] Indeed, the dancers discussed the choreography and dance aspects on "equal footing" with Chinese dancers and choreographers. Observers emphasized the equal prowess of the two cultures, Soviet and Chinese, in this moment of exchange. As with every new national encounter, in order to support a view of communism as a productive system, the Soviet coverage emphasized how the dancers competed with local culture and usually became seen as equals or as superior.

The Moiseyev exchanged not only friendship with the Chinese people but knowledge of their dance and culture, the "the rich, vivid and unique art of China, which inspires the people of that great country who are building a new socialist world." The ensemble felt certain the Chinese would utilize art much as the Soviet Union had in the development of a new communist society.[73] The visit to China became an opportunity to underscore a message of fruitful artistic and cultural development under communism with the Moiseyev Dance Company as a prime example of that development.

Similarly, on their tour of Egypt in 1957, Moiseyev noted that the Egyptians eagerly welcomed the ensemble's tour and that it would help cement friendship between the two nations. The dancers learned how earnest the Egyptians were to maintain a positive relationship with the Soviet Union on both the political and cultural level.

Despite the uproarious successes in Egypt and elsewhere, in certain places the reception was not wholeheartedly positive, usually because of political issues. In Greece, people formed long queues for tickets in anticipation of the Moiseyev's performances. Some members of the Greek press criticized the Moiseyev as pure propaganda. However, "The attacks leveled by some hostile newspapers were not able to damp the high spirits of the dancers as a result of their great successes and of their acquaintance with the beauties that Greece had to offer." The newspaper *Efnos*, criticized "spectators up in the gallery [who] were 'full of enthusiasms for the Soviet Union.'"[74] With its numerous tours across the world, the Moiseyev became an international phenomenon and an "envoy of peace and friendship."[75] In total, between 1945 and 1960 the ensemble toured thirty-three countries on four continents. Everywhere the company visited, it met with an overwhelmingly positive reaction and exchanged both goodwill and dances. The ensemble subsequently added dances to its repertoire from many countries, including China, Germany, and Mexico to show how the exchange was not one-way or Soviet dominated.[76]

Travel to Western Europe

The Moiseyev's use as a diplomatic tool increased as Western Europe and countries with democratic regimes opened up to cultural exchange with the Soviet Union in the 1950s. In 1955, the Moiseyev toured both France and England and contemporary Soviet writers enthusiastically responded by describing how the Moiseyev dancers conquered the West. In France, the French audience in particular already knew of the excellence of Russian ballet. Even so, by the time of the Moiseyev's tour in 1955, it had been almost fifty years since a Russian ballet troupe visited, and the French audience had never viewed Soviet ballet. Despite the potential obstacles—particularly because of political events in Vietnam and Algeria which may have tainted the French audience's perspective—the performances were a "triumph." This kind of success in Paris, as an international center of culture, meant international recognition of the Moiseyev as a prestigious, noteworthy group. Even prior to arriving, the tickets to performances almost completely sold out. This was especially consequential, as "Paris was a city with no less than 50 theatres and 300 cinemas where the appearance of world-famous artists was quite a commonplace." The local newspaper *France Soir* noted that "when three million francs worth of tickets had been sold for a play at the Madeleine Theatre before the première, this had been considered a fantastic figure. Yet before the Moiseyev company's first performances sales had run to 25 million francs."[77] The French people were clearly eager to see the dance troupe and no doubt Soviet authorities relished how their cultural representatives garnered such enthusiastic interest.

While some among the French audience may have had their doubts about the Moiseyev because of its communist origins, "Prejudices and doubts entertained in regard to Soviet art were dispelled soon after the curtain rose on the opening performance held in Paris on October 3, 1955." The dancers won over the French audience, and even the French press had to pay the ensemble "ungrudging tribute." Given the strong historical French ballet tradition, this tribute is emphasized by Soviet coverage, feeding into the Soviet narrative of cultural development and superiority over its American and other Cold War enemies. Additionally, the dancers traveled around Paris seeing the sights and spoke with everyday Frenchmen, which once more contributed to both the cultural and political aspects of the Moiseyev's victorious tour in France. A radical deputy in the French Parliament, M. Forcinal, "said that the company had conquered the French capital and by so doing had sown fresh seeds of friendship between the French and Russian peoples."[78] The impact on individual people is given heavy emphasis in Soviet coverage, as it would be in the American tour by both Soviet and American press.

In Britain, though the Moiseyev wondered if the dourer British audience would receive the Moiseyev with similar enthusiasm, the performances were again an unmitigated success: "Unrestrained enthusiasm had seemed natural from the impulsive and exuberant French, but from the English it came as a surprise to the Soviet dancers." Once more, according to Soviet writers the performance was not simply an artistic victory but a political one too in the form of impact on British individuals. The dancers received many letters during their tour from everyday British people. These letters expressed adulation for the performances but also the "British people's longing for friendship with the Soviet Union." For instance, one British mother of five wrote about how she hoped the Moiseyev's tour and the success it achieved would lead toward greater friendship and understanding between the Soviet and British people.[79]

After World War II and more so after the death of Stalin, the Moiseyev became an external propaganda tool as part of Soviet cultural diplomacy. The ensemble's performances reflected a positive image of the Soviet Union and of a peaceful, happy existence for the different peoples living within it. Additionally, Igor Moiseyev and the Soviet regime emphasized how the ensemble not only wanted to perform for international audiences, but also to learn from them. Given the Moiseyev's domestic and international popularity and its carefully coded multicultural message, it proved a perfect selection as the first cultural representation sent to the United States after the signing of the Lacy-Zarubin Agreement for cultural exchange in 1958.

PART
TWO

PART
TWO

CHAPTER 3

Paving the Way for the 1958 Tour

So completely en rapport were dancers and audience at the end of the evening that when the Russians stood smiling and waving, Americans stood up—smiling—and waved back. . . . For two-and-a-half hours last night at Masonic Auditorium, the Iron Curtain melted away, and people on both sides—discovered again that humanity—like music and dancing—transcends geographical borders, outlasts political change, and above all—loves itself.

—Dick Osgood (DJ), "Show World" on *WXYZ Radio*, May 1958

The Moiseyev garnered incredibly positive feedback from its American audience, to the point where "the Iron Curtain melted away" and Soviet and American people could relate to each other in their universal humanity. This opportunity to see and, for some Americans, even directly interact with their Cold War enemy underlines how the Cold War was a lived experience by individuals. Americans felt the Moiseyev tour revealed Soviet citizens to be likeable, genuine people who were similar to Americans; Americans saw their Cold War enemy as human. This empathy on the part of Americans complicated the Cold War narrative of incompatibility but also glossed over the troupe's purpose as a Soviet propagandistic tool, showing multicultural solidarity in a nation that in reality targeted its own people.

While the troupe was not tailor-made for an American audience, its dances' focus on heteronormative relationships and idealized view of multiple ethnicities and nationalities living together offered a visually engaging escape to contrast with the reality of gender and race issues in post–World War II America. The dances and dancers comforted Americans and assuaged anxiety. In this chapter, the focus in on the initial events and anticipation leading up to the Moiseyev Dance Company's 1958 tour as well as the ways reception to the tour can be gauged.

Gauging American Reception

Given the enormous amount of press coverage and political concern regarding the Moiseyev Dance Company's tour, its every move and the audience's subsequent reaction became amplified. Americans of 1958 attached significance to all aspects of the dancers' visit, providing an opportunity to examine the critical, political, and personal responses to this Cold War event. In order to draw out the nuances of American opinion of cultural exchange and its impact on Cold War political relations, this middle set of chapters will examine the initial reception in 1958 in detail. While responses certainly exhibit variety, viewed as a whole, Americans lauded and celebrated the Moiseyev dancers and their performances and, correspondingly, the American embrace of the Moiseyev dancers demonstrates several important aspects of the American Cold War experience.

First, this conflict was not just black and white, democracy versus communism, American versus Soviet.[1] The American reaction to the Moiseyev complicates a Cold War narrative emphasizing differences between the American and Soviet ways of life and ideology. The intense response American had to the dancers highlights the power of culture in this moment and in this conflict: most commentators observed that the Moiseyev Dance Company proved able to change Americans' opinions.

Additionally, the admiration expressed for the Soviet people is striking. The visit provided an opportunity for Americans to see Soviets "in the flesh," articulating the differences between the two nations' cultures as played out onstage and off. Americans expressed a fascination with the abilities of the Soviet dancers and a desire to learn more about them as people. For many Americans, the tour defused the characterization of the Soviets as enemies, as can be seen in the below description and analysis of press coverage and Americans' personal notes and writing. Indeed, Americans saw in the Soviet dancers people who were not so unlike themselves, despite their political, ideological, and cultural differences.

The impact of the Moiseyev provides a window into how Americans felt about their own identity and culture, especially as compared to their Soviet counterparts, and their views of the Cold War and its imprint on American life. While this chapter outlines the theoretical and contextual factors impacting the tours' reception, chapters 4 and 5 do the work of categorizing responses to provide evidence of the nuances of this overwhelmingly positive reception. Here, the buildup and the moment of the Moiseyev's American premiere is the focus while the following chapters demonstrate how this moment functioned as an important juncture of political, racial, and gender issues in America.

In assessing American reception of the Moiseyev, multiple aspects of the performances are taken into account in order to understand as fully as possible the American experience of this moment of cultural exchange in the Cold War and what meaning Americans drew from viewing the Moiseyev. Identifying, much less attaching specific meaning, to markers of reception like applause, coughing, or silence, can be uncertain and problematic. It is helpful to consider how the spectator experience is made up of both intellectual and emotional reactions to a performance. Scholars Jacqueline Martin and Willmar Sauter assert that understanding audience reception must take four aspects of performances into account: what are the important elements of the performance (such as the movements and plot) which the audience takes note of, how are these elements interpreted differently by different audience members, what emotions does the audience experience, how does the audience evaluate the performance, and finally, to recognize that the audience's experience begins prior to the performance in the form of preconceived notions that influence reception.[2] In analyzing reception of the Moiseyev Dance Company on its 1958 tour, the latter two aspects are of particular interest and in this chapter. Accordingly, below is an examination of how reception began prior to the performance itself in terms of the Cold War context and the initiation of official cultural exchange through the Lacy-Zarubin Agreement.

The audience can affect performance and reception but also, through the performance experience, the audience can learn something about "their own emotive lives." In personal notes written in response to seeing the Moiseyev, as will be explored later on, Americans articulated the personal and emotional reaction to and connection with the dancers they felt after viewing a performance. An audience's idea of culture and what it means to go to performances forms part of reception as well.[3] In the case of the 1958 tour and the Moiseyev tours after that, dance took on an enhanced role as a Cold War weapon and the American audience would have recognized the corresponding propaganda role the Moiseyev performers took on. What is striking is the efficacy of the troupe's message and Americans' positive response in spite of the overtly propagandistic nature of the tour.

The Moiseyev reached many Americans through press coverage, adver-tisements, and the personal experience of seeing the company perform. Their tour was highly publicized and was widely discussed before, dur-ing, and afterward. Keeping in mind that reception theory can have its difficulties, reaction to the Moiseyev Company is gauged based on several factors. First of all, critical reception is taken into account. Several types of critics, including theater, dance, and music critics—even radio DJs—attended Moiseyev performances and published their evaluations in local and national newspapers. Their reactions to the Moiseyev's performances and the terms they used to describe the dancers are highlighted, revealing how intellectuals and prominent members of the American arts commu-nity perceived the Moiseyev, both politically and artistically. Reception is also gauged through attendees' interest or lack of interest as determined by reports of individuals' reactions to the Moiseyev, anecdotes, and ticket sales. The emotions the American audience expressed and how they evalu-ated the Moiseyev's success also form a vital part of reception. The above aspects of reception also can be used to determine what the American audi-ence learned about itself as a result of the Moiseyev tours and the mean-ing Americans attached to the performances. Finally, reception is gauged by looking at the US government's reports on the success of the Moiseyev tour, by examining Igor Moiseyev's accounts of the tour, and by analyzing reports to assess whether the tours were successful in disseminating a pos-itive image of the Soviet Union.

American Experience of Ballet

One factor that certainly influenced American reception to the Moiseyev was the American understanding of and experience with ballet. Ballet's presence in American culture can be traced to the founding of the United States itself, starting primarily with French dancers and teachers.[4] George Washington "cultivated social and theatrical dance as part of the civilizing process of the young republic" with the help of cultural figures like ballet master Pierre Landrin Duport.[5] Ballet performances grew into the nine-teenth century, though ballet usually would be seen as part of a program of other dance forms or kinds of performance rather than as part of a program solely devoted to ballet. *The Black Crook*'s wild success as not only arguable America's first musical but a widespread opportunity for Americans to see ballet on stage, spurred revivals and further ballet interest. American initial preference for and deference to European ballet dancers reflected how ballet became enshrined by the American middle class as high culture. Accordingly, though the 1893 Chicago's World Fair included a ballet featuring the Statue of Liberty, the latter nineteenth century marked ballet moving into more elite performance venues and an increasing separation between more popular art forms and ballet.

Indeed, the 1909 founding of the Metropolitan Opera Ballet School reflected this trend by tying ballet to opera as both high culture art forms. Though American ballet schools and companies were slow to get started in general, European touring ballet dancers did increase American exposure to and awareness of ballet. Russian touring companies in particular made their mark, sending so many dancers to the United States between 1911 and 1913 that domestic performances in Russia were impacted by short staffing. Anna Pavlova became the image of ballet for many Americans and toured across the country, again increasing exposure.

In the 1920s with both the founding of dedicated periodicals like *American Dancer* and newspapers in areas like New York hiring dance writers, Americans could learn more about dance, including ballet. Russian or Russian-influenced ballet continued to find an eager audience in the United States, including Michel Fokine's ballets and Sergei Diaghilev's *Ballets Russes* and its offshoots. Both the founding of the new ballet schools, such as the School of American Ballet, in 1934 and ballet on display in Disney's *Fantasia* in 1940 reflected continued American interest in ballet. Domestic American dancers and dance companies grew, such as the Littlefield Ballet, and similarly toured across the United States, as when the Littlefield ballet performed in forty-two cities to a cumulative audience of 115,000 Americans. Indeed, the creation of regional ballet companies mirrored these other areas of growth with the first regional ballet founded in Atlanta in 1929, and eventually leading to regional ballet festivals starting in the 1950s.[6]

As the United States grew its role globally speaking in the twentieth century, members of the upper and middle class influenced culture including ballet and its association with high culture. Indeed, the United States had to choose how to define itself and present itself and its culture as it grew in its global influence and presence, which would influence both America's cultural exchange efforts in the Cold War and how Americans received the Moiseyev Dance Company in its 1958 tour.

America Presents Itself to the Post–World War II World

The movement towards culture as Cold War weapon and the cultural exchange efforts predating 1958 primed the scene for the Moiseyev tour. The significance of this tour—and the agreement for cultural exchange allowing for the tour—stems from the cultural and propaganda warfare the United States and Soviet Union engaged in before and throughout the Cold War.

For the United States, these cultural exchange endeavors were part of a larger post–World War II effort. As it emerged as a superpower, the United States felt it had to present itself to the world in a way it had not before and intentional infrastructure would be necessary to accomplish this presentation. Correspondingly, President Truman did not shut down propaganda as the Wilson administration did after World War I. After reading a report by Arthur W. MacMahon that suggested peacetime propaganda was necessary to present a "fair picture" of the United States to the world, Truman had propaganda organs moved to the State Department to create and disseminate this "fair picture."[7] To conduct the process of creation and dissemination, Truman enacted the United States' first peacetime propaganda initiative in 1945. The goal of Truman's formation of the Interim International Information Services (IIIS) was "to see to it that other people receive a full and fair picture of American life and the aims and policies of the United States government."[8] Though the United States traditionally shunned peacetime propaganda, with increasing tensions between the United States and the Soviet Union, the American approach changed.[9] Now the United States had to show the world what it meant to be "American."

The successor to the IIIS, the United States Information Agency (USIA), began its work in 1953 and utilized a broad range of media to share its definition of "American" internationally. Activities by the USIA and its predecessors included translation of "useful" books—such as George Orwell's *Animal Farm*—into different languages and encouraging international book distribution. The USIA also sponsored exhibitions, such as *The Family of Man* which featured 503 pictures of marriage and family life from 68 countries. Such efforts were intended to sway non-Americans around the world to support democracy and the United States—or at least to create a negative image of communism and the Soviet Union. The USIA and State Department efforts were sometimes more overt in nature when responding to contemporary events. For example, in 1958–1959, when Khrushchev began stepping up pressure on West Berlin, the USIA widely publicized the way Khrushchev contradicted the "Peaceful Coexistence" policy the USSR touted. Accordingly, the International Press Service put together a story entitled "A Tale of Two Cities" using pictures to make visible the differences in everyday life between East and West Berlin.[10]

President Eisenhower took further steps with regard to cultural diplomacy, at least partially in reaction to Stalin's death in 1953. Shortly after Stalin's death, Secretary of State John Foster Dulles stated "The Eisenhower era begins as the Stalin era ends." These words reflected international and domestic changes in both the Soviet Union and in the United States. The atmosphere between the two nations relaxed somewhat and a greater desire for openness came to be expressed by both nations' governments.[11]

As the new leader of America's Cold War enemy, Khrushchev was different from Stalin in appearance and demeanor; he seemed less harsh and less brutal. He also expressed interest in Hollywood and Disneyland and wanted to visit the United States. Khrushchev set a new tone for the Soviet regime in the wake of Stalin's death. In his "Secret Speech" to the Twentieth Party Congress on February 25, 1956, Khrushchev enunciated how his regime would differ from Stalin's. While maintaining an admiration for Lenin, Khrushchev took the opportunity to distance himself from Stalin and even criticize him outright. "Stalin acted not through persuasion, explanation, and patient cooperation with people, but by imposing his concepts and demanding absolute submission to his opinion. Whoever opposed this concept or tried to prove his viewpoint, and the correctness of his position—was doomed to removal from the leading collective and to subsequent moral and physical annihilation." He claimed Stalin hurt the Soviet people and the Soviet system. Khrushchev characterized Stalin as overly suspicious and fickle; those working with him personally never knew where they stood and feared what their futures held. These characteristics only increased after World War II as Stalin became more brutal and more suspicious of those around him, as evidenced by his fear of the doctor's plot. Khrushchev concluded that Stalin hurt the Soviet Union, and accordingly he would try to compensate for the damage Stalin had done.[12]

Khrushchev expressed an interest in "peaceful coexistence" with the United States and other Western countries. His view of culture also differed; he supported Soviet culture but also was very interested in the culture of the capitalistic West. Khrushchev believed that "the Soviets did in fact have a great deal to learn from the world beyond their borders." Additionally, there could be other benefits including a "leading to greater understanding of the Soviet system abroad" and keeping international relations calm.[13] Cultural openness could achieve multiple political goals for Khrushchev and his regime consequently pursued cultural exchange in a way Stalin had not.

On the American side, Eisenhower had already enhanced propaganda like the campaign "Crusade for Freedom" in which private organizations conducted cultural events and activities in Europe in conjunction with the CIA.[14] He took a step further by creating the President's Emergency Fund for the Arts. This fund, created in August of 1954, authorized the State Department to send cultural representatives to places selected for "maximum psychological impact."[15] In practice, this meant direct government sponsorship and funding of tours, including $2,225,000 designated for dance, music, theater, and sports tours, and another $157,000 at the disposal of the USIA to advertise and publicize.[16] The Eisenhower administration believed that exchange would create a positive understanding of the United States and influence the "minds and hearts of men" abroad.[17] In the late 1950s, President Eisenhower stressed the need for greater exchange between the United States and the Soviet Union as well through his support of the Lacy-Zarubin Agreement (1958) which ensured regular exchanges with the Soviet Union.

In addition to the American and Soviet governments, impresario Sol Hurok represented a third party interested in cultural exchange. Hurok endeavored for years to facilitate cultural exchange between the two superpowers. He worked in the arts for over sixty years and "S. Hurok Presents" became a well-known sight on billboards, programs, and advertisements for entertainment events. "Under his name the great singers, musicians and dance troupes of the early and mid 20th century toured the United States," including the likes of Galina Ulanova, Marian Anderson, Richard Strauss and others.[18] Though the Bolshoi Ballet may have been Hurok's most desired target for exchange, the Soviet Ministry of Culture insisted on the Moiseyev dance troupe touring the United States first.[19] Hurok met Igor Moiseyev personally in Paris while the Moiseyev toured Western Europe in 1955. Both men expressed a desire for the Moiseyev to tour the United States, but admitted they had their doubts as to whether or not this would ever actually occur.

Hurok, however, assiduously pursued his efforts by contacting both American and Soviet officials and demonstrating the value of cultural exchange on a larger scale. Through his cultivation of a relationship with Edward Ivanyan in the Soviet Ministry of Culture (and by persuading other Moscow officials through personal encounters and the visits of famous American artists), Hurok secured an agreement in 1956 for the Moiseyev to tour the United States. One political factor stood as a barrier, however. The Soviets requested that the American government remove the fingerprint clause of the McCarran-Walter Immigration Act, which would entail all the dancers being individually fingerprinted for US entry.

The State Department took careful note of Hurok's efforts. In a March 1956 memorandum, State Department official Robert O. Blake related how Frederick Schang, President of Columbia Artists Management, contacted him to let him know that Hurok had requested booking dates for the Metropolitan Opera in September of that year for the potential Moiseyev tour. Schang expressed concern about Hurok's actions and wanted to confirm that the State Department had not changed its policy with regard to "large cultural groups" being admitted to the United States (perhaps to ensure that if its policy had changed, Columbia Artists would be part of the cultural exchange initiatives). Blake reassured Schang that nothing had changed that would allow for Soviet cultural representatives to tour the United States.[20] A month later, Robert O. Blake reported that Hurok had communicated with the Soviet Embassy about a possible Moiseyev tour in the United States. The memo noted that "Mr. Hurok is apparently undertaking a private campaign to build up support for repeal of the fingerprint requirement. During the last few days he has, to my knowledge, interviewed Congressman Celler of New York, Mr. Maxwell Raab and Mr. Jack Martin of the White House."[21] The State Department did not prevent Hurok's negotiations, but at this point it did not actively aid this kind of cultural exchange.

The 1956 agreement fell through, and the obstacles to establishing a viable cultural exchange agreement continued to mount, including American concern over the potential landing of Soviet planes on American soil to transport the artists. Finally, after securing another agreement with Moscow that included the tour not only of the Moiseyev, but also of the Bolshoi Ballet, violinist David Oistrakh, and composer Aram Khachaturian, the American government repealed the fingerprinting clause, so the planned tours could move forward.[22]

In a National Security Report dated June 29, 1956, the role and goals of cultural exchange were discussed in relation to future policy.[23] Exchanges aimed at the Soviet Bloc were intended to accomplish several goals, among which were the following:

a. To promote within Soviet Russia evolution toward a regime which all abandon predatory policies, which will seek to promote the aspirations of the Russian people rather than the global ambitions of International Communism, and which will increasingly rest upon the consent of the governed rather than upon despotic police power.

b. As regards the European satellites, we seek their evolution toward independence of Moscow.

The US government concluded that the impetus behind cultural exchange initiatives was partly a response to changes in the Soviet Union following Stalin's death in 1953 and Nikita Khrushchev's rise to power. The Security Council noted "visible signs of progress" in the Soviet Union recently along with "increasing education and consequent demand for greater freedom of thought and expression."[24] Under these new conditions, the dissemination of American ideas and cultural products might prove more effective as they would receive the greater attention and reception.

While the Cold War policies at the time were for the most part defensive, this moment marked a realization that "they can be *offensive* in terms of promoting a desire for greater individual freedom, well-being and scrutiny within the Soviet Union, and greater independence within the satellites." To grow this desire in Soviet and satellite peoples, US cultural products and representatives should endeavor to combat negative images of the United States and challenge Soviet ideals. On a more mundane level, the Security Council encouraged initiatives to "stimulate Soviet desire for more consumer goods by bringing them to realize how rich are the fruits of free labor and how much they themselves could gain from a government which primarily sought their well-being and not conquest."[25] For their part, the Soviets through cultural representatives like the Moiseyev, similarly sought to demonstrate the benefits of a communist system and that peoples were included, not conquered. However, with the repression of the Hungarian Revolt in November of 1956, the State Department suspended any exchange initiatives because of the Soviet government's actions, consequently adding further but not indefinite delay to the initiation of the Moiseyev Dance Company tour.[26]

Official Cultural Exchange Established

After the obstacles and difficulties along the way in the post-Stalin period, on January 27, 1958, the United States and Soviet Union signed the Lacy-Zarubin Agreement. Special Assistant to the Secretary of State William S. B. Lacy and USSR Ambassador Georgi N. Zarubin functioned as negotiators and signatories on the agreement. The planned cultural exchanges included films, radio and television broadcasts, students, professors, scientists, and athletes. The *State Department Bulletin* announced that "this Agreement is regarded as a significant first step in the improvement of mutual understanding between the peoples of the United States and the Union of Soviet Socialist Republics, and it is sincerely hoped that it will be carried out in such a way as to contribute substantially to the betterment of relations between the two countries, thereby also contribute to a lessening of international tensions."[27] Though the purported goal was calming of tensions, it should be kept in mind that both sides saw exchange and an opportunity to combat negative perceptions of their own country and demonstrate their own superiority to gain international power.

The proposed radio and television broadcasts focused on science, technology, industry, agriculture, education, public health, sports, music, and politics. Accordingly, exchange utilized representatives in iron, steel, mining, plastics, agriculture, forestry, lumber, and medical delegations. To gain more personal knowledge of each nation's way of life, students, writers, artists, and other professionals would be sent.

Section VIII of the agreement identified the first cultural representatives who would travel between the nations: the State Academic Folk Dance Ensemble of the USSR would arrive in the United States in April or May of 1958, and in exchange, the Soviet Union "will consider inviting a leading American theatrical or choreographic group to the Soviet Union in 1959." The Philadelphia Symphony Orchestra would travel to the Soviet Union in May or June of 1958 and the Bolshoi Ballet would come to the United States in 1959. With respect to individual artists, Soviet musicians E. Gilels, L. Kogan, I. Petrov, P. Lisitsian, Z. Dolukhanova, I. Bezrodni, and V. Ashkenazi would visit the United States in 1958 in exchange for American counterparts B. Thebom, L. Warren, R. Peters, L. Stokowski, and others. In addition to the artists and performers, athletes (representing sports including basketball, wrestling, track and field, weight lifting, hockey, and chess) took part in competitions with each superpower alternating as hosts.[28] While these agreements were official government matters, they also involved private sector industries, including agriculture, film, athletics, and more.[29]

These cultural exchanges were renewed throughout the Cold War by a series of agreements over the years. The final agreement, signed in 1985 by President Reagan and Premier Mikhail Gorbachev, was designed to last until December 31, 1991, but essentially ended with the fall of the Soviet Union on December 25 of that year.[30] The significance of these exchanges in terms of their specificity to the Cold War is underlined by the fact that, after the fall of the Soviet Union, the US government deemed such agreements no longer necessary. Some historians, like Yale Richmond, argue that culture and cultural products led to the end of the Cold War and the fall of the Soviet Union. While supporting this argument is not within the purview of this case study, here culture is similarly highlighted as having a major impact on Cold War relations. The Moiseyev Dance Company led to a greater interest in Soviet citizens and a more reasonable view of Soviet people as fellow human beings with similar hopes, dreams, and worries.

One of the better known early cultural exchanges occurred when the American pianist Van Cliburn won the Tchaikovsky International Piano competition in Moscow in 1958.[31] American newspapers highlighted how enthusiastically the Russians acclaimed the Texan pianist and admired his skill; he "needed just an hour and a half to change this country's opinion of culture in the United States." Americans felt that Van Cliburn's reception demonstrated the vibrancy of American culture, particularly since his performance yielded a "display of technical skill that Russians have long considered their own special forte."[32] Russian audiences dubbed him "the American genius," and "Malchik [the little boy] from the South." The press in particular focused on how Russian women allegedly adored Van Cliburn, who was "mobbed everywhere by fans, autograph seekers and girls bearing flowers."[33] Van Cliburn's successful tour was a feather in the cap of American cultural identity and cultural exchange.

This could not have happened during Stalin's rule. For instance, in the 1930s, Sol Hurok, who had arranged tours of artists from Russia prior to the 1917 Revolution, tried to initiate tours again but without success. Similarly, American scholars could not study in the Soviet Union from 1936–1958 and very few American tourists were able to travel to the Soviet Union.[34]

A new era of exchange began with Khrushchev and would be maintained for the duration of the Cold War.

Soviet Preparation for the Moiseyev's 1958 Tour of the United States

The Soviet regime carefully selected the State Academic Folk Dance Ensemble of the USSR as the first representatives sent to the United States after the signing of the Lacy-Zarubin Agreement. The government emphasized the cultural and political importance of the tour, and sent the ensemble with a thorough list of instructions. The government told the ensemble to telegraph the Ministry of Culture as soon as they arrived in New York and to stay in a hotel near the performance venue, the Metropolitan Opera House. Throughout the tour, the dancers and musicians had to allow for four hours, usually from 10 a.m. to 2 p.m., to rehearse and to allow for enough time to get enough sleep at night.[35]

While the Soviet government endeavored to keep a close eye on the dancers with KGB agents to control interactions with Americans, Igor Moiseyev sought to prepare the dancers in a different way. In a communication to the Ministry of Culture, Moiseyev requested several things so the dancers would be at their best as performers and could take advantage of learning opportunities. Moiseyev asked for a series of lectures about America to be held for the ensemble's benefit, as well as access to books about America and American films. Additionally, he wanted the dancers to study English, with lessons to be continued on the Ukrainian tour just before they left for New York. Moiseyev also requested an increase in the dancers' pensions. Moiseyev felt comfortable making all these requests given the gravity of the Cold War situation and the fact that the Soviet government chose the Moiseyev to be the first cultural representatives to the United States. Moiseyev noted that the ensemble "represents Soviet art not only inside the Soviet Union and . . . democratic countries, but also in the tours of the most capitalistic cities."[36]

American Anticipation of the Moiseyev

In the wake of the signing of the Lacy-Zarubin Agreement, Americans questioned the Soviets' sudden willingness to engage in cultural exchange with the United States. At first, Americans expressed suspicion of Soviet motives, seeing the agreement as purely a political, propagandistic maneuver. However, once the Moiseyev arrived it swept away most Americans' doubts and suspicions.

Still, it is worth unpacking further Americans' perspective on what the Soviet motives for exchange might have been. The Soviet Union's "sudden" embrace of cultural exchange related to the current Soviet regime, its tone and its issues. The American press noted that under Stalin exchange was out of the question, but with Khrushchev at the helm things had changed. Additionally, as *The Pittsburgh Press* emphasized, "The Russians have been trying hard to overcome the cultural black eye they got in crushing the Hungarian students' revolt" and cultural exchange was an avenue to improve the Soviet Union's international image. Americans theorized that Soviet artists were eager to see the rest of the world and what it had to offer artistically and thus had pressured the Soviet government into negotiating the exchange agreement. The artists "realize they have some things to learn from other countries."[37] Some felt that the repressive Soviet regime was desperate to be seen in a positive light. This last reasoning partly originated from a sense of American cultural superiority; in the United States, artists supposedly did not experience the same amount of government interference and could take advantage of an open global exchange of ideas and cultural products.

Even while questioning the Soviet motives behind the Lacy-Zarubin Agreement, anticipation grew as the dance troupe's April arrival neared. Despite the excitement, some Americans felt that the Moiseyev was not the right choice for American audiences, arguing that the Bolshoi Ballet was a better representation of Soviet culture, and that the Moiseyev did not represent "high" Soviet culture. Americans were more familiar with the Bolshoi because of its longer history and international renown and its easily recognizable focus figures like *prima ballerina assoluta* Galina Ulanova.

Critic Walter Terry attempted to allay such criticisms of the choice of the Moiseyev, asserting that Americans should not be disappointed in a folk rather than classical ballet troupe touring since it was well known that the Moiseyev dancers were highly skilled and quite entertaining. He reminded Americans of a recent television broadcast of the *Bob Hope Show* from Moscow that gave Americans a taste of the Moiseyev with "fascinating glimpses of Russian folk dancers leaping through space, racing about with flashing spears, whirling at unbelievable speeds and tossing off those knee-shattering 'prisyadkas' with communicable abandon." Terry claimed that the Moiseyev would be just as worthy of an American audience and that Americans were already excited for this "artistic invasion."[38]

Once the tour dates were announced, anticipation turned frenzied as Americans clamored for tickets to the first performances in New York. *Dance News* reported that "If the demand for tickets for the Moiseyev Dance Company from Moscow, which opens April 14 at the Metropolitan Opera House, continues as it has until the end of March the company will sell out nearly all tickets before the show opens." Indeed, even before the box office opened on March 27, mail orders totaled $180,000 (roughly $1,820,000 when adjusted for inflation in 2022).[39] On the day the Metropolitan Opera House opened for in-person ticket sales, a line formed, beginning at 7:30 in the morning.[40] While some may have initially been disappointed in the choice of the Moiseyev, nonetheless Americans were extremely eager to see representatives from the USSR.

Americans were not completely unfamiliar with the Moiseyev. Some had read newspaper accounts of the troupe's exploits at home and abroad during and after World War II. As the dance troupe began to extend its tours to include Western Europe in the mid-1950s, American press coverage increased of its performances as well as its impact on the Soviet Union's international image. In Paris and London, critic Mary Clarke relayed in *Dance Magazine* how "the dancers were received with joyful enthusiasm not only for their dancing, brilliant as it is, but also for their tremendous vitality, gaiety and the infectious pleasure in dancing which they communicate to an audience."[41] This kind of coverage contributed to the anticipation as the Lacy-Zarubin Agreement came to fruition and America waited for the arrival of the Moiseyev. Moreover, the evidence of the prowess of the Moiseyev, by winning over Western countries like France and Britain, contributed to how Americans received the Moiseyev in their turn.

The First Performance

The Moiseyev's 1958 American tour began April 9 with their arrival in New York and ended with their last performance at Madison Square Garden on June 28 and their departure back to the Soviet Union on July 1. The April 14 premiere performance became a nationwide event, reported widely in the press with numerous details of the attending audience, performance, dancers, and Americans' reactions. The Moiseyev stunned Americans, who vociferously expressed their response:

> The Metropolitan Opera House nearly burst its aging seams last Monday when the Moiseyev Dance company from Moscow made its American debut. On stage, approximately one hundred dancers performed with explosive exuberance and stunning virtuosity while on the other side of the footlights, the audience exploded with applause and cheers.[42]

The press agreed that the Moiseyev was riveting and that the American audience could not help but applaud and praise the troupe. The tremendous premiere at the Met swept away any doubts about the Moiseyev being ill-suited for the role of first cultural ambassadors. Indeed, many critics felt

FIGURE 2. From The Russian Suite. Source: M. Chudnovsky, *The Folk Dance Company of the USSR: Igor Moiseyev, Art Director* (Moscow: Foreign Languages Publishing House, 1959), 24.

themselves at a loss for words in trying to relate the nature of the Moiseyev's performance: "The excitement generated in the audience about equaled the breathless pace at which the Soviet dancers performed. They gave an incredible performance fast, fantastic and fabulous. . . . This is not something to describe but something to see." Journalists noted that the ushers actually watched the show as well as the audience because it was so engrossing.[43] Newspapers emphasized again and again that the Moiseyev was something special that Americans had not seen before.

The premiere, in addition to being widely covered by New York newspapers, was also reported across North America. The American national press coverage agreed with local coverage as to the exuberant reception of the troupe and audiences' visible excitement during its first performances. The *Toronto Daily Star* reported that "The company was cheered with uninhibited delight throughout the program, which went in heavily for unmitigated gusto, virtuosity and exuberance."[44] The makeup of the first-night audience was also commented upon: among the 3,600 attendees were prominent New Yorkers as well as celebrities and representatives of the State Department and United Nations diplomats.[45] The Moiseyev premiere was certainly not a typical performance at the Met; it was a celebrated, politicized event that garnered American interest nationwide than usual because of the Cold War political implications.

Popularity Gauged by Ticket Sales

After the initial success at the Metropolitan Opera, Sol Hurok recognized that "New Yorkers can't get enough of the Moiseyev." He decided to add more New York performances to the troupe's tour in late June and to change the venue to Madison Square Garden, which would allow more people to attend each performance. Hurok announced additional performances for June 20–22, but even this was not enough, and so he added four more performances on June 24, 25, and 28.[46] In total, New Yorkers alone would pay $365,000 (roughly $3,690,000 when adjusted for inflation in 2022) for the Metropolitan Opera House performances. In the added-on performances at Madison Square Garden, the venue experienced the largest advance mail order sale (receiving 18,000 ticket order requests) in its history.[47]

In New York, the Moiseyev clearly had no trouble selling tickets in abundance. Elsewhere, the Moiseyev proved similarly popular, soliciting sell-out performance and new box office records elsewhere, including in Detroit, Chicago, Los Angeles, San Francisco, Washington, St. Louis, Cleveland, Philadelphia, and Boston.[48] The Boston Garden sold over 6,000 seats in the first possible day to purchase tickets and sold a record $30,000 in advanced tickets.[49] The ticket buying frenzy made for good press. One Eugene Groden of Belmont, Massachusetts, told the *Boston Globe* his story of struggling to get a ticket. Mr. Groden, an army veteran and a "devotee of the ballet since he fought the Soviets in Russia," greatly desired to see the Moiseyev perform. However, he was unable to buy tickets in advance because of work. The article goes on to relate how in a desperate attempt, he showed up at the Boston Garden the night of the performance. However: "There were no tickets. Well-dressed folks were streaming through the lobby[,] and he watched them enviously." The article highlights Mr. Groden's misery at being unable to attend this highly anticipated event and how disappointed he felt watching other Americans pour in through the Garden's doors. Happily, Mr. Groden was able to buy a ticket from a well-dressed lady, and though he paid a hefty price for it, was finally able to see the Moiseyev.[50] The ticket sales numbers and press coverage indicate that the Moiseyev was the "must see" event of the time period and an American obsession and that the event garnered interest from multiple social classes.

Exposure to the Moiseyev

Newspapers offered different estimates of how many people saw the Moiseyev during its first American tour. *Dance Magazine* reported that more than 100,000 people attended the performances at the Boston Garden alone.[51] Soviet records carefully counted the number of tickets sold and also the number of estimated viewers who watched the one-hour special featuring the Moiseyev on the *Ed Sullivan Show*, a nationally televised Sunday evening variety show.

The Moiseyev appearance on the *Ed Sullivan Show* at the end of the 1958 tour functioned as the culmination of the troupe's success. Sullivan's aggressive tactics to connect with the troupe for a performance further demonstrated this success. He spent $200,000 to engage the Moiseyev (even though he usually had a limit of $100,000)[52] and he featured the ensemble for the entirety of his show, the first time this had happened since the program's inception in the late 1940s.[53] The hugely increased expenditure

TABLE I. Transcribed and Condensed RGALI Chart of Attendance during 1958 Tour

PERFORMANCES	CITY	VENUE	TOTAL ATTENDEES
21 performances from April 14–May 3	New York	Metropolitan Opera House	78,256
4 performances from May 5–8	Montreal	Forum	28,588
3 performances from May 9–10	Toronto	Leaf Garden	22,557
3 performances from May 12–14	Detroit	Masonic Auditorium	14,055
7 performances from May 15–21	Chicago	Opera House	24,783
7 performances from May 25–30	Los Angeles	Shrine Auditorium	44,975
7 performances from May 31–June 5	San Francisco	Opera House	22,387
1 performance on June 8	St. Louis	Keel Auditorium	8,919
1 performance on June 10	Cleveland	Cleveland Opera	9,522
2 performances from June 11–12	Philadelphia	Convention Hall	19,632
2 performances from June 13–14	Boston	Boston Garden	22,406
3 performances from June 16–18	Washington, DC	Capitol Theatre	10,062
8 performances from June 20–28	New York	Madison Square Garden	100,459
Television program	New York	*Ed Sullivan Show*	More than 40 million viewers

Source: Chart of Moiseyev Performances during 1958 American Tour, RGALI, f 2483 0 1 d 267, 71, p. 1.

highlights the importance of the tour to Americans and the Moiseyev appeared on June 29, 1958, with an audience spanning North America.

The New York audience received the Moiseyev with wild enthusiasm. Throughout the tour, the Moiseyev encountered "enthusiastic audiences and ultra-laudatory reviews in every city of its tour."[54] Despite the audience's potential foreknowledge of the group, the dances it performed, and its virtuosity, audiences were freshly surprised by what they saw on stage. Critics and reporters across the country described the Moiseyev as alternatingly indescribable and explosive. In Chicago, the music-dance critic Claudia Cassidy, wrote of the premiere: "There were times in the Civic Opera House last night when so much rocket power exploded on stage that I suspected those sputniks had been launched by especially selected Moiseyevs."[55] The explosive nature of the Moiseyev dancers could be directly tied to Soviet space capabilities and Soviet advances in the space race and clearly the acrobatic skills of the dancers impressed the audience.

Indeed, the dancers would be noted as indescribable but as will be analyzed further later on, as incredibly happy and emotive. The *Toronto Telegram* reported: "The spoken or written word is hardly adequate to describe the details effects of these superbly trained dancers, most of them in their early twenties who danced unmistakably with joy last night at Maple Leaf Garden."[56] Across North America, Americans reacted with awe and fascination to the Moiseyev performances. Another Toronto journalist confessed to listeners on WXYZ Radio: "I think what I witnessed at Masonic Auditorium last night will live in my memory with the top half dozen theatrical events of my life, for the appearance of the Moiseyev Dancers generated an electric charge that went deeper than dancing itself."[57] The Moiseyev functioned as a significant event in North Americans' lives. Those who saw the company felt changed by their experience and grew this appreciation not just of dance, but of Soviet people.

While some reporters had been critical of the fact that it was the Moiseyev, a folk dance troupe, rather than the Bolshoi, a classical ballet troupe, which had been sent, they were quickly silenced by the performances. Rather than criticizing the folk dances on display, they noted how Moiseyev proved able to make the dances not only entertaining, but also fascinating.[58] At the San Francisco Opera House, the audience "stood up and roared some of the longest, loudest bravos in local stage history"[59] while the Chicago Opera House, "There were more than 10 curtain calls and the dancers seemed as moved by the applause as the audience by the performance. . . . From the opening suite of old Russian dances to the rousing Ukrainian suite finale there was a rising roar from the packed 3,600 seat Opera House."[60] Americans responded loudly and without restraint to the performances and were not shy in sharing their appreciation for these representatives of their Cold War enemy.

The advent of official cultural exchange through the Lacy-Zarubin Agreement in 1958 marked a change in the Cold War atmosphere and a new level of openness between the United States and Soviet Union. While both superpowers desired to relax Cold War tensions through the use of cultural representatives, the United States may not have been prepared for just how enthusiastically the American audience would react to the State Academic Folk Dance Ensemble of the USSR's first tour in 1958. The desire to see Soviet people for the first time certainly explained the high level of anticipation leading up to the ensemble's arrival. However, the company's success was based more on American's fascination with the Soviet dancers' skill and Americans' ability to see past the Cold War narrative and view the dancers as people, rather than as polar opposites in their ideals and way of life.

The Soviet response, discussed in further detail in the next chapter, reflected the Moiseyev's success as establishing the effectiveness of cultural exchange and especially the American interest in the Moiseyev in particular. This led to the many cultural exchange initiatives thereafter and the Moiseyev's continued numerous tours to the United States and across the globe. Even as the Moiseyev returned other times and performed many of the same dances, Americans continued to find the troupe incredibly engaging onstage and off; the troupe had a particular hold on the American audience. In order to better understand this American fascination with the Moiseyev, it is helpful to break down and categorize the kinds and patterns of American reception, both positive and negative.

CHAPTER 4

Reception and the Cold War Narrative

For three hours a gaily caparisoned and festive gathering forgot about
hydrogen bombs, intercontinental missiles and space-girdling satellites.

—Thomas R. Dash, *Women's Weave*, April 15, 1958

To say that Americans positively received the Moiseyev company would be
a huge understatement. Regardless of political leanings and affiliations, critics across the board praised the Moiseyev and noted the incredibly enthusiastic reception on the part of the American audience. "The reception given
by the American people to the Moiseyev Dance Company is a sensational
one," was a typical comment, while rave reviews described the Moiseyev
in superlative terms, acknowledging that the dancers were full of "super-
human vitality and unbounded charm."[1] Responses to the Moiseyev were,
for the most part, passionate and fervent with praise.

However, this recognition of overwhelming enthusiasm does not present the full picture. To gain access to American mentalities and ideas in this
time period, responses to the Moiseyev can be broken down thematically
in order to better understand the nuances of the response, and what it tells
us about American Cold War life. The responses are found in press coverage, contemporary interviews, official American and Soviet documents,
personal notes and remembrances and, finally, Igor Moiseyev's own report
of the Moiseyev's experience in America. While here the response is broken down categorically, it should be emphasized that, in terms of overall
reception, Americans actively received the Moiseyev. This active reception
meant, at the basic level, curiosity to see the group perform and a desire to
learn anything and everything about the dancers. On a higher level, active
reception meant communicating with Igor Moiseyev personally, asking
to meet the dancers, and interacting with them offstage. Given the way in
which the tour was embedded within Cold War cultural exchange and the

narratives each superpower established, the political nature of this active response is unpacked here first.

Political Reception

The Lacy-Zarubin Agreement, which allowed for the arrival of the Moiseyev dancers (as well as future exchanges and American counterparts visiting the Soviet Union) was a carefully negotiated political maneuver by both superpowers—this form of exchange functioned both a way to encourage friendly relations and to "fight" the Cold War through cultural representatives' successes in the nation visited. As with other aspects of the Cold War, politicians' words became magnified and examined carefully to determine who currently was "winning" this indirect conflict. Reporters felt that the way in which politicians reacted to the Moiseyev was important. Indeed, it was during a Moiseyev performance that Secretary of State John Dulles first heard the news that the Soviet Union executed Hungarian political leader Imre Nagy for his role in the 1956 Hungarian Uprising.[2] So taken was the secretary with the dancers that he went so far as to make a surprise visit backstage to meet the dancers during intermission. He told the dancers he felt the best term to describe the ensemble was "happiness," which he then compared to the Declaration of Independence's "phrase about 'pursuit of happiness,'" and emphasized that the dancers were "giving a good deal of happiness to the American people."

Dulles' reaction is significant; he identified the dance troupe as sharing an ideal put forth by America's founding fathers. These enthusiastic sentiments contrasted strongly with the execution of Nagy. Upon learning of the execution during this same intermission, Dulles simply said how it was "tragic, tragic."[3] Dulles noted the solemnness of this news but did not let it interfere with his appreciation for the Soviet cultural representatives who were sent over by the same government instigating the execution. While the reason behind his deprecatory response can only be guessed at, it is interesting that, compared to the response to the Hungarian Revolt itself, which delayed and could have derailed the Moiseyev's visit, in this instance, the response is quite diminished. Perhaps the dancers had an ability to assuage or at least distract from Cold War concerns; or Dulles felt the value of cultural exchange higher than sharing public disapproval for the execution.

The dancers certainly functioned here to distract general American concerns and fears about the Soviet Union and its people.

The impact of the cultural exchange on American relations with peoples living under Soviet rule did not escape the State Department. In a foreign service dispatch from Budapest on July 3, 1958, a US official reported to the State Department that the Americans' favorable reception of the Moiseyev Dance Company did not go unnoticed behind the Iron Curtain. In Hungary, local papers related the great success of the Moiseyev in the United States, which could create an unfavorable view of the United States. Such reporting could serve as a:

> fairly subtle reminder to the general reader that although the U.S. professes great horror and shock at the execution of Imre Nagy and compatriots, it does not feel called upon to take action to stop U.S.S.R. cultural attractions from appearing in America. At another level, which only the more gullible Hungarian would swallow, it appears to prove that the U.S. public in general holds no regard for the hostile statements of the "U.S. ruling circles"; by patronizing Soviet cultural exhibitions the American public is showing its basic sympathy with the Soviets.[4]

Viewing the American actions as hypocritical could lead Hungarians to feel abandoned by America and its promise to support Hungarian claims to freedom. Up until this point, the United States had pledged to support resistance to communism. It was in light of conflict and rebellion in Greece and Turkey that President Truman promulgated the Truman Doctrine in a speech in 1947, promising to defend all free peoples across the globe. Once more, the question remains why Dulles and the United States chose not to demonstrate disapproval or take responsive actions like changing their attendance at or support of the Moiseyev's performances. The dancers' popularity may have been a factor and/or a desire to strongly support the nascent official cultural exchange effort started with the Lacy-Zarubin Agreement.

Despite the political reasons for the Moiseyev's visit—which implicitly included improving relations through the fostering of cultural exchanges between the Soviet Union and United States—some viewed the arts as functioning in a non-political space. Such critics argued that Americans received the Moiseyev without a thought for politics: "Completely ignoring the political implications," wrote *Dance Magazine* editor Lydia Joel, "the U.S. public has lovingly accepted the dancers from Soviet Russia."[5] However, recognizing the reception as nonpolitical also involved using Cold War rhetoric to note its absence. Indeed, the Cold War narrative was inescapable in the context of the Moiseyev tours, given the fact that the dancers' visit was part of an officially sanctioned exchange, in addition to the company's subtle yet inescapable propagandistic veneer. Cold War terminology penetrated the way both the press and individuals described the audience's reactions, and opinions of the artistic value of the performances often went hand-in-hand with opinions of their political value.

Americans were not unaware that the selection of the Moiseyev Dance Company as a cultural exchange representative to the United States was a politically savvy one. Many admired the Soviet Union's choice in sending the Moiseyev because of its huge impact. Dance critic Walter Terry wrote in the *New York Herald Tribune*, "The Russians have made a mighty effective move in sending us a mass of smiling, richly talented ambassadors. For it is quite impossible not to like these spirited folk dancers."[6] Rabbi Mordecai Levy of Temple Beth Hillel in Mattapan, Massachusetts, wrote a letter to the editor of the *Boston Globe* lauding the Moiseyev's performance as "sheer artistry; superb entertainment," but also mentioning its political significance. In viewing the Moiseyev as an expression of folk culture, political differences seemed to ebb. Rabbi Levy encouraged further exchange: "If such endeavors were to increase, the chasms that divide people would be bridged. Every effort must be made to utilize the cultural values of the two great nations, the Soviet Union and the United States, to bring about such a reality upon man's desire to accept his fellow man."[7] The Moiseyev brought with it a certain confidence that world peace could be obtained and that culture was an avenue through which to accomplish this. Americans thought it was an effective political tool, and some applauded its use and success.

The Moiseyev and cultural exchange generally came to be portrayed as a more effective way to calm tensions and encourage friendship, rather than traditional diplomacy. Based on its New York reception, Alice Hughes of *The Reading Eagle* believed the Moiseyev far superior to any prior diplomatic moves:

> The Russian Moiseyev Dance Company . . . did more to unfreeze Soviet and American relations . . . than all the planned propaganda and striped-pants diplomacy that has served to keep our two countries apart

these many years. Some believe this cultural interchange . . . may effect [sic] more harmony between Moscow and Washington than a blizzard of white papers flying between the two capitals.[8]

The ineffective and flurried political diplomacy of "striped-pants" politicians and diplomats represents a sharp contrast to the colorful, costumed diplomacy of the Moiseyev dancers. Americans, according to Hughes, found the Moiseyev a more accessible way to learn about and understand the Soviet Union and she even contrasts them with "planned propaganda" rather than fitting them within other Soviet and American propaganda efforts. The Moiseyev appeared to be able to reach people more successfully and on a different level than more customary political representatives. Reaction to the Moiseyev was so strong that some reporters implied that this troupe's reception could lead to a relaxation in Cold War tensions or even a further step toward more permanent peace. Immediately after the performance, "Bouquet after bouquet was delivered to the dancers, until it looked like a thing called the cold war could be only a myth."[9] The positive American reception to the Moiseyev seemed to have great implications for the current political situation rather than simply cultural or social repercussions. The Moiseyev had an ability to reach the American audience in an effective, accessible way within the Cold War context.

The claim that the Moiseyev had this kind of power to sway American minds was not just one made by newspapers, magazines, and other publications. Like members of the press, Americans on an individual basis were very much aware of the artistic and political impact of the Moiseyev performances. This knowledge is apparent in the notes and letters sent to the performers. For example, Jeanette McCoy wrote: "Your very presence and magnificent performance has brought to our hearts new inspiration and deeper love for your people and country. We are infinitely honored, and it is our dearest hope that one day we can all live as one." Indeed, she insisted that "you have shown us new life."[10] Jeanette felt that she and other Americans received the positive message of mutual appreciation and friendly relations from the Moiseyev's performance. For her the impact of the Moiseyev was huge; it brought a new perspective to light that was both artistically and politically inspiring.

Letters like Jeanette McCoy's represented the majority of Americans' view of the Moiseyev as a wonderful example of the benefits of cultural exchange. However, some Americans doubted the validity of any positive political outcomes because of which Americans actually attended the performances; namely the middle and upper classes. One American (who left his letter to Igor Moiseyev unsigned) felt he had to tell the troupe's leader the "truth" about who attended the company's performances: "the audience you have been playing before here in America is not representative of the true American working class. But rather the upper-middle class and privileged few of our Capitalist Society. Only about 20% of your audience has been made up of workers and artists." The author reveals Marxist influence in the way he described who was able to attend the performances and who did not. He derided this state of affairs and noted how the Moiseyev performances sold out far in advance making it difficult for the everyday working man to purchase tickets and see the performances. This, he felt, was to the detriment of the dance troupe and meant that the message the dancers hoped to convey was not reaching those who would most appreciate it and learn from it.

Additionally, the letter's author shared how, due to scalping, the cost of tickets grew too high for many Americans.[11] Once more, America's capitalistic society was preventing the more deserving parts of American society from attending the performances and this simply served to demonstrate the problems with capitalism. The author of this letter criticized the American way of life and American capitalism. He saw Americans as greedy and materialistic and that the kind of American who had the opportunity to see the Moiseyev represented the bourgeoisie rather than the average American worker. His critique did not include the dancers themselves but instead represented his views about what was wrong with America and Americans in contrast to the Soviet Union and its citizens living under communism.

American Protests against the Moiseyev

Not all Americans agreed that the Moiseyev helped make leaps and bounds in international relations between the superpowers. Nor did all agree that even encouraging cultural exchange and allowing the troupe to come to the United States was a good idea. Though the positive reception of the Moiseyev is underlined above, there is another side of the story worth noting. In several cities, the Moiseyev encountered picketers outside their performance venue holding up a variety of signs condemning the exchanges. In

Los Angeles, picketers held signs with slogans such as "Free Hungary!" and "Red Butchers!"[12] The picketers at the Los Angeles protest were made up of "anti-Communist Russians" who peacefully held up their signs but then left once the performance started. Inside the concert hall, one person did shout as the Soviet national anthem played, and some of the audience refused to stand during its performance. However, this was soon forgotten once the show started: "The rest of the evening was pure harmony between the lithe dancers and the rapt audience. The amazing leaps drew cheers and the humor evoked guffaws."[13] While the protests were part of the press coverage, reporters claimed that seeing the performance would change people's minds.

The protests appeared minor in comparison with the effects of the performances and did not impede Americans' abilities to enjoy the dances. In terms of the dancers' reactions to protests, many did not entirely understand what was going on. One English speaking member of the company, upon viewing the protestors, expressed himself baffled, noting that "Yet nowhere [in Russia] do we have this—the peekets [sic]."[14] Moiseyev, in his brief report of the trip to the United States to the Soviet Ministry of Culture, noted the presence of the protestors but did not feel they represented the majority of American opinion.

Los Angeles was not the only city which witnessed protests. Boston proved to be another city in which picketers very much made their presence known. Prior to the June 13 performance, two hundred picketers, including many Soviet refugees, protested outside of Boston Garden. The press noted that Baptist Reverend Oswald A. Blumit of Quincy, Massachusetts, had smuggled bibles into countries behind the Iron Curtain. He claimed that the troupe included among its members several secret servicemen. Reverend Blumit, however, led a peaceful protest and, once the performance started, left. At the end of the performance, a man got up on stage with a banner proclaiming "Wake Up, America! Now Moiseyev Dances, Next Khrushchev Bullets!" The man, later identified as a "Polish freedom fighter," had his banner pulled down by another member of the audience and the "freedom fighter" fled the scene.[15] Yet again, while this incident proved significant enough to be included in reviews of the performance, it did not appear to have a major impact on the positive reception the troupe received in Boston.

In addition to some protests, the Moiseyev was unable to completely avoid American fears and tensions regarding domestic communism. Arthur

Lief, an American guest conductor playing with the Moiseyev and Hurok's son-in-law, was fired by CBS-TV (he was to appear with the Moiseyev on the *Ed Sullivan Show*) after he would not tell HUAC whether or not he was a communist.[16] A backdrop to this incident was the fear that Soviet spies might be using the Moiseyev tour to enter the United States. The *Boston Globe* reported that the CIA sent an agent to New York to attend a Moiseyev performance and that he was able to identify a dancer as "Col. Alexander Kudryavstev, a leading intelligence officer in the NKGB, who was immediately placed under surveillance by the FBI."[17] American fears of Soviet spies was present during the Moiseyev tour but did not become a focus of American interest or reception.

One additional incident occurred during the Moiseyev's appearance on the *Ed Sullivan Show*. At the end of the performance, Igor Moiseyev gave a speech, and a loud snort could be heard. Mr. Sullivan, while looking stern, did not comment upon what happened. The *Boston Globe* claimed that this snort may have been the result of "A lunatic fringe [which] persisted in regarding the Moiseyev Dancers as Communist plotters planning the overthrow of democracy."[18] The *Globe* picked up on the overall American sentiment that these dancers were here in a friendly capacity rather than for more sinister purposes—only those who were not mentally competent could possibly believe that the dancers had strategic or militaristic goals in addition to their numerous performances. Despite this snort in protest, the audience lauded the performance and "there were fifteen curtain calls."[19] The lack of serious concern about Soviet KGB agents or spies is another instance of the dancers escaping the American Cold War narrative.

When there were protests, pickets at the Moiseyev performances usually reflected current events (such as the "Free Hungary" sign noted above during the 1958 tour). For instance, the Moiseyev returned in 1965 and picketers at a performance in Toronto specifically protested the "Russian occupation of the Ukraine."[20] In Boston during the 1970 tour, picketers protested discrimination against Jews in the Soviet Union. This time the signs proclaimed: "'Freedom for the 3 Million Soviet Jews,' 'Save Soviet Jewry,' 'USSR, Let My People Go Now,' and 'Never Again.'" This protest, carried out by dozens of Bostonians, was sponsored by the Boston chapter of the Jewish Defense League, a group concerned with the plight of Jews in the Soviet Union. Even so, the pamphlets handed out by protesters "welcomed the dancers and dwelt on the importance of their performances in promoting friendship and goodwill." It is only after making this point clear that the pamphlets went on to describe the discrimination experienced by Soviet Jews who were unable to practice their religion, celebrate their own culture, or emigrate should they so choose.[21] While the presence of the picketers was noted by the press, their behavior was described as peaceful.

Later on, during the 1970 tour, things turned violent. The Moiseyev was scheduled to perform at Chicago's Civic Opera House in August. Prior to the performance, protesters from the Community Council of Jewish Organizations stood outside the Opera House with signs. Abbot Rosen of the Anti-Defamation League of B'nai B'rith led the protest.[22] However, the performance was canceled after a tear gas grenade was set off in the audience forty minutes into the performance.[23] The fire department had to extinguish a fire created by the grenade. The dancers and audience were evacuated, and five people were treated for complications due to inhaling tear gas fumes.[24] Leading up to the grenade detonation, the *Chicago Tribune* received a phone call in which the speaker claimed that "'the next one will not be a smoke bomb,'" and demanded that the Moiseyev leave Chicago.[25]

Despite the incident, the Opera House announced that the season's six scheduled performances would be given.[26] The State Department reacted by apologizing to the Soviet Union after Valentin M. Kamenev, cultural counselor of the Soviet embassy, lodged a formal protest with the State Department.[27] As a result of this event, the Soviet Union ended up canceling a future tour of the Bolshoi Opera and the Bolshoi Ballet.[28]

Tension was greater on this later tour because of the recent defection of a Moiseyev dancer while the company was on tour in Mexico. The press hastened to cover this story. The Mexican government granted asylum to Aleksander Filipov, and he became one of the many Soviet defectors of this era whose situation was closely examined in American newspapers.[29] Later, the Pittsburgh Ballet Theater would offer Filipov a position as a permanent guest-artist-in-residence. His defection was depicted with sympathy and the understanding that there were valid political and personal reasons to leave the Soviet Union. However, Filipov, when interviewed, claimed that he did not defect for political reasons, but because he had fallen in love with a Mexican dancer, Lucia Tristao.[30] Americans found Soviet defections (especially more dramatic ones involving acts such as physical leaps to sanctuary) intriguing—this once more was a way to gauge who was "winning" the

Cold War. If citizens of the Soviet Union chose to risk their safety in order to leave their home country, Americans felt this indicated the superiority of democracy and capitalism.

Fear of Cultural Inferiority and American Dance

Recognizing the power and impact of the Moiseyev also meant questioning what could possibly be America's cultural equivalent. In terms of political reception and rhetoric, discussing the political impact went hand in hand

FIGURE 3. Hora from Moldavian Suite. Source: M. Chudnovsky, *The Folk Dance Company of the USSR: Igor Moiseyev, Art Director* (Moscow: Foreign Languages Publishing House, 1959), 48.

with discussing what America would send to the Soviet Union. Walter Terry recognized that "the Soviet government has made both a shrewd and pleasant move in sending the Moiseyev dancers here," and that America needed to decide what to send back to the Soviet Union that would have a similar impact.[31]

While Americans received the Moiseyev with great enthusiasm, at the same time some people expressed a sense of inferiority after such an impressive performance. Americans questioned how American culture compared with Soviet culture in light of the awe-inspiring dance troupe. The *New York Herald Tribune* dance critic Walter Terry maintained that American and Russian dancers displayed many traits and skills in common but at the same time he questioned who the United States would send to the Soviet Union, noting that he overheard "some rather panicky remarks, following the Moiseyev debut, to the effect that we should round up our own folk dance group and pack it off to Russia."[32]

Terry questioned this proposed course of action, saying that the folk material for American dancers was not as rich as that in the Soviet Union because it was so much younger and did not contain as many nationalities. Additionally, in his opinion, Americans did not take their native folk dance as seriously but rather deemed it a recreational pursuit. In contrast, the Americans felt Russian folk dance, with its professional state-sponsored groups, was taken far more seriously and displayed a certain virtuosity not seen in American folk dance. Despite these negative observations, Terry encouraged his readers not to despair. He felt American folk sources, "and more important, our heritage of freedom as a people are incorporated in many of our theater dance works, ballets and dance-dramas by Agnes de Mille, Jerome Robbins, Michael Kidd, Doris Humphrey, José Limón, Martha Graham and many others." These artists' works could be sent to the Soviet Union and "do America proud." He suggested that America should not try to compete with the Soviet Union's unfamiliar artistic forms, but that America should stick with what it knew and did well.[33] Demonstrating the similarities between their cultures might not be the best form of cultural exchange between the peoples of the Soviet Union and America. Instead, Terry claimed that greater admiration would be elicited by highlighting differences and the different art forms in which each country excelled.

Even so, the United States did send American dancers abroad as part of cultural exchange. Like with cultural diplomacy and exchange efforts broadly, dance exchange had earlier precedents to draw on. For instance, President Roosevelt created the Office of the Coordinator of Inter-American Affairs (CIAA) which, in 1941, sponsored America's first official overseas performing arts event: a South American tour by the American Ballet Caravan.[34]

As mentioned previously, the creation of the Special Emergency Fund in 1954 included a designated $2,225,000 for support of State Department sponsored dance, music, theater, and sports tours. The State Department had multiple divisions to support such tours, including the Bureau of Educational and Cultural Affairs (ECA), the USIA and partnered with institutions like the American National Theatre and Academy (ANTA). While the federal entities dealt with the logistics and publicity, non-federal institutions like ANTA conducted more of the selection and artistic aspects. This would change in 1963, when the State Department moved on to utilize its own Advisory Committee on the Arts, though current and former ANTA members continued to take part in the cultural exchange selection process.[35]

Through the State Department and entities like ANTA, the United States debated what kind of dance would be most effective in presenting a positive image of American culture and the United States itself. Modern dance became one such dance genre it chose. José Limón's modern dance troupe toured Latin America in 1954 and in 1955, Martha Graham's modern dance group conducted a State Department–sponsored dance tour of Asia which started in Japan and included Korea, Thailand, Malaysia, Indonesia, Burma, and India. The US government saw modern dance as effective given the post–World War II claim that it had a specifically American origin (a claim which neglected the more international origins of the form). At first there was some concern about the accessibility of modern dance especially for diverse audiences, but these concerns were eventually allayed. For instance, the government's view of modern dance started to change with works such as *Appalachian Spring* (1944), which Graham choreographed. *Appalachian Spring* presented a "high-art yet accessible American message" which would work well in cultural exchange.[36] Additionally, the Soviet Union's usage of ballet convinced the United States of the need to do likewise.[37]

The government furthermore focused on geographic areas like Latin America and Asia as part of growing concern of communism spreading, especially in light of the recent Bandung Conference of decolonized countries and a desire to ensure they avoided communism.[38] American dancers also toured the Soviet Union, especially after the signing of the Lacy-Zarubin Agreement, such as when the New York City Ballet visited Moscow in 1962, to further American propaganda aims.[39]

The fear of cultural inferiority on the part of America often coincided with admiration for the Moiseyev. Reporter Glenna Syse lauded the Moiseyev for their "sheer physical virtuosity, acrobatic excellence and ease of execution." At the same time, however, she admitted some discomfort over how the Moiseyev dancers would compare with American representatives of culture and admitted that she found Van Cliburn's recent success in the Soviet Union reassuring, since without it, "the Moiseyev program might have left us feeling slightly inferior to the U.S.S.R."[40] Certainly many Americans expressed doubt about America's ability to directly, dancer-to-dancer, compete with the Moiseyev performers but this did not lead to any souring of reception.

Similarly in a *Sarasota Herald-Tribune* article discussing art as a universal language and reporting about the Moiseyev's New York performances, the reporter also mentioned Van Cliburn and his own successes as a representative of American culture. While admitting that the Moiseyev gave a "magnificent performance" and that this cultural exchange "can melt the Iron Curtain," the reporter quoted a Muscovite as saying, after hearing Van Cliburn, that "now America has a sputnik that beats ours."[41] Though the reporter himself did not state a definite opinion as to whether American or Soviet cultural representatives were superior, he did note the discourse that existed regarding fear of cultural inferiority on both sides.

The Moiseyev Dance Company as Middlebrow Culture

The concern around American cultural inferiority paired with the overwhelmingly positive reception to the Moiseyev Dance company speaks to how this cultural product was a well-chosen propaganda tool on the part of the Soviet Union; Americans found the dancers accessible and easy to understand while still impressive in terms of demonstrating Soviet cultural development. The dance troupe comforted Americans; it permitted them (as will be discussed in chapters 6 and 7) to see a depiction of simplified, heteronormative romantic relationships and idealized view of multiple ethnicities and nationalities living together offered a visually engaging escape to contrast with the reality of gender and race issues in post–World War II America. Beyond the depiction of gender and sexuality, race and ethnicity, which Americans found comforting was the nature of the art form itself and Americans' perceived ability to understand it; the Moiseyev Dance Company can be examined as a "middlebrow" cultural product and this "middlebrow" nature as contributing to its propagandistic success in its Cold War enemy's home.

There are twists and turns to the understanding of and value attributed to "middlebrow" in American cultural discourse, first popularized by reporter Will Irvin in 1902, but here it is helpful to touch on examples of the idea of "middlebrow."[42] As scholars and commentators note, it can be difficult to define middlebrow and to have artists and critics agree on which cultural products fall under this category but broadly speaking, we can speak about middlebrow as educational, accessible, and reaching [multiple classes] of Americans.[43] Middlebrow could take on negative connotations; Virginia Woolf lamented her sense that middlebrow contributed to a perceived tension between highbrow and lowbrow that, noting that "The middlebrow is the man, or woman, of middlebred intelligence who ambles and saunters now on this side of the hedge, now on that, in pursuit of no single object, neither art itself nor life itself, but both mixed indistinguishably, and rather nastily, with money, fame, power, or prestige." To drive her point home, she stated that if any person (or dog or cat) labeled her as middlebrow, she would promptly stab them with her pen.[44]

In moving into the Cold War period and notions around "middlebrow," Dwight Macdonald's *Masscult and Midcult* from 1962 harshly criticized "midcult" artistic expression which aimed for lofty, high culture ideas but which got dragged down by its consumerist nature; "midcult has it both ways: it pretends to respect the standards of High Culture while it in fact waters them down and vulgarizes them."[45] Macdonald identified specific American cultural products which fell into this "midcult" category, such as John Steinbeck books and magazines like *Saturday Review*.[46] Joan Shelley Rubin examines middlebrow after World War I, noting how for several decades "Americans created an unprecedented range of activities aimed at making literature and other forms of 'high' culture available to a wide reading public."[47] The *Book of the Month Club* was one form this middlebrow production took, and the texts selected for the club were ones which had Enlightenment values and were not too challenging in terms of their form and ideas.[48]

As Steven Mintz notes, middlebrow cultural products aimed to "introduce unevenly educated adults to somewhat diluted versions of high culture in accessible, engaging and unthreatening ways."[49] It was into this mix that the Moiseyev Dance Company entered, in addition to functioning as part of Soviet cultural ideas and norms.

While middlebrow is not a term utilized by the Soviet Union at the time of the Moiseyev Dance Company's founding nor in the 1950s with the advent of official Soviet-American cultural exchange, Pauline Fairclough argues that we can examine certain cultural products from this time period within the frame of middlebrow. Given that socialist realist art encouraged artists to create accessible and educational works and that the Soviet regime promoted the idea of *kul'turnost'*—the quality of being an educated, polite, and civilized Soviet citizen—middlebrow can be an effective way of discussing the works, particularly symphonic works with no program or text like Shostakovich's Fifth Symphony. That being said, this notion of "Soviet middlebrow" is not the same as its American counterpart but a different version.[50]

The Moiseyev can be viewed in this framing of Soviet socialist realism as highly accessible and educating and improving Soviet and other citizens and in light of American notions around middlebrow. For instance, the dancers appeared in both more "high culture" venues like the San Francisco Opera House as well as those that could be used both for "high" and other level of cultural performance, such as Madison Square Garden. Indeed, in a program for one of the New York performances in 1958, the text describing the Moiseyev takes time to highlight how the Moiseyev, like middlebrow American cultural products, existed in that middle, gray area:

> Critics observed that one must place such [the Moiseyev Dance Company] folk dances on the same plane as classical ballet. Others suggested that Moiseyev had created a new, theatrical genre. Impresario S. Hurok succinctly commented: "Moiseyev has brought folk lore to the theatre and the theatre to folk lore."[51]

The dance company could not be easily defined as "high" or "low" culture but functioned in this middle arena and this contributed to Americans' response. Americans could feel they could understand and engage with the Moiseyev dance phenomenon and that they were viewing something that was culturally impressive and educational (in addition to being entertaining).

In her examination of the role of ballet in America in the Cold War period, scholar Lauren Erin Brown argues that cultural products like ballet should not just be labeled as either highbrow and lowbrow culture but rather the cultural hierarchy is far more variable and not a simple dichotomy. She demonstrates that ballet in postwar America shows the malleability of the cultural hierarchy and in fact, the popularity of ballet in America was derived from the fact that it could navigate between lowbrow and highbrow ends of the cultural spectrum. Ballet appeared in America in highbrow venues but also in stadiums and on television. Ballet therefore could be deemed popular, though "part of ballet's allure was its perception of privilege."[52]

The Moiseyev was a cultural product that similarly navigated between lowbrow and highbrow culture. Attending the Moiseyev similarly had that "allure" of being a highbrow event with some of its performances at corresponding highbrow venues like the Metropolitan Opera House and Moiseyev's own Bolshoi background. At the same time, the Moiseyev dances took a more crowd-pleasing, flashier form than a classical ballet performance and more middlebrow in nature. In a New York program for the 1958 tour, the program text works hard to tie the Moiseyev to a lengthier history of Russian folk tradition and endeavors to point to how it is part of more high culture products. For instance, the text alludes to how Beethoven used Russian folk music in his own compositions and how it appears in familiar ballets like *Sleeping Beauty*.[53] Upon viewing the Moiseyev on its 1970 tour, Margo Miller concluded: "So much for the common notion that Russian folk dance is all thigh-slapping hijinks, armless catherine wheels, stomping, grinning and clapping." Instead, Miller was stunned by the performance's virtuosity and complexity.[54] Like others, Miller became convinced that the Moiseyev Folk Dance company presented a different kind of dance and certainly not lowbrow, overly slapstick traditional folk dance.

Igor Moiseyev's Response to the Tour

Reporters clamored to know what Moiseyev and his dancers thought about American culture. Moiseyev explained that he wanted not only to demonstrate Soviet culture and art but also to "absorb" American cultural idioms and expressions. In particular, he was eager to see the New York City Ballet, having heard a lot about it and having met the sister of NYCB ballerina Maria Tallchief in Paris. He noted how glad he was that Sol Hurok had invited him to see a Martha Graham production, since he wanted to recount American choreography back home in the Soviet Union and he claimed: "I want to discover America as much as I want to have America discover our form of choreographic art."[55] Moiseyev's stated desire to learn about American dance builds upon the preparation he did with his dancers before the tour to learn more about America and Americans. Here he is certainly reflecting the Soviet Union's officially stated support of cultural exchange as allowing the Soviet Union to learn from its Cold War enemy.

In a June 1958 interview, Moiseyev commented how much he had enjoyed the Martha Graham concert and her work as a specifically American product with an "exciting, unique and a very positive artistic expression." The *Dance News* editor, the Russian born Anatole Chujoy, asked Moiseyev what he thought would be best for the United States to send to the Soviet Union. Moiseyev replied that the musical *My Fair Lady*, then playing on Broadway, would be easy for Russians to understand and that *West Side Story*, another Broadway musical, would be a wise choice as well given its contemporary context and display of American talent. Moiseyev did, though, criticize the United States for sending *Porgy and Bess*, as it had been misunderstood by some and elicited some negative reaction. He concluded by saying that the United States should send dance companies performing American works, "not established classics which could not come up [to] the level of production and execution of the Moscow Bolshoi Theatre Ballet." At the same time, he warned against sending works like those of Martha Graham, since he was not sure if her work would be accessible to a Soviet audience.[56] In other words, the US should send cultural products that were middlebrow pieces, like the Moiseyev, in order to solicit a similar response.

Moiseyev chose to address the American people directly in a lengthy article in *Dance Magazine*. He acknowledged the enthusiastic reception the Moiseyev received and that he and the dancers did not arrive expecting such a reception, but instead had a certain number of misgivings: "We really had no idea of what we could expect. We were afraid, for one thing, that Americans would not understand our dancing and perhaps might not take to it." This fear, Moiseyev claimed, was justified due to the dearth of interaction between the superpowers recently. Moiseyev did not know what Americans would like and dislike and whether or not they would be able to "understand our national art." Accordingly, the hugely positive reception surprised the dance troupe and throughout the tour, Moiseyev felt welcomed and well received by the Americans.[57] Again drawing on the Soviet Union's rationale for supporting cultural exchange, Moiseyev identified the tour as teaching the world more about the Soviet way of life and he posed his approach to folk dance as a prime representative of the Soviet nation and its art.

Indeed, despite his fear that Americans might be unable to understand Soviet national art, Moiseyev instead found that Americans had a thorough understanding of the dances' artistic merits. Like the American reporters, Moiseyev felt there was a lot in common between Americans and Soviets: "We found the same warmth, the same openness and expansiveness, the same feeling for humor. It was a constant astonishment to us to see how similar the reactions were [to the Moiseyev]." The *City Quadrille* number "evoked the same spontaneous laughter in America as it would in any Soviet city. There was the same kind of understanding applause of the *Suite of Old Russian Dances* . . . the same delighted chuckles for our comic *Two Boys in a Fight*."[58] This surprised Moiseyev; he observed that he did not have to change the dances whatsoever in order for them to be understood by the American audience.

Moiseyev, too, picked up on the discourse of the fear of cultural inferiority. Prior to coming to the United States, he knew a little bit about American dance but nothing very specific. While on the tour, he took the opportunity to learn as much as possible about American dance and culture. He observed a variety in folk dance in America and that, like for his own choreography, American folk dance was a worthy source. In the same way, he had created the Moiseyev's dance repertoire using such folk material. However, in order to accomplish this in America, research needed to be done.

Moiseyev himself wanted to study American folk dances and add American dances to his repertoire. He was able to try out the "Virginia Reel" in New York. Here a group of Americans demonstrated the dance and the Moiseyev dancers gradually joined in, after which the Americans withdrew, leaving the Soviet dancers performing alone on the dance floor. Within two days the Moiseyev added the "Virginia Reel" to their own repertoire as the encore to their performance in New York and other cities. Moiseyev found it amusing that this essential American dance, which was performed after the finale dance "Hopak," was performed in "Ukrainian national dress" and that the audience reacted quite positively. Americans, Moiseyev remarked, could accomplish similar feats in folk dance using their own folk material.

But at the same time, in relating his experience with the "Virginia Reel," Moiseyev made it clear that the Soviet dancers had already mastered American folk dances, and quite quickly and easily too.

Moiseyev felt that the peoples of the Soviet Union were curious about America, Americans, and American culture. He observed that while many in the Soviet Union knew about American cultural expression in the form of literature, theater, and art, and "all of this helps us to get a picture of American life . . . without direct contact, it is necessarily an incomplete picture." It is interesting that Moiseyev highlights specifically how "direct contact" is necessary and otherwise the superpowers cannot truly understand each other as people. Moiseyev seems to imply the argument being made more broadly in this book; that the Moiseyev Dance Company's tour allowed Americans to navigate and negotiate the Cold War narrative. Moiseyev saw the impact the troupe had on their American audience, though it should also be noted that by underlining the need for direct contact, he supported continued cultural exchange endeavors and his troupe's continued employment therein.

This problem of the "incomplete picture" did not just concern the Soviet Union, but other countries. Countries with which the United States *did* have more contact did not necessarily know much about the positive aspects of American culture, but instead still held "certain misconceptions." Drawing upon the experiences from his many tours in different countries, Moiseyev related how Europeans told him the US did not have a well-developed theater culture and that American films, while entertaining, actually "harmed the theater art." Moiseyev hoped to allay American fears of cultural inferiority—he commented that he himself had seen many plays while in the United States and that he, as mentioned above, greatly enjoyed them. *West Side Story*, *The Diary of Anne Frank*, and *My Fair Lady* were all quite well done, in Moiseyev's opinion, and should be considered wonderful representations of American culture.[59] By noting the parallel development of American and Soviet culture, even noting positive comparison of American culture with French and his own artistic approach, Moiseyev again underscored the value of cultural exchange for enabling Soviet and American people to relate to one another.

In an undated letter, Moiseyev drew positive conclusions about the impact of the American tour overall and the ensemble's international presence. He felt that cultural exchange would result in increased friendly relations between the superpowers and emphasized that its impact was two-ways. Both Van Cliburn and the Philadelphia Orchestra's successes in the Soviet Union showed that cultural exchange held huge potential value. On the other side of things, the State Academic Folk Dance Ensemble of the USSR met with wonderful success in the United States and Americans expressed much interest in the ensemble and in the Soviet Union in general. Moiseyev felt he could identify a "desire among ordinary Americans to strengthen international ties . . . Americans want to know more about the country which astonished the world with its satellites, [and] whose contribution to the world treasury of art and literature earned the recognition of all humanity." During the US tour, Americans of varying economic and social backgrounds "often expressed the thought of how good [it would be] to do away with the Cold War and substitute it with an atmosphere of friendship, which [already] surrounds the performances of Soviet Artists in America and American artists in the Soviet Union." Moiseyev concluded that if cultural exchange continued and if both superpowers wholeheartedly supported it, it could lead to the end of the Cold War.[60]

Moiseyev's Report of the American Tour Results

Moiseyev deemed the tour a "thundering success" and a triumph.[61] The Soviet government also recognized it as such. After returning to the Soviet Union, Moiseyev presented a short report of the tour in the United States and Canada. He summarized first the number of Americans reached, namely that during the tour, the ensemble gave seventy performances to approximately 519,000 viewers as well appearing on the *Ed Sullivan Show* to an additional forty million viewers from across North America. Moiseyev noted that the American audience expressed curiosity and strong interest in the ensemble long before the group actually arrived on American soil. He related the scramble for tickets, adding that the first day of in-person ticket sales for the Metropolitan Opera performances featured "nasty rain" but still, "several thousand people stood in line for their turn [to buy tickets]."[62]

Moiseyev emphasized the political and cultural significance of the tour's New York debut. The first-night audience included major political figures, such as the Soviet ambassadors, State Department representatives, and ambassadors from India, Indonesia, Iran, and other countries, as well as cultural figures, including the president of the Metropolitan Opera Anthony

Bliss, choreographer Martha Graham, pianist Arthur Rubinstein, actor-activist Paul Robeson and others.[63] Other important political figures made appearances at later Moiseyev performances, including General Secretary of the United Nations Dag Hammarshel, who attended two performances by the ensemble. Unable to attend, President Eisenhower sent a personal letter expressing his regrets.[64] The performance began with the American and Soviet anthems, which the audience met the first dance with a "thundering" response. An "explosion of applause" greeted each new dance, and when the final piece ended, "the hall from the gallery to the orchestra/parterre applauded for almost 15 minutes."[65] Moiseyev emphasized how much the Americans were impressed by the dancers as clear evidence of the efficacy of cultural exchange.

The reception continued after the performance, when the audience "did not head home, but rather to the artist's exit. They flooded between Broadway and Seventh Avenue and in the flood [of people] waited forty minutes for the artists of the ensemble."[66] Relaying this information again supported a view of cultural exchange as effective for reaching the American people and demonstrating the Soviet way of life and implied superiority of its system.

Moiseyev made sure in his report to note how much the dancers learned during the tour. He remarked that during their free time, the dancers "dedicated [themselves] to the acquaintance with life and culture of the American people. They visited all the great museums of the country—the Met, the Frick in New York, the National Museum in Washington, Chicago, Boston, the Philadelphia museum, etc." Their American education also included tours of factories, film studios, and theatres. They viewed American films and shows including *West Side Story*, *My Fair Lady*, and *The Music Man*. While acknowledging a widely held impression that the United States had a less developed theatrical culture and indeed, when speaking about American culture, foreigners usually thought of jazz, Moiseyev praised works like *West Side Story* and *My Fair Lady* as representing a "subtlety of directing . . . and high taste [which] strongly rivals the most refined French samples."[67] The performances left a "huge impression," especially after Moiseyev met *West Side Story* choreographer Jerome Robbins. Moiseyev praised Robbins, who had worked with the Russian choreographer Michel Fokine in the early 1940s and considered him an inspiration. Robbins, Moiseyev believed, had achieved the same balance of drawing on classical ballet paired with a more contemporary style which Moiseyev himself tried to achieve. Indeed, after viewing *West Side Story*, Moiseyev later recalled, "I had my doubts about the correctness of the statement that our [Soviet] ballet is 'ahead of the rest.'" New York, in particular, impressed Moiseyev as the cultural center of America and he saw in American cultural products many things to be admired.[68]

Moiseyev reported that the audience's enthusiasm for the Moiseyev continued throughout the tour, and in some places, the price of a black-market ticket cost as much as eighty dollars. However, in his report, Moiseyev also noted less positive responses. Utilizing his rudimentary English skills, Moiseyev overheard reporters at the premiere phoning in their reactions, which included, "They [the dancers] were forced to dance so well, because if they danced badly, when they returned to Russia they would be banished to the salt mines," and "These artists, of course, the KGB, trained to be a success."[69] Though Moiseyev relayed this Cold War narrative view, it was not a view widely expressed in the press or by individuals in response to seeing the dancers perform.

In Los Angeles, "a group of anti-Soviet organizations" marched in front of the venue holding posters calling for the boycott of the performances. At the same time Moiseyev emphasized that the picketers were not violent, welcomed an invitation to view the show, and did not appear again the next day. In Boston similar protesters appeared, and this time, members of the audience angrily yelled "Beat it!" at them. One young audience member grabbed a protestor's sign resulting in a "Mighty buzz off [*sic*] approval in the audience."[70] When there were protests to the ensemble's performances, Moiseyev underlined that welcoming Americans far outnumbered the disapproving Americans and that the protestors were not particularly stubborn. Similarly to Americans, Moiseyev did not see the protests as off-putting or representing the American view as a whole.

Moiseyev's emphasis on the enthusiasm and the majority of Americans' disapproval of protestors served Moiseyev's personal agenda. His report to the Ministry of Culture demonstrated the effectiveness of cultural exchange in general and the American adoration for the Moiseyev specifically. This solidified the Moiseyev's position as a continued diplomatic tool and Moiseyev's position as head of the troupe—indeed, Moiseyev's success in establishing the victory of this first tour no doubt informed continued cultural exchange generally during the Cold War and the Moiseyev Dance

Company's role as regular exchange representative within it. The Soviet view of cultural exchange as successful would further be dependent on seeing the logistics of cultural exchange as feasible.

As impresario and organizer of the tour in all its details, Sol Hurok did everything in his power to make the tour a success. Hurok ensured that all the requested rehearsals took place and that the dancers had enough time off and time to travel without getting too worn out. Though the ensemble had feared the quality of accompanists during the tour, "our fears were unfounded. American musicians played flawlessly everywhere, and they only had one hour to learn our repertoire."[71] Choosing to emphasize the smooth coordination with accompanists is again helped express how effective and easy cultural exchange could be.

At the same time, not everything was within Hurok's power. The Moiseyev ran into problems with American officials. For instance, before the tour a great deal of heated discussion took place about whether or not the dancers should be permitted to fly on Soviet planes into the United States. This discussion ended with the dancers being forced to take commercial flights on other airlines. Moiseyev sensed that the police assigned to the performances agreed with the protestors and were accordingly less eager to keep them under control and from interfering with the dancers and the audience. Finally, officials sometimes prevented the dancers from visiting places they wanted to learn more about. For instance, Jack London's house north of San Francisco was off-limits.[72] However, these challenges did not negate Moiseyev's overall message of success, efficacy, and ease of cultural exchange.

In addition to creating and sharing his short report, after returning to Russia Moiseyev made statements in which he expressed open admiration of America and its culture, for which he was then censured. For three hours, in front of "600 leading creative artists in Moscow," Moiseyev claimed that the Soviet Union had no idea American culture was well-developed and thriving. Moiseyev's report caused an "uproar" in the Soviet Union. The Boston Globe, in terms similar to those used to describe the Moiseyev itself when it was in America, noted that the Moiseyev had taken "dynamite" home with it. The Ministry of Culture censured Moiseyev for his speech, which the Boston Globe described as "the full expression of a free spirit." Poetically, the Boston Globe article ended, "In the glare of that sort of cultural exchange the dark flowers of tyranny are likely to wither more quickly than other recent events have encouraged us to hope."[73] It should be stressed that during the Cold War, any experience of American culture by Soviets was problematic. Especially in the late 1950s, with cultural exchange so new, those few Soviet people who traveled to the United States had to be careful how they related their experience abroad once they returned home. The United States remained the capitalistic other that Soviet people were expected to criticize, not praise, and accordingly Moiseyev's talk came under much scrutiny.

This is certainly an instance where Igor Moiseyev's careful handling of promoting his troupe as an exemplar of Soviet artistic expression and a worthy cultural exchange representative was perhaps not as skillful. In the Ministry of Culture's records, multiple Soviet officials responded to Moiseyev's eager speech to the six hundred Soviet artists on December 11 and his report itself. The Head of the Main Directorate for the Protection of State Secrets in the Press, Pavel Romanov, wrote in a letter that same month how Americans, particularly in the *New York Times* coverage of the speech, were pleased by Moiseyev's positive depiction of American culture. According to Romanov, Moiseyev exaggerated, especially when saying that American theater could in fact compete with its European counterparts and that American music was rich in its development. Indeed, Romanov points out that Moiseyev's enthusiasm demonstrated that exposure to the United States actually could hurt the Soviet's own message; that what artists saw when they were abroad simply did not give them the full picture of the reality of the capitalist society and its faults.[74]

Moiseyev responded fervently to the criticism he received from Soviet officials; in back-to-back letters to the ministry on February 19 and 26, he shared how he was summoned by Minister of Culture Nikolai Mikhailov to meet with the Deputy Minister to discuss his report and speech. Moiseyev insisted that his words flowed from the purpose of culture exchange; to connect with the United States; and thus he did not focus on the negatives of American culture as this could hurt future exchange endeavors (and that the negatives were well known in the Soviet Union already). He claimed his framing should have made this apparent to his audience since he shared that he purposefully focused on the positive so as to inform Soviet artists and intellectuals about American cultural products to inform future exchange. In both letters Moiseyev expressed dismay at the criticism he received and about being summoned to the Ministry of Culture. He emphasized his many years of work for the government and contributions to Soviet art and that the Minister of Culture was in fact mispresenting him and tarnishing his reputation. In the second letter, Moiseyev underscored how he always carried out whatever he was asked to do by the government, even signing the letter "national artist of the Soviet Union."[75]

Two Soviet officials, including Dmitri Polikarpov, Head of the Department of Culture of the Central Committee of the Communist Party, highlighted how Moiseyev was "complaining" about the Minister of Culture's depiction of him and pointed again to the *New York Times* article emphasizing Moiseyev's positive view of American culture after the 1958 visit. The officials chastised Moiseyev, noting the praise of American culture as "excessive" and careless of Igor Moiseyev; he essentially provide a one-sided view of the state of art in America which hurt rather than helped the Soviet's own cultural exchange goals.[76]

Though there is no indication of it in Moiseyev's contemporary report on the tour or other official documents included as part of the American tour files, in his memoirs Moiseyev filled in the details about his talk and struggled to understand the censure it incurred. He remarked that as soon as he returned from the United States, people in Moscow pressured him about the tour, which was understandable given the lack of communication and travel between the Soviet Union and United States. This led to Moiseyev giving a talk at the Society for Friendship with Foreign Countries. After giving a speech of his impressions of the United States and Americans, Ministry of Culture Minister Nikolai Mikhailov criticized Moiseyev for "crawling on his belly in front of American culture." Moiseyev claimed he had only spoken of interesting aspects of life in America and that he did not overly praise America or American ideals, and thus he did not understand Mikhailov's criticism, especially given the amount of praise Van Cliburn, a representative of American culture, received in the Soviet Union.[77]

Official Soviet Reaction to the Ensemble's 1958 American Tour

Censure aside, the Soviet government agreed with Moiseyev's report and his opinion of how well the tour had gone. The Ministry of Culture reported on the results of the tours to North America, noting the complex conditions under which the ensemble worked and noting the number of viewers who experienced the company through its live and television performances. The Ministry of Culture said the concerts were "a huge success" and furthered the "development of cultural ties between the Soviet Union, United States and Canada and of the feeling of sympathy [among them]."[78] In the ministry's view, the tour accomplished its stated goals for cultural exchange, including permitting them to learn more about the United States and creating a positive image of the Soviet Union and its system. Accordingly, the Soviet government awarded the ensemble bonuses of 75,000 rubles for its contributions to Soviet art and cultural exchange.[79] The government also awarded the dancers awards recognizing the ensemble's contribution to presenting a positive image of Soviet art while Moiseyev himself received the Order of Lenin among other awards.[80]

Soviet books published in the wake of the tour emphasized the extremely high anticipation Americans felt toward the ensemble's arrival. This anticipation included numerous photographs, articles, and discussion of the potential for breaking down barriers. The first few performances in New York "exceeded all expectations. American audiences cheered and applauded wildly. Everywhere the press paid ungrudging tribute to the Soviet dancers." They also emphasized the impact of the tour on Americans. Wherever the Moiseyev dancers went, "An atmosphere of friendship, good cheer and hospitality surrounded the dancers."[81] The Soviet amplification of the positive American response fed into their goals for cultural exchange but also undergirds how the dancers escaped the Cold War American narrative's depiction of the Soviet enemy.

Soviet writers took note of how average Americans wanted to meet the Soviet dancers and felt the ensemble accomplished its goal of easing tensions between the Soviet Union and United States. Betty Conrad, a mother of ten, for instance, wrote to the company and invited the dancers to her home to meet her family. She wrote that "We shall never forget the Sunday performance you gave," and that she wanted to learn more about the dancers on a personal level. Indeed, after the ensemble's television performance, the "'Sibias' television company [CBS] was literally deluged with letters and telegrams in which spectators expressed their appreciation and gratitude." For Conrad, and for other Americans, the Moiseyev performances calmed their fears regarding their Cold War enemy and enabled them to negotiate with the Cold War narrative and see the dancers as people, rather than as potential species or causes of nuclear war.

While there were some protestors, contemporary Americans did not take the Moiseyev protestors seriously and claimed they did not represent the majority of the American populace. Americans dealt with the protestors promptly, forcing one audience member to leave after "disrespectful behaviour during the playing of the Soviet Union's national anthem." Most Americans loved and adored the dancers. Sol Hurok summed up that the Moiseyev "was the most talented dance group which had ever visited the U.S.A."[82] Contemporary Soviet accounts depicted Americans bowing down before the superior Soviet cultural skill and expression, supporting the Soviet Cold War narrative in this case.

In another instance of the tour's success from the Soviet perspective, Americans recognized Igor Moiseyev individually for his superb work in folk dance with a *Dance Magazine* Award in 1961 in recognition of his choreographic achievements but also for his political achievements.[83] Moiseyev was the first non-American to receive this award and it served as fodder for the Soviet regime's depiction of Moiseyev's success as a diplomatic tool.[84] Clearly the American audience viewed the Moiseyev as something they had never seen before and that the ensemble's skill elevated folk dance to a whole new level. The ensemble "brought to the American stage the breath and spirit of a vast faraway land and its many peoples who were full of creative virtue and unconquerable optimism."[85] While Americans saw an escape from the Cold War narrative, for Soviets the reported response reinforced it.

In addition to the instances Igor Moiseyev relayed, the dancers received many invitations to view American cultural expression, which the Soviet regime would have recognized as fulfilling their goal of learning from other nations through exchange. For instance, the dancers visited the New York studio of Michael Herman (originally Mikhail Gherman from the Ukraine) and learned the American Square Dance, which became a popular encore in the ensemble's North American performances. Indeed, Americans expressed an avid interest in Soviet folk dance, and throughout the tour begged the ensemble "for advice, for a lesson, or a lecture." Igor Moiseyev complied in New York, where he held a lecture on folk dance for choreographers and dance instructors.[86] Contemporary accounts emphasized how much Americans desired to learn from the Moiseyev and to try to imitate the dancers' skills, similarly achieving yet another Soviet goal of teaching others about the Soviet way of life.

Soviet accounts concluded by noting that, "the American press had never paid such unanimous tribute to any form of artistic endeavour. . . . All the newspapers and magazines, regardless of their political sympathies, al reviewers, whatever their standing, spoke in such high superlatives as 'fantastic,' 'superb,' 'magnificent' of the Soviet dancers' preferences." The ensemble was a highly effective diplomatic tool, more so than any ambassador or traditional means of forming a political understanding between countries. Additionally, Americans admired Soviet accomplishments in the arts and in science and technology and wanted to learn more about Soviet people. They wanted peace and friendship with the Soviet Union. The cultural exchange initiative proved incredibly successful and, as Moiseyev put it, "It is to our mutual cultural advantage . . . [to continue cultural exchange] to consolidate ties of friendship between peoples. . . . The Cold war retreats before the advance of art."[87] Moiseyev demonstrated how successful cultural exchange could be and cemented his dance company's continued role in it.

American reception of the Moiseyev did not reflect a black and white world divided between American and Soviet, but instead demonstrated a more nuanced understanding of the Cold War world and of Soviet people. The ensemble received overwhelmingly positive response but with certain complexities. Americans still viewed the Moiseyev (for the most part) with politics in mind and often used Cold War terms or events to describe the dances and dancers. As will be explored in greater depth in the following chapter, Americans complicated the Cold War narrative by viewing the dancers as people similar to themselves rather than as Cold War enemies. There were those critics and individuals who could not escape the Cold War narrative view of Soviet people and communism as inherently negative or evil but both the American press and Igor Moiseyev himself labeled this as a minority view and one which did not interfere with the overall American population enjoying the ensemble's performances and taking their multicultural message to heart.

CHAPTER 5

Fascinating Human Beings

On behalf of my husband and children as well as for myself, I want to
thank you for sharing with us your extraordinary talents and artistry.
The enthusiasm, happiness, humor, friendliness, and love expressed
so magnificently through your dancing, will be long-lasting with us.

—Letter from Debby Jacobs to Igor Moiseyev, May 28, 1958

The Moiseyev Dance Company's 1958 tour profoundly affected its American audiences and, as will be examined in-depth in this chapter, enabled them to see the Soviet dancers as human beings. However, along with this personal connection felt by Americans was a heavy dose of fascination and voyeurism to the point of the dancers becoming celebrities during their visit. News reporters and individual American citizens did their best to learn as much as possible about the dancers on and offstage. Much of this fascination and view of the dancers as human beings stemmed from the pairing of the dancers as the first Soviets many Americans had ever seen in person and a widely expressed response of being able to relate to the dancers and the folk dances they performed, despite the openly articulated cultural and political differences between American and Soviet peoples.

Cultural exchange broadly and in the form of the Moiseyev Dance Company's tour specifically can be viewed as "pseudo-events" in which consideration not only of the performance itself but how it was covered in the media came to the fore. Given the sponsoring superpower's awareness of the amount of media coverage involved due to the inflated sense of impact any cultural exchange moment could have in this Cold War, both the Soviet Union and United States brought a great deal of intentionality to every aspect of their cultural exchange moments, the resources and literature about the cultural diplomats, and how they framed the propagandistic message inherent in the exchanges. As scholar Danielle Fosler-Lussier traces in her study of American cultural exchange efforts in music, this also entailed an emphasis on the performers themselves and what they and their performances could impart about the United States. Thus, in addition to permitting audience members to feel they were viewing a true representative of the United States, cultural diplomats' "manners, appearance, and interactions would be open to view, interpreted as evidence about America by eyewitnesses and in the press."[1] With Soviet cultural diplomats, Americans similarly felt they could understand the Soviet people as a result of viewing a performance or media coverage of exchange moments like the 1958 Moiseyev Dance Company tour. And again, similarly, Americans clamored to observe and learn more about the dancers offstage in addition to onstage, once more feeling the details gleaned filled in the picture of Soviet peoples and way of live even further.

Privileging of the Moiseyev Dancers' Opinions

Americans very much wanted to know what the Moiseyev dancers thought of America and of American culture. The dancers, as the first Soviets visiting the United States in many years, were viewed as representatives of the entire Soviet population. Their opinions, therefore, would offer insight into prevailing Soviet opinions and illustrate how typical Soviet citizens would react to America. Americans privileged the dancers' opinions and clamored for their reactions to all aspects of American life. For instance, W. G. Rogers of Hanover, Pennsylvania's *The Evening Sun*, asked Igor Moiseyev about any purchases Mr. Moiseyev had made (a camera "and all the fixings" for $1,200) and also whether or not he liked modern art, to which Mr. Moiseyev replied "no," though the reporter noted he did like "Picasso (the Communist)."[2] Igor Moiseyev's likes and dislikes were part of wide coverage afforded the dancers for an eager American public and again, thought to be representative of more than just Igor Moiseyev himself.

The dancers' thoughts on America and what they encountered on their visit was a large part of this coverage. In an interview with female dancers, reporters asked dancer Galina Korolkova to compare New York to Chicago. She replied, "'In New York it is impossible to differentiate one skyscraper from the other. . . . There is more harmony here, more space.'" This statement, no doubt, delighted Chicago reporters but also exemplifies how highly Americans valued the dancers' perspective. Americans were curious about the Soviet viewpoint, and the dancers became arbiters of Soviet taste as it resembled or diverged from American taste. They received special status and functioned as representatives for the Soviet people overall, being asked everything from opinions on pointed toe shoes to New York City streets.[3]

Reporters prompted the dancers to draw comparisons between Soviet and American lives, just as Americans did in reaction to the Moiseyev. No doubt they hoped the dancers would love America and think it better than the Soviet Union. In grilling the dancers about their leisure time, reporters discovered that they loved rock 'n' roll but preferred visiting museums above all else, and they liked to drink vodka ("But they're always on the job the next morning"). As for their opinion of American folk dance, which will be discussed further below, they proclaimed it "'Zamylitchatinoya' . . . Wonderful."[4] Given the impressive nature of the Moiseyev dancers own performances, no doubt Americans would be flattered by this positive opinion. Though these compelled comparisons could feed into the American Cold War narrative, the consistent view expressed was the dancers as human beings, similar to or the same as their American counterparts. When reporters told anecdotes about Soviet-American interactions, they frequently emphasized the dancers' emotions and especially when Americans and Soviets smiled at each other or laughed together. The press highlighted positive exchanges between Soviets and Americans and assigned the dancers not just an official cultural role, but also a social, personal one.

The focus on offstage experiences of American life and culture continued with later tours. Evidence abounds of the American audience's continued obsession with what the Moiseyev dancers did, not only on the stage, but off as well. The 1965 tour featured news reports describing the Russian dancers' visit to the "Whisky A Go-Go" nightclub in San Francisco and joining in the dancing. In particular, reporters noted how quickly the Russians learned the newest dances like "The Swim"—the dancers "didn't invent the swim dance, but took to it like capitalists."[5] Indeed, one of the male dancers danced "The Hunch" with a Go-Go girl, who convinced him to dance in a suspended glass cage. He improvised on "The Hunch" by adding dance moves from the Cossack squat dance. The Go-Go dancer, whose name was Colleen Costello, raved, "'Everything—the minute I did it, he could do it.'"[6]

The Dancers as Celebrities

The Moiseyev dancers became celebrities in 1958 and even American celebrities wanted to meet and talk to them. In Hollywood, reporter Bob Thomas observed that film stars became fans of the dance troupe as well and attended their performances, numbering among them Jack Benny, Burt Lancaster, Gene Kelly, Milko Taka, and Mel Ferrer. He then went on to quote from the famous stars of the day:

> Raved Anthony Quinn "This is the greatest thing I've ever seen." "Fantastic," said Kirk Douglas, and Lauren Bacall remarked, "Unbelievable." Said Debbie Reynolds: "I'm speechless. It's a trendous [*sic*] emotional experience." Oscar Levant cracked "they're marvelous—too bad they're Russian."[7]

The Hollywood stars agreed on the amazing nature of the performances. Even Debbie Reynolds, a singing and dancing star herself, claimed to be overwhelmed by the display.

Hollywood admiration did not end with the performance itself. Civic officials hosted a post-performance party at the Beverly Hills Hotel for the dancers. Among the guests were the mayor of Los Angeles, the president of the Hollywood Bowl Association, and celebrities like Danny Kaye, Gregory Peck, and Clifton Webb. Everyone had a marvelous time—the Soviet dancers even spontaneously danced to the jitterbug, Charleston, and rock 'n' roll.[8] Elizabeth Taylor and Eddie Fisher hosted a late party for the dancers as well, with one hundred celebrity guests such as Tony Curtis, Janet Leigh, Mel Ferrer, and Lawrence Harvey and featuring jazz music.[9] The celebrity status of the Moiseyev dancers allowed them to mix with America's own celebrities. In Hollywood, and throughout their tour, they encountered a genuine desire to see them perform and to know all about them but, more importantly, a genuine desire to interact with them offstage on a personal level and to encourage them to experience American life for themselves. Though American fascination did take on the form of fandom, the emphasis on the individual dancers, as discussed below, framed them as human beings.

This latter desire is demonstrated by the Moiseyev dancers' inability to leave California without also visiting its great tourist attraction—Disneyland. *LA Times* reporter Cordell Hicks related all the details of this visit, from the observation that "the only way you could tell them from the rest of the throng in appearance was when they spoke" to the fact that "They rode everything. Twice." Typically, they also reported that the dancers shopped at Disneyland, and all bought souvenir hats "with 'Disneyland' in large letters across the crowns."[10] Additionally, reporters wanted to know if the dancers felt that the Soviet Union had anything like Disneyland. The dancers responded that they had many things to entertain children like ballets and puppet theaters and trained animals. But upon being asked again if any of these things were like Disneyland, they finally responded "Nyet." Reporters described this visit as a victory for America's amusement park. While their enthusiasm was expressed by riding each Disneyland ride twice, the consumption of treats, and the purchase of souvenirs, the dancers returned to the stereotypical image of the serious, unsmiling Russian after the conclusion of their visit to Disneyland.

Though each city devoted articles to what Moiseyev dancers ate, shopped for, and admired in America, later on in the tour reporters did note that some of the dancers were getting tired of these kinds of interactions with reporters. The *San Francisco News* reported that:

> Soviet Russia's stupendous Moiseyev Dancers are it turns out, only humans—and young ones, at that. They're getting mighty weary of doing the hick shopping-and-sightseeing routine to please those quaint American newspapermen, they confessed today.

The younger members in particular were "fed up" with this sort of routine.[11] This is not reported as rude or as a negative on the part of the dancers. Instead, the commentator remarks that the dancers are human too and growing weary the press's gimmicks. According to the *San Francisco News*, the dancers could only endure so much; here the dancers came off as sympathetic figures while American journalists came off as trying too hard to make the dancers' every move part of the capitalism versus communism debate.

Personal Notes to the Moiseyev

Perhaps even more telling than the published accounts of American curiosity about the Moiseyev dancers are the personal letters, notes and thank you cards sent to Igor Moiseyev and the company during their tour. These were carefully gathered and archived by the Soviet Union along with the documents related to the tour. A typical example: Ona Storkins Mama-roneck, in a note addressed to Igor Moiseyev, proclaimed that "On Satur-day, May 3, I had the greatest thrill of my life" (this, of course, being the day she saw the Moiseyev at the Metropolitan Opera House). "The dancers' reactions to the audience's applause in the end was so friendly that it made a perfect ending to a perfect performance." Wanting to ensure she would never forget this exciting moment, Ona asked Moiseyev to send her the pic-tures and names of all the performers (or at least those of the soloists). She was more than willing to pay for these and thanked Moiseyev once more for the performance.[12]

Ona's note further underlines positive American reception to the Moiseyev—but also the perception of a personal connection that Ameri-cans felt toward the dancers. Certainly, Americans viewed the dancing as wonderful entertainment, but their reception went deeper than mere appreciation for the dances. Americans did not view the Moiseyev in a strictly bifurcated manner, as audience versus performers, Americans ver-sus Soviets, and democracy versus communism. They presented a more nuanced view of the dancers and of themselves and how the two fit together. Though the dancers could have been perceived as purely exotic, instead they became identified as welcome visitors that Americans felt they could personally reach out to—and with the expectation that surely the dancers would reciprocate.

On an individual basis, Americans wrote to Igor Moiseyev in the same way they might write to an American they admired and wanted to know better. They did not view him as unapproachable or as someone who would not be able to understand Americans' thoughts, needs and concerns. A few assumed that if they wrote to Moiseyev, he would be able to help them get tickets to performances. Mrs. Seymour M. Hallbron wrote a long letter in which she mentioned repeatedly how well connected she was and remind-ing Moiseyev that they had met during a reception at Ambassador Lall's house. Through this connection, she hoped to obtain tickets for a doctor friend in Philadelphia for the troupe's performances there: "You will be there with your troupe on June 11 and 12 and he [the doctor] cannot get any tickets for love or money. He says they are all sold out. He wants three tick-ets and he has been so good to me that I would like to present them to him. Would it be possible to have someone send me 3 tickets and I will be very happy to send the check for them." She went on to say that the good doctor would additionally like to have backstage access for himself, his wife, and friends in order to meet the dancers. She noted that the doctor called the Moiseyev the "crème de la crème" and explained, for Igor Moiseyev's benefit (perhaps not knowing he was fluent in French) that this meant the best of the best.[13]

Even those who had not met Moiseyev personally felt they could write to him pleading for tickets. Mr. Sherley Ashton wrote saying that he had studied Russian for three years and was very eager to see the troupe perform. However, he could not get a ticket at the San Francisco Opera House and asked Moiseyev for "any form of ticket, at any price."[14] Mr. Ashton related how several years before he had worked with a member of the Soviet delegation to the UN and attached his own biography to his letter to reinforce his Russian background. Americans felt they could write to Igor Moiseyev and appeal to his good nature. Mrs. Halbron, for example, was certain he would want to ensure that people with a certain position in American society saw the performances. Ashton claimed to have a special need for tickets based on his previous experience with Soviet people and the Russian language, an appeal to which he was certain that Moiseyev would respond.

Many expressed a desire to meet Moiseyev and his company. One couple from Chicago wrote Mr. Moiseyev a letter, describing themselves as "young Chicagoans interested in the arts, and in your country and its relations with ours," requested to meet the dancers, especially those of similar age, even though neither husband nor wife knew any Russian. They hoped the Moiseyev could spare two to four dancers so that the couple could entertain them in their Chicago apartment. Mr. Ludgin noted that he and his wife led "surprisingly typical lives": he was the editor of an encyclopedia and she was a housewife. They wanted to meet young Russians in order to show them a typical American lifestyle, but also because, despite an inability to speak Russian, they could communicate their cultural interests.[15] The Ludgins believed that Americans and Soviets could communicate and relate to one another despite the language barrier; the Moiseyev had already demonstrated this through their performances.

Audience members found their enthusiasm grew immediately upon viewing the dancers, as did the urge to express thanks. Mr. Roger J. Durmont penned a letter on June 2, noting, along with the date, that the letter was written at 1 a.m. Addressing Igor Moiseyev directly, he said that he had only just arrived home from the San Francisco Opera House and the Moiseyev program and, upon his arrival, immediately sat down to record his reactions. He congratulated Moiseyev on the skill and success of the troupe, observing, "It was a memorable evening one that I shall not soon forget."[16] Americans found the Moiseyev instantly electrifying, an impression that endured over time. This active positivism toward the dancers is striking, with many Americans indicating the need to share their admiration for the dancers with the dancers themselves, as well as with anyone else who would listen.

By the time of the first tour by the Moiseyev in America in 1958, the "iron curtain" had fallen; communism dominated eastern and parts of central Europe; and to Americans it appeared as if the Soviet Union was bent on global domination. Americans heard peoples living in the Eastern Bloc described as oppressed; the regime change to communism being viewed as a compulsory change and reinforced by direct and indirect Soviet control. Various moments of rebelliousness in these areas, such as the Hungarian Revolt in 1956, provided the evidence Americans needed to support this view.

Once more, however, the reaction to the Moiseyev stepped outside the Cold War narrative of communism as oppressive and devoid of anything that could possibly appeal to free people. Immigrants and those of Russian and Eastern European heritage expressed this in writing to the troupe. Peter Gawura of Dearborn, Michigan wrote: "On behalf of the Ukrainian people who were born in Western Ukraine, and those who were born in United States, I wish to thank you for your wonderful dance performances in Detroit, Michigan."[17] Mr. Gawura regretted that the Ukrainians did not get to meet the dancers and emphasized that he would have liked to invite the dancers to his home also, so that his family and friends could meet them. In lieu of this, he sent this "letter of friendship" and hoped to hear back from the troupe in the near future.

Americans wanted to interact with Igor Moiseyev and the Moiseyev dancers on a personal level. They did not view the dance troupe as just a piece of propaganda meant to change Americans' opinions of the Soviet Union and communism. Rather, they reacted to the Moiseyev with great empathy and expressed the desire to communicate with them on a level that was more intimate and individualized.

In addition to individuals, local and national groups invited the Moiseyev to receptions, talks, and performances, hoping to meet and interact with the dancers. The Folk Dance Federation of California invited the Moiseyev to a three-day event in which folk dances would be performed and folk dancers

FIGURE 4. Tamara Zeifert and Lev Golovanov in the Russian Suite. Source: M. Chudnovsky, *The Folk Dance Company of the USSR: Igor Moiseyev, Art Director* (Moscow: Foreign Languages Publishing House, 1959), 25.

from the United States and Soviet Union could meet.[18] The Folklore Education and Research Institute in Chicago similarly wrote to the Moiseyev in order to try to meet the company's dancers. The Institute wanted to discuss Russian folk dance and asked for a future meeting in order to accomplish this.[19] The Ethnic Dance Theatre of Los Angeles, which had served as host to other groups like the Armenian Ballet Company, Kansuma Kabuki Theatre, and Afro-American Dancers similarly invited the Moiseyev to attend performances.[20] All these groups emphasized that the cultural exchange promoted by the Lacy-Zarubin Agreement should not just consist of official performances by the Moiseyev Dance Company. Rather, exchange should be taken to the next level, and folk dances and folklore should be exchanged on both sides.

Hungry for Details

American audiences did not receive the Moiseyev passively. They wanted to know every little detail about the dancers: what they liked to eat, what souvenirs they bought, if they were married, if they liked American music—the list goes on. Indeed, journalists chose to highlight these likes and dislikes in their reports of the Moiseyev experience in America. Commentators devoted entire articles to the dancers' reactions to everything American—especially the food—in comparison to what they enjoyed at home in the Soviet Union:

> They grew terribly fond of American pie, which they call "priog." [*sic*] They have gone in rather heavily for the hotdog. They discovered waffles, and like them. They are also pretty happy over American pancakes, which they call "blini." In Russia, they have caviar and sour cream with a similar cake. They've gone ca-razy about milkshakes, especially chocolate-flavored.[21]

The idea of Soviets enjoying American hot dogs and even labeling American foods with their Russian equivalents tickled Americans. In particular, the press emphasized the collective sweet tooth of the ensemble, noting how the dancers happily consumed numerous desserts yet remained physically fit. The American audience soaked up details of Soviet eating habits with just as much enthusiasm as they had received the dancers' performances. They very much appreciated the opportunity to learn what Soviets liked about American life and American products. Accordingly, every small thing the dancers experienced in the United States became intriguing news in the American press and the American audience readily welcomed such reports.

This discussion of food included health and healthy living choices. While the details of Soviet food selections amused most Americans, others worried about the impression the Soviet dancers would draw about American food preferences and lifestyles. Elizabeth Palmer, an American nutritionist, wrote to Igor Moiseyev personally to express certain concerns regarding the dancers' diets. Palmer mentioned that press coverage of the dancers featured them consuming candy bars, ice cream, and soda, and advised the dancers to note that American health standards (and corresponding food options) needed improvement so the dancers should look to eschew some of the foods they appeared to eagerly consume.[22]

Palmer warned against "refined bakery products" and hot dogs ("poor man's food"). She went on to note that in the cities, specifically in Chicago, the water was not the cleanest and that the dancers should instead purchase bottled spring water as it tasted better and was healthier. Palmer feared that the Soviet dancers would be corrupted by this aspect of American life. Like other Americans who encountered the Moiseyev, she offered to explain American food traditions and fads to them, but enhanced her analysis with opinions as to what formed the basis of a good, healthy diet. The tone and emphasis by Palmer, as in other instances, was of seeing the dancers as fellow humans who, in this case, might need help in the form of diet advice just as her American clients did.

American Desire for Soviet Admiration of Capitalism

The Cold War narrative, which underlay American-Soviet perception in 1958, emphasized the vast divide between communism and capitalism, with America touting capitalism as far superior. Unsurprisingly, how the Moiseyev dancers viewed capitalism, their nation's alleged antithesis, fascinated Americans. A tour by the dancers of the Ford Automobile Factory in Detroit, a bastion of American capitalism, had greater meaning than a simple tourist activity for the American audience, and received particular political emphasis. This tour was covered not just in the local press, but also in national papers like the *New York Post*. The dancers were quite polite during the tour, made notes, and took pictures. Many journalists commented that the Russians were "typical" tourists, acting like "a senior class from Dubuque." The fact that the dancers were "typical" proved a disappointment for some. The tour's bus driver, Bill Mulroy, "groused" that "I can't tell them from the regular tourists." The dancers came off as normal human beings visiting the factory as any American might.

However, this should not give the impression that everyone was necessarily in agreement. Though most of the dancers left the impression of being like any other tourist group (or even a high school basketball team), "Two of the girls, with waist-length pigtails and sad Russian eyes, made you want to hum, 'Ochi Chornie.'"[23] This no doubt was an allusion to the Ukrainian song "Ochi chyornye" (Black Eyes), which was usually identified as Russian. This view reflects perhaps the more expected American reaction to the dancers, as it emphasizes the idea of Russians as sad and somber—emotions reflected in Russian cultural products of the time. It is in direct contrast to Americans' reaction to the dancers as the vibrant, joyful personalities they had witnessed onstage.

Given Ford's established role as a cornerstone of American manufacturing, Americans were curious about how Ford's production method would compare with its Soviet counterpart. Stalin's five year plans to push the Soviet Union's economy forward and increase industrialization on a mass scale elicited production and growth numbers that were awe-inspiring, particularly during the Great Depression and America's own difficulties in that time period. While the US had provided supplies and aid during the Lend-Lease Program as the Soviet Union rapidly prepared its military for war with Germany, once underway the Soviet war machine ground out impressive numbers of armaments—and this continued emphasis on military and industrial production persisted into the Cold War. What would the dancers, therefore, think when comparing their industrial sector with America's? When asked his impressions, one dancer claimed, "We have never seen anything like this before," while another noted, "The factory is so clean" but refused to compare it with the Soviet equivalent (despite prompting by American reporters).[24]

The American press yearned for direct comparisons between capitalism and communism, ideally with capitalism being labeled the superior of the two. However, the dancers were not willing to oblige in this instance. The dancers were most interested in seeing the automobiles coming off the assembly line completed and ready to go. A blond dancer, Susanna Agranovskya, loved the convertibles and exclaimed how "You just push a button and the top folds back!"[25] The American press vied for Soviet reactions to this model of American capitalism. They hoped to draw out, not just positive opinions toward the factory, but also comparisons with Soviet factories and products, likely hoping the Soviet dancers would conclude that America's factories and cars were better.

The presence of KGB agents in their midst no doubt contributed to the dancers' reluctance to draw direct comparisons between American and Soviet industry. Sending KGB agents, or "companions" was an aspect of Soviet exchange programs that continued through the fall of the Soviet Union. These agents accompanied the Moiseyev dancers on this tour, future tours and tours undertaken by other cultural groups and figures. Communist Party officials and the KGB did careful background checks on all the dancers prior to their departure from Moscow. The accompanying KGB agents imposed a curfew on the dancers and made sure no one got out of line or traveled alone.

These KGB agents did not precisely blend with the rest of the dancers and other supporting personnel. As Edward Ivanyan, a Ministry of Culture official, put it, "It was even funny, because they were immediately noticeable to both sides, and had meaningless titles like Personnel Director or Director of the Raising of the Curtains."[26] For the dancers, the message was clear: everyone was to conduct themselves in a manner befitting a representative from the Soviet Union to its rival country. This meant presenting a positive image of the Soviet Union at all times and minimizing exposure to possible harmful influences.

Whether Americans recognized the KGB presence or not is debatable. Some critics and members of the audience thought the presence of the KGB was inevitable and that they could even identify specific KGB agents among the dancers. Other critics and reporters did not take this at all seriously, and felt that the cultural exchange agreement was being followed to the letter, which precluded the need to send intelligence agents with the dancers. Most newspapers did not comment on the potential KGB presence and instead simply noticed that the dancers went out on their own during their free time.[27] This, however, did not tell the full story of a Soviet cultural exchange representative's experience abroad during the Soviet period. In a recent interview, singer Dmitri Hvorostovsky recalled his two female "companions" who accompanied him on a trip to the Toulouse Singing Competition in 1988. Hvorostovsky did not find the two women too much of an encumbrance, but this changed when he won the competition and, after receiving an ovation and prize money onstage, had to hand the money over to "the KGB boss lady" so "the Soviet government could take its share."[28] Though the Soviet regime selected artists like Hvorostovsky to represent Soviet culture and identity, this did not necessarily mean the regime allowed the

artists greater freedom or favors. Rather, these artists experienced difficulties in their travels and a need to be ever-conscious of toeing the approved
government line.

Thus when the Moiseyev dancers visited the United States and spoke
with reporters, they had to be careful what they said and who they spoke to
because of the KGB presence and the intense scrutiny they experienced as
part of the tour. Accordingly, when American reporters questioned the dancers about what they liked about America and how it compared to the Soviet
Union, the dancers could not answer without carefully considering their
responses and how the KGB and the Soviet regime would react. The message
Americans received from the dancers was always negotiated via the policies
dictated by the Soviet regime. While this means that the dancers should be
viewed with this influence ever in mind, it does not mean that their reactions
and responses to their American tour experience cannot be used. Rather,
the focus is on American reactions, as well as how most Americans did not
appear to be aware that the dancers could not be entirely honest and genuine.

Dancer-to-Dancer Exchange

Along with the official performances, Americans were sometimes treated to
spontaneous exhibitions of contrasting, side-by-side dance cultures. There
are several anecdotes of Moiseyev dancers watching and learning American
folk dances. In New York, sixty Moiseyev dancers attended an "American
'hoe down'" at Folk Dance House. There they watched and learned how
to dance traditional folk dances like the Virginia Reel, Texas Schottische,
and New England Square Dance. A reporter observed that Igor Moiseyev
wrote notes throughout the performance and dance lessons and posited
that Moiseyev would likely share these American folk dances back in the
Soviet Union.[29] The implication of such a statement was twofold. The Soviet
troupe could easily learn American folk dances and Igor Moiseyev would
be able to produce a wonderful version of the American dances, as he had
with folk dances of so many other cultures. Indeed, at the final performance
in New York at the Metropolitan Opera House the Moiseyev performed
the Virginia Reel to "Turkey in the Straw."[30] Though the reporter could have
expressed fear or disappointment from witnessing how easily American
culture could be imitated and adapted by the Moiseyev, instead he and the
American audience in general delighted in this form of cultural exchange.

In another instance, Moiseyev (along with lead dancer Lev Golovanov) offered a master class for New York dancers in June of 1958. Five hundred dancers attended the class and from all different dance backgrounds and experiences:

> There were modern dancers, ballet dancers, tap dancers, ethnic dancers, choreographers, performers from Broadway shows, members of folk dance societies, distinguished teachers (some of them Russian born), neophytes, balletomanes, photographers, journalists. High school students rubbed elbows with teachers of forty years' experience. There were expert professionals and there were amateurs barely able to distinguish the left foot from the right.

The critic-historian and former dancer Lillian Moore attended the class. It began with Moiseyev describing how the Soviet Union consisted of many different peoples and many different cultures and how the dances served as expressions of these cultures. With Golovanov he then went on to demonstrate a variety of steps, and the dancers in turn imitated him, "jigging enthusiastically, tripping over the toes of their neighbors, digging their elbows into each other's sides, and having a perfectly marvelous time." By the end of the class, all the students remained enthusiastic, and Moiseyev himself commented that "We have found a common language. If we want to understand each other better, let us dance together more often."[31] Like the many Americans who wrote to him, Moiseyev pointed to a way to communicate despite language differences and encouraged the view frequently expressed by Americans in reaction to the tour; that they could and should relate to the Soviet dancers as human beings.

Reporter Bob Thomas noted that many Americans, after seeing the Moiseyev, wondered why (in his opinion) there was no American equivalent that could compete with the Soviet dance troupe. Thomas turned to Marjorie Champion (a dancer and choreographer) and her husband Gower Champion (a dancer, director, and choreographer) Champion to answer this question. They replied, "Serious dancing in America is sick and can take some lessons from the Russians" and agreed that America did not have anything that could compete with the Russian dancers at that time.[32] However, he also left the door open for American artists to improve. He claimed that American dancers had the potential to perform as well as the Soviet dancers that the folk source material for Americans was "just as rich" as that for the Soviets, listing Mexican, Native American, and jazz dances as possible points of departure for American folk dance. Marjorie asserted that "our dancers are as good as theirs." She noted that the problem was, these dancers were not always recognized.

In part, this lack of recognition came from gender connotations associated with American dancing. In the Soviet Union dancing was associated with "vigor and masculinity," while in America dance was "feminized and sick." The Champions regarded American dance as homosexual in a pejorative sense. They furthermore characterized American dance as weak, even though the American dance boom was well under way and there were a wealth of dance companies, such as Martha Graham's, and dance productions, such as *West Side Story*, with a large following in the United States. In contrast to the reality of the American dance scene at this time, both Champions felt the Moiseyev's visit offered an opportunity for American dance to grow healthier and that the impact of the Moiseyev might be immeasurable. Now it was up to American society and culture to take advantage of this great opportunity.[33] Igor Moiseyev felt the Moiseyev's tour had more than just a performance role to play. For him, cultural exchange would lead to better political relations and further cultural development for both superpowers.

Reception to Later Tours

The Moiseyev toured the United States several times during the Cold War, with return visits in 1961, 1965, and 1970. While here the focus is on the first 1958 tour and the initial renewal of contact between the United States and Soviet Union, it is worth noting whether the popularity of the Moiseyev continued or if interest faded as the company became more familiar. The heightened anticipation described above in 1958 stemmed from certain factors that influenced the company's initial reception. First of all, the Moiseyev Dance Company was the first Soviet cultural presentation of the Lacy-Zarubin Agreement. Second, Americans had never seen the troupe perform live before. Third, Americans were eager to see "real" Soviets in person. This anticipation and the later overwhelmingly positive reception could easily have dissipated once the Moiseyev itself, and Soviet peoples in general, became familiar elements in American culture and life.

As the United States readied for the 1961 tour by the dance troupe, advance press for the later tours once more stoked anticipation and politically tinted language: the *Lakeland Ledger* noted before the 1961 tour that "Moscow is preparing a new 'cultural offensive' against the United States in the form of the popular Moiseyev Ballet." However, anticipation was also framed as the continuation of a personal relationship, with Igor Moiseyev reported as proclaiming, "'Our hearts are beating wildly . . . America has given our company many new friends and we have been working hard in preparation for this trip overseas."[34] Americans continued to be fascinated by the Moiseyev during the 1961 tour. The audience once more applauded its performances as at the Metropolitan Opera House, with critics lauding how Moiseyev's choreography was superior to that of any other dance company.[35]

The Moiseyev continued to impress critics on its return visits, and greater familiarity did not seem to diminish reception or anticipation. In 1961, the initial New York performances were again sold out.[36] As before, Americans clamored for tickets to the Moiseyev and once more, "In response to the overwhelming enthusiasm shown by audiences," four performances at Madison Square Garden were added onto the already scheduled tour.[37] Journalists reported that it appeared the Moiseyev's 1961 tour would be just as successful as its 1958 tour. The *Herald-Tribune* reported how the Moiseyev again broke advance sales record at the Metropolitan Opera in New York, "and will, undoubtedly, leave the $1,000,000 mark far behind when their tour's gross is totaled."[38] Though the Moiseyev had toured a few years earlier and since that 1958 tour, the Bolshoi and other Soviet representatives visited, this did not negatively impact interest in the 1961 tour.

Critics admitted attending performances with the foreknowledge of what they were going to see, and yet, came away yet again floored by the dancers' performance and with the same positive response. Similarly, Americans went to performances feeling that perhaps the Moiseyev dancers would be less thrilling now that they were a known quantity. However, this did not dampen their enthusiasm: "We did not expect the same impact, the same sense of utter surprise as the first time the company appeared in this country just three years ago," wrote *Dance Magazine* critic Doris Herring, "But there it was again! New-sprung, newly endearing."[39] In Boston as well as New York, the Moiseyev again "captured" the city's attention and "added Boston Garden to their satellites." As with critics, the American audience did not falter in their positive reaction to the new tour.

Enthusiasm for the Moiseyev was described in similar terms as before: "From the moment the company of 100 men and women took stage," wrote the *Boston Globe*'s Kevin Kelly, "they held the vast audience captive and breathless in a breakneck display of folk dance that, once again, proved the vigor of the Russian spirit in the perfection of an art form."[40] While critics and audiences continued to be amazed by the Moiseyev on these later tours, some did admit that Americans reacted most strongly to the first tour.[41] This conclusion, however, does not reflect the majority of coverage, which claimed that once more Americans reacted in the same way as they had in 1958.

As with the first tour, Cold War associations continued and flavored the reception, even as it continued to be quite positive. For instance, Igor Moiseyev attended a reception in Philadelphia during one of the later tours intended to honor the Soviet ambassador Mikhail A. Menshikov. Americans clearly saw Igor Moiseyev as inextricable from Cold War relations and diplomacy. Though that being said, Moiseyev continued to be framed as a positive figure (for instance, in invitations to the reception, he is labeled "World famed director of the Moiseyev Ballet").[42]

The 1965 tour elicited similarly positive reviews. On the New York performances: "Inconceivably, the company seemed even stronger and more energetic than its previous visits, with the male contingent noticeably strengthened by the addition of a number of steel-sinewed youths." Critics were impressed by the addition of a new dance, "Exercises," which introduced audiences to the company's training. Though dance critic Jacqueline Maskey pondered if the other dances could compete with "Exercises," such concerns were quickly allayed as "a smooth succession of a national dances from the Ukraine, Hungary, Byelorussia, Bulgaria, and Poland, alternately swift-moving and stately, flowed across the stage."[43] While others noted that their reviews would not be as detailed as their previous ones, this did not take away from critics' admiration for the skills and creativity displayed on stage. The Moiseyev was frequently compared with other folk dance groups that visited the United States, and was held up as the highest standard, with other groups judged as inferior.[44]

Indeed, in 1965 as before, the Moiseyev sold its tickets easily and quickly. In an interview by WNYC radio show host Marian Horosko (a former Ballet Russe de Monte Carlo and New York City Ballet Dancer) with Igor Moiseyev and Sol Hurok, Hurok noted: "We have sold out all over. . . . It is evidence [*sic*] how much they [Americans] remember the Moiseyev company. It has planted in their mind itself." The troupe sold out the first two weeks of performances, with about $100,000 in ticket sales.[45] Americans continued to be eager to see the Moiseyev, despite greater familiarity with the troupe and access to other Soviet artists. While enthusiasm continued with this tour, there was mild criticism offered as well. Jacqueline Maskey, writing in *Dance Magazine*, felt that the second half of the performance lagged in comparison to the first, though this was compensated for by the finale, *Gopak*, that "brought a roaring audience to its feet."[46] The familiarity with the dance repertoire did solicit minor critical comments, though the skills of the dancers continued to impress critics and Americans clearly continued to desire to see the troupe perform and continued to be enthralled by the Moiseyev.

Americans did not always react the same way to other groups that came to the United States. When the Leningrad Kirov Ballet toured the United States in 1961, again with the guidance of Sol Hurok, it did not meet with the same success. One of Mr. Hurok's associates, George Perper, wrote to the Ministry of Culture noting how the company "sustained heavy losses during the tour of the [Leningrad Kirov] ballet . . . [by] Mr. Hurok's estimate, . . . $175,000."[47] In comparison with the Moiseyev, the Kirov did not fascinate Americans in the same way. While certainly the repertoire of the two groups was different—the Moiseyev utilizing folk dance creations and the Kirov classical ballet—the differing American response does demonstrate that Americans did not just respond wholeheartedly to any Soviet cultural representation in this time period. The Moiseyev had a particular appeal for Americans which was not easily duplicated by other dance troupes, including troupes utilizing folk dance as well. There are, no doubt, several factors for the Moiseyev's meteoric success while others troupes fared poorly by comparison. That being said, it is argued here that the Moiseyev's particular appeal to Americans in this time period stemmed in large part from the accessibility of the Moiseyev dances and their middlebrow form of entertainment and specifically, as follows in the next two chapters, the simplified and conservative view of gender and multicultural societies which comforted American audiences in the contemporary context of gender and race upheaval.

PART
THREE

CHAPTER 6

American Notions of Gender

A number of these Moiseyev reconstructions of folk dances have to
do with the familiar boy-meet-girl theme, indicating that Russian
art is not all dedicated to boy-meets-hydro-electric plant. Another
theory exploded by the visiting Muscovites is the one that Russian
girls are built like tractors. There are some mighty pretty ones here, in
impressive numbers, too.

—Harry MacArthur, *The Evening Star*, Washington, DC, June 17, 1958

The preceding three chapters, making up part two, provide evidence for
how the Moiseyev Dance Company proved so successful in its tour due to it
accessibility which enabled Americans to relate to the dancers on stage and
absorb their propagandistic message; the savvy choice by the Soviet Union
to use this middlebrow art form paid off. The next and final section of chapters here contain further exploration of why that message was not only so
accessible but most effectual for the American audience in this time period.
Beginning with an examination of notions of gender articulated by the dancers followed by a parallel examination of notions of race and ethnicity, the
Moiseyev Dance Company presented an idealized, simplified view of gender norms and of different races and ethnicities living happily together that
comforted Americans. In the context of American anxiety about emasculation, changes in traditional gender roles, and homosexuality, Americans
found the Moiseyev's depiction of heteronormative relationships soothing. Similarly, the Moiseyev's multicultural message and alleged appreciation for people of all backgrounds provided reassurance in the context of
the civil rights struggle and racial violence in 1950s America. The troupe's
almost Disney-like depiction of heterosexuality and diversity made Americans extremely receptive to this simplified vision of love and cooperation
among peoples, as it seemed more attractive than the reality of America's
contemporary gender and racial issues.

Gender and Sexuality in the Cold War

The tours of the Moiseyev Dance Company represented more than a view of Soviet–American relations and notions of American and Soviet culture. In the Cold War context, Americans engaged in a debate about defining American identity and the role of masculinity, femininity, and sexuality therein. American responses to the dancers reflected these contemporary discourses, especially as the dance troupe presented idealized heteronormative relationships. Consequently, part of the positive reception by Americans consisted of the Moiseyev's ability to assuage contemporary concerns about American gender norms.

In viewing the dancers onstage and offstage, Americans compared the dancers to themselves and their ideas of American and Soviet identity. Based on the Cold War narrative that political figures espoused, as well as preconceived notions about gender and the Soviet people, the American audience found the male Moiseyev dancers intimidating in their masculinity and the females surprising in their expression of femininity. That being said, despite even the intimidating masculinity, Americans found the dancers to be similar to themselves as people even with their inherent cultural, political, and ideological differences. American reception to the Moiseyev offers an opportunity to examine the debate of American identity. In terms of showcasing masculinity, femininity, and gender roles, the Moiseyev presented dances with specific steps assigned to men, women, the expression of love between men and women, and national identities.

Sexuality and gender played a major role in American self-identity and concern during the Cold War, with men who had communist leanings or more liberal ideas often depicted as effeminate while conservative figures depicted as more masculine. Scholar K. A. Cuordileone identifies a pervasive anxiety regarding masculinity during the Cold War that expressed itself in both cultural and intellectual discourse. While a general unease grew out of the fear of atomic bombs and the spread of communism, it also indicated a concern with the "modern self."[1]

In particular, concerns about the self and masculinity impacted politics and culture in the Cold War era. Films and books such as *12 Angry Men* and *The Lonely Crowd*, which focused on the "self" and the need for approval by others, are evidence of such concerns. A way to address this anxiety was an increased stress on American manhood and masculinity to avoid producing "soft" and conformist children.[2] The concept of American man-hood included heroism, especially in the post–World War II world, and thus politicians emphasized their time in military service or even embellished it.[3]

At the same time, this need to have "manly" politicians and male role models also meant labeling what was not masculine. In particular, homo-sexuality became a symbol to represent the un-masculine. In addition to those who had alleged communist connections or leanings, HUAC (the House Un-American Activities Committee) and Senator McCarthy also questioned those who were allegedly homosexual. HUAC and McCarthy apparently thought that homosexual people posed the same security risk as someone with alleged communist connections. In 1950, as McCarthy made his Wheeling speech about communists in the US government, Deputy Undersecretary John Peurifoy of the State Department testified in front of a congressional committee that the State Department fired ninety-one employees because they were homosexual, leading to a growing concern about the number of homosexual people in the State Department and in the US government.[4] As part of the panic over homosexual employees in the US government, individuals were brought in for questioning about their sexuality, based on refusal to respond or speculative evidence of their homosexuality. These employees were considered a security risk because it was felt that they would be more susceptible to blackmail and thus could be coerced by other governments to reveal secrets or betray their country.[5]

It should be noted that fear of homosexuality was not limited to males. A corresponding set of expectations of American femininity existed as well for State Department employees—these included being properly attired and presentable, being concerned with one's appearance, and also taking care of one's home. Thus when a Miss Blevins, a secretary clerk in the State Department, became frustrated with her boss, a Miss McCoy, she wrote an anonymous note to State Department security about Miss McCoy's hab-its. She noted that Miss McCoy did not overly concern herself with her appearance and appeared to spend time with another female employee who had a "mannish voice." Based on this evidence, McCoy was brought in for questioning.[6]

The general anxiety regarding gender, and especially masculinity, appeared outside the contemporary political arena. In 1963, Stanley Milgram published "Obedience to Authority," the results of his experiments to explore the actions of SS officers in the Holocaust in which test subjects thought they were employing electrical shocks on fellow subjects.[7] This study is a further example of the pervasive nature of the Cold War narrative in American life and, in particular, how it plays into American concerns over gender and identity. Fear of "enfeeblement" of American character and masculinity drove the popularity of experiments like Milgram's and fed the fire of this anxiety.[8] Milgram's experiment "revealed American masculinity to be disconcertingly passive and compliant"; two-thirds of the participants were willing to continue with more and more intense shocks up to the point of causing death.[9] In addition to fearing enfeeblement of American masculinity, Americans found Soviet masculinity intimidating. America envied the Soviet Union's military conduct and chose to ignore the sacrifices made on the part of the Red Army and Soviet people after the end of World War II and into the Cold War.[10] Part of this envy stemmed from reports of Soviet masculinity and bravery in the field. Americans viewed Soviet men as tough, strong, and willing to die for their country. America, with its homeland intact and with fewer deaths during the war, did not demonstrate the same level of commitment and sacrifice to the World War II conflict or level of masculine prowess.[11] Americans could not help but be envious of the Soviets' abilities and the way Soviet men fought.

As for femininity, post–World War II America featured the interplay of the fears and anxieties stemming from changes in gender roles during the war with the "celebratory mood" of suburbia, wives, and family. To be a properly feminine woman in this atmosphere often meant marriage and domesticity.[12] As for feminism, it became associated with lesbianism during the Cold War and became part of a homophobic narrative in which homosexuality became un-American. Indeed, scholar Robert Corber underlines how "like the communist, the lesbian allegedly threatened the American way of life." Social scientists and politicians were concerned that educated women who could make enough money to live alone would no longer see marriage and family as important goals. Those who did marry might then neglect to emphasize the importance of these goals for their own daughters, which "[would] weaken . . . the nation's ability to defeat totalitarianism." Accordingly, maintaining traditional gender roles was thought to be a vital part of preserving democracy and American identity.[13]

The image of the domestic American wife and mother contrasted with the Cold War narrative's depiction of Soviet women. Lenin and other members of the Bolshevik party proclaimed gender equality as one of their goals in forming a communist state.[14] While certainly this ideal did not play out simply in terms of policy execution in the work place and in Soviet society, it remained a part of American perception of Soviet life. Hand in hand with this notion of gender equality in the Soviet Union was the notion that Soviet women were deprived of the niceties American women enjoyed. For instance, reports of Soviet women clamoring for gowns, perfumes, and furs from Paris and New York at a Christian Dior show in Moscow in 1960 furthered this impression. Soviet women reportedly fought for tickets to the fashion show and were physically overwhelmed by the luxury items they saw.[15]

Americans, as evidenced through cultural products like the films *Ninotchka* (1939), *Comrade X* (1940), and *Jet Pilot* (1957), were curious about the Soviet ideal of gender equality.[16] In these films, a Soviet woman is introduced who epitomizes the ideals of gender equality; she dresses in simple, militaristic clothes, she is somber and serious, and she prefers to be addressed as "comrade," rather than by a female-specific term. The female character, however, is "converted to womanliness and is sexually liberated through exposure to the products available in a market economy: hats, perfume, champagne, steak, jewelry, room service."[17] Ninotchka, for instance, is a strong supporter of gender equality until she arrives in Paris and meets Count Leon d'Algout, who introduces her to the pleasures of capitalism. Her "conversion" is complete when she purchases a hat which, when she first arrived in Paris, had struck her as frivolous.[18]

The American View of Soviet Men

The press consistently portrayed the men of the Moiseyev Dance Company as incredibly athletic and as very masculine. The American audience did not view the male dancers as feminine because of their ballet-like steps or for their ballet training, but instead found them to be "astoundingly agile and robust."[19] Indeed, the dancers were regarded as performing steps outside of classical ballet's domain, as this was understood at the time in the West: "Such leaps are never seen, nor required, in classic ballet, as were performed by the men of the Moiseyev Company. During the final number one of the men was catapulted from behind the chorus line in a high flight."[20] The male folk dancers of the Moiseyev, though they had extensive classical ballet training, were viewed differently by the American audience than American male ballet dancers. The Moiseyev men brought dancing to

FIGURE 5. The Leaping Male Dancers of "Partisans." Source: M. Chudnovsky, *The Folk Dance Company of the USSR: Igor Moiseyev, Art Director* (Moscow: Foreign Languages Publishing House, 1959), 81.

a new level of athleticism and skill, leaving their masculinity in no doubt. They were able to escape stereotypes associated with male ballet dancers because of their dance moves, costumes, and folk dance associations.

Reporters found the male dancers more skilled and more engrossing, though often this observation went hand in hand with noting that folk dances afforded a "more spectacular part"[21] for male dancers. Reporters did not downplay the skills of the female dancers, focusing on their grace, beauty, and "fleetedness of foot."[22] The women, rather than being viewed as masculine or particularly muscular, maintain their femininity rather than playing into the Cold War American narrative that emphasized gender neutrality. The skills of both men and women were acknowledged, but in the end:

> whatever [dance] you choose [as your favorite] you will always come back to the fabulous feats of the men. They bring down the curtain at intermission and at the end with a display of prisyadka of every imaginable variety which left us more breathless than the dancers.[23]

Such moves bordered on the unbelievable and the perfection with which they were executed awed the American audience. Moreover, in addition to being more dazzling than the women, as one journalist noted, the men could do the same gliding step as the women.[24] Americans credited the men with greater abilities than the women and as quite versatile in their ability to do a woman's dance move while remaining very masculine.

The men's ability to perform the women's steps is not seen as effeminate or emasculating. Instead, once more it demonstrated just how skilled they were. In particular, the *prisyadka*—or squat dance—was extremely popular. Americans were fascinated by how the dancers could perform kicks "done from what appears a sitting position" while "spin[ning] like dizzy dervishes."[25] Again and again reporters tried to explain this dance to their readers, noting how "fantastic" it looked.[26]

While the description of the male dancers always expressed admiration for their superior abilities, there is no explicit commentary noting potential deficits of American men in comparison to their Soviet counterparts. However, as discussed earlier, praise of Soviet male bodies and masculinity occurs in the context of a general fear of American emasculation. Furthermore, there is an outright questioning of the ability of American male dancers to compete with the Soviet display of prowess on stage. It is clear that the male dancers proved the most intriguing and it is only when they are on stage and performing the *hopak* that "the stage sizzles."[27]

Though there is no articulated questioning of whether American men were as virile or masculine as the Soviet men on display, the descriptions of the male dancers do play into another area of perceived American inferiority—the space race. As discussed above, describing the Moiseyev's performances very often involved using "explosive" terms. Along similar lines, reporters compared the Moiseyev to the space race and to rocket power:

> If Russia soon puts a man into space it is quite likely to be one of the agile, gravity-defying artists of the Moiseyev Dance Company. . . . And one of these fellows would need no rocket or missile propulsion—just his own.[28]

Reception to the Moiseyev reflected and reinforced American concern that the US position in the space race was behind that of the Soviet Union. Similarly, when the Moiseyev dancers noted that they had traveled so much that their total traveled distance would cover a trip to the moon and back, reporter W. G. Rogers likened the distance to "Sputnik III."[29] Again, though American men are not explicitly compared to their Soviet counterparts in the dance troupe in terms of masculinity, certainly implicit comparisons are present in how the male dancers are described and how they are framed within the space race, a largely male endeavor at that point in time.

After the first Moiseyev tour, American commentators acknowledged that they now could understand why the Soviet Union was able to launch Sputnik before the United States launched its own satellite. Later tours fostered similar rhetoric. The male dancers could "leap to heights only recently reserved for spacemen and hang suspended," wrote critic Kevin Kelly in 1961. " They spin on their knees, jump on their toes, invert themselves in mid-flight, dance en pointe, execute split-jumps."[30] The skills displayed by the male dancers reminded Americans of the perceived space and missile gap, and the political context colored their impressions of the dancers in the later tours as well.

Offstage, Moiseyev men did not seem to fit in with American society as well as their female counterparts. It proved much easier to pick the men of a crowd as they did not shop for American clothing as much as the women and continued to wear more of the clothing brought from home. The men did prove interesting in their desire for cameras and camera accessories: "Almost every male member of the troupe arrived at Boston Airport this morning with at least one camera and gadget bag slung over his shoulder."[31] The men did not present as many opportunities to comment on their likes and dislikes but this, nor their interest in cameras did not receive negative nor positive comment.

Though more fascinating than the women onstage, offstage the men received far less press coverage. This is no doubt due to the fact that they seemed less approachable and less friendly than the women and less willing to submit to the reporters' questions on their likes and dislikes, shopping adventures, and dating habits. The men were quieter and less willing to try to communicate with reporters, with or without an interpreter. A male dancer speaking to Americans at all was deemed a surprising, noteworthy event: "One of the male dancers seemed virtually capable of delivering a major address [in English]. He put together: 'It is the rule.' This virtual filibuster was uttered when an American woman on the tour, directed to accept his seat on the crowded plane, questioned him concerning why he always so eagerly abandoned his squatter's rights."[32] With cultural products like the film *Comrade X* in mind, Americans were probably surprised that a Soviet dancer offered to give up his seat to a woman. Almost as astonishing as the dancer's words was his gesture, which contradicted the principle of gender equality.

The curiosity about male–female relationships in the Soviet Union continued with press coverage of all aspects of male–female interactions, including how males expressed appreciation for the opposite sex. The *Boston Globe* informed its readers of a "gem of information": "Russian blades don't whistle at them [women] on the street. Instead, they drop a few lines of poetry out of the corner of their mouths as they walk by."[33] This revelation emerged as part of an interview with female dancers, who mentioned that they were whistled at on American streets and wondered what it meant. Upon being informed of the intent behind the whistles, the dancers appeared somewhat ruffled, and explained how in the Soviet Union, expressing admiration for the female form was quite different. Americans were surprised that Russian men recited poetry to women—an older, more romantic mode of expression—when the American Cold War narrative emphasized the Soviet Union as committed to going against traditional gender norms.

The American View of Soviet Women

Impressions of the Moiseyev men as masculine and athletic remained constant during the 1958 and later tours. Reactions to the female dancers contained a bit more variety. American descriptions of the dancers primarily utilized terms like "pretty" and feminine;[34] adhering to American notions of appropriate female gender expression. However, there are a few, though not dominant, descriptions that likened the female dancers more to their male counterparts and described them as far too muscular: "Girls in the company are pretty but heavy of hip and thigh. Hair is frizzy and they could learn precision from the Rockettes."[35] Here the Soviet female dancers are the worse for their comparison to their American counterparts. This view perhaps better aligns with the stereotypical American view of Soviet women: they lacked feminine niceties because of Soviet culture and the Soviet construction of gender.

For the most part, though, the dancers were seen as very feminine, contrasting with the conventional American view of Soviet women. The feminine side is emphasized in descriptions of the more graceful, slower dances in the repertoire, or numbers with colorful costumes:

> A close-knit line of girls in pink, blue, orange, cerise, green, and deep red came upon the stage. Theirs was a gentle modesty. Their steps were small and absolutely precise. Their feet had a ballet-trained articulateness. Their turns, too, were balletic. And yet they maintained a beguiling air of folk simplicity.[36]

The women were depicted as graceful and modest; they evoked a nostalgic country scene through the different colors of their costumes and their peasant-like simplicity.

Costumes dramatized their femininity in the Bulba dance, "in which the horizontal stripes of the whirling skirts spun gorgeous patterns and high spirits filled the stage."[37] For each dance, and to represent gender in each culture, the Moiseyev used costumes with different ranges of color and eye-catching designs. Indeed, the *Detroit Free Press* felt American Broadway costume designers could learn a thing or two from the Moiseyev's costumes. The costumes functioned as another way in which the dances and dancers differentiated men from women and their corresponding, clearly defined heteronormative gender roles. The costumes made it easy for Americans to understand the roles, in addition to the specific steps for men versus women and the ways the women and men's costumes (in addition to the steps) complemented each other.

Though usually depicted as modest (or somewhat coy) peasant girls, the women were occasionally described as seductive. Critic Claudia

FIGURE 6. Female dancers in the Bulba dance. Source: M. Chudnovsky, *The Folk Dance Company of the USSR: Igor Moiseyev, Art Director* (Moscow: Foreign Languages Publishing House, 1959), 40.

Cassidy noted that when the female dancers came on stage, they initiated the "come-hither of courting the world over" to which the male dancers responded with a "defiant game of 'anything he can do, I can do better.'"[38] The women functioned as goals for which the men competed. Descriptions of the women did not include terms like "erotic" or "provocative," however. Their type of seduction was one known "the world over" as part of courtship leading to marriage. Though some articles emphasized the prettiness and beauty of the female dancers, they did not come across as lustful or sexual. Instead, they fit comfortably within a traditional, heteronormative set of values.

Unlike the surprisingly consistent perceptions of the Soviet men, perceptions of the Soviet women varied somewhat, eliciting descriptions of shy peasant girls, manly women, and women with a certain seductive power. The majority of press reports concurred with the peasant girl depiction. However, though the men's physical abilities were noted again and again, the women's athleticism was by no means overlooked and "the girls proved that they were just as limber."[39] Indeed, in the Bulba dance, "the line of girls rolls itself into a ball and goes merrily bowling off at the end."[40] Even in these acrobatic on-stage roles, press depictions framed the female dancers as feminine and adhering to a view of women as desirable romantic partners for men.

Americans observed Soviet notions of femininity onstage and offstage. As with the men, what the women wore when not performing came under scrutiny. At Disneyland, for example, the women wore skirts: "Every time. No shorts no pedal pushers or other bifurcated attire."[41] Wearing a skirt at this time was not a surprising or particularly conservative choice; while certainly more formal than pants, it more likely demonstrates how the dancers were under such scrutiny during their tour that they always tried to appear at their best. Given the Soviet ideal of gender equality, it is perhaps understandable that Americans were curious about what Soviet women wore and how they acted, especially (as in this instance). This curiosity allowed writers to lend greater significance to what women wore and for the writers to feel they could use the women's appearance to demonstrate whether or not Soviet women adhered to the Soviet ideal of gender equality.

Compared to the males, the female dancers were more personable offstage. Reporters were able to get them to "warm up." The women smiled more readily and would even laugh. With this kind of breakthrough, "The crew of reporters and photographers following the troupe around resorted to physical gyrations, pantomime and ridiculous antics to make themselves understood. This probably was the ice breaker."[42] The interactions are depicted as amusing to the Soviet women and that the women reacted in an understandable way, namely appreciating these, at times, ridiculous efforts and responding with receptiveness and opening up. Again, when describing the dancers' experience at the Ford factory tour, it is the female dancers who were more enthusiastic and more willing to express their feelings. One reporter relayed how some of the "girls" so admired the color Walker's gold Continental that an employee at the factory promised to send a bucket of paint in that shade to them in Moscow.[43] The female dancer found a personal connection with their American enemy in the admiration for the Walker's gold Continental color and clearly reporters and the worker felt tickled by this admiration.

The men remained, for the most part, more stoic towards the reporters. When speaking to the dancers during their first breakfast in San Francisco, reporters noted that the female dancers were friendly and they looked and acted like American women: "They could have been American women—until they began to speak." The press chose to emphasize how alike American and Soviet women could be. In contrast, the male members "began to saunter into the dining room . . . nibbled at their heavy breakfasts, watching staring American diners with a wary yeye [*sic*]." The men came across as unfriendly and even suspicious of others while "The girls were different. They were well mannered, reserved, but laughter always bubbled just under the surface."[44] In terms of interaction with Americans, the female dancers proved more engaging and likeable—seemingly more like their American counterparts.

The Life of a Soviet Woman

Americans wanted to know what life was like for Soviet women in general. Reporters noted that the female dancers "consider home, marriage and motherhood 'very important, of course,' but are lured by the 'vast open horizons of art and travel.'" The women prioritized the same goals as American women and no doubt American women could relate to temptations to pursue other or additional goals like "art and travel." Personal relationships, career, and motherhood were correspondingly frequent topics of conversation. Americans wanted to learn how Soviet women functioned within their society. Dancer Liubov Khruliova, "was moved to tears when asked if she misses her 5-year-old son. She does."[45] Reporters felt Americans would be interested in hearing about the Soviet view of family and children but also again emphasized how the dancers were human beings and parents with the same kinds of feelings towards their children as Americans.

Reporters emphasized how many of the female dancers manage "a career and home much as do women here."[46] The American press chose to emphasize the ways in which Soviet women were similar to American women. The life of a Soviet woman was not entirely divorced from the way an American woman would live her life; rather the press claimed that the Soviet woman put the roles of career and family in similar perspective. They claimed for

American women a strong desire for marriage and family, but that these goals could be accomplished in conjunction with a career.

An in-depth interview at the Fort Wayne Hotel coffee shop in Detroit with dancer Olga depicted an appealing young Soviet woman akin to her American counterpart. Olga "looks as if she were a senior at Cooley High School or a sophomore at Wayne State University. But her hometown is Moscow, Russia." The interviewer noted that many Americans had a different idea of what Russian women looked like and Olga defied this preconceived notion because she was "a trim, smartly dressed young lady whose winsomeness overcomes the language barrier."[47] Olga emphasized how much she loved to dance. At home, she went on dates like any young American. The interviewer learned that Olga's father was an architect and that her mother ("as do many mothers in Detroit") had encouraged her to pursue her interest in dance.

Naturally, the interviewer noted how much and what Olga ate and how this contrasted with her fit frame. At the breakfast interview, Olga ate "two fried eggs sunny-side up two pieces of buttered toast a piece of apple pie and one cup of coffee" yet she only weighed 108 pounds. Her clothes included a Soviet "gray tailored suit, a pink plaid blouse and a pair of red shoes" complete with matching red purse. When asked about her thoughts regarding what she had seen in America, Olga mentioned that while she enjoyed the Ford factory, she was confused when she heard that "Americans buy new cars every year," yet it appeared that they did not all buy new cars this year, since there was unemployment in Detroit. Olga said that she much preferred Niagara Falls to the Ford factory.[48]

Olga clearly contradicted the stereotypical image of a Soviet woman. In appearance, she was just like any American girl of the same age. Her parents acted just as American parents would, encouraging her ambition to pursue a career in dance. Again and again, the article emphasized how Olga and the life she chose corresponded to American counterparts, thus belaying American prejudices about Soviet people. When a potentially political topic was introduced—the Ford factory—she acknowledged a prejudice of her own which she had come to realize was not accurate. Even when given the opportunity, Olga did not adopt a political posture. The interview with Olga is representative of the persistent way the press and individual Americans viewed the dancers as similar to average Americans with the same kinds of experiences, dreams, and ideas.

The Soviet Wife

As the Moiseyev toured the United States, Mrs. Moiseyev became a resource for those who wanted to learn about Soviet culture and gender roles. Her name, in fact, was Tamara Zeifert and not Tamara Moiseyev, though in newspaper articles she was referred to as Mrs. Moiseyev. She was one of the lead dancers of the Moiseyev and famous in her own right. Newspapers referred to her as Tamara Zeifert, though with the caveat of "in private life [she] is Mrs. Moiseyev."[49]

Despite keeping her maiden name, Tamara Zeifert fulfilled rather traditional roles as a wife and mother. During interviews she described summer vacations with her husband and their teenage daughter, Olga, at a villa near the Black Sea: "At the memory of the view of the sun on the water, rimmed by the pleasant Crimean coastline, Mrs. Moiseyev's round brown eyes begin to dance and her ready smile seems to bubble up from a deeper well of internal mirth." The fact that she had a "ready smile" and describing her as mirthful would contrast with the stereotypes the American Cold War narrative promoted of Soviet women as dour or emotionless.

When asked if she liked to entertain, Tamara admitted that during the dance season she was usually too tired, but during the summer break, she loved to host "whole colonies of friends."[50] If she were at her usual summer home at that moment, for breakfast she would be serving "fruit, milk, or cream" because during the summer the dancers were on a strict diet. The article initially idealized Tamara's proper duties as a wife and mother who (though her career was never forgotten) enjoyed entertaining and vacationing with her family.

Interestingly, one interviewer's positive impression changed somewhat when Tamara described how the Black Sea had "wonderful fish," claiming, "You have nothing like it here." The interviewer, slightly offended (and noting that "patriotic pride stirs in a U.S. citizen's blood"), asked the name of the fish. Tamara again insisted there was no American equivalent. Finally she offered up the name: "schav." The American reporter—certain that this fish did in fact exist in American waters—replied that Tamara referred to "sorrel made into a cool, greenish white puree and served most often cold with sour cream." Tamara responded that it was most definitely not the same thing, and began to lament all the foods she missed from the Soviet Union, like fruit and meat pies. She particularly craved a certain fruit "though in the U.S. it is probably not known, she feels certain." Tamara went on to describe it for the benefit of the reporters present who felt certain the fruit was simply a raspberry but even amongst this culinary jostling, "all three of us beam happily at one another."[51]

However, Tamara escalated things when she added that Russia produced the best champagne in the world. The interviewer thereafter refused to take her opinions seriously, and portrayed her as a biased, frivolous woman who simply did not know any better. Even so, Tamara did not come across as gender-neutral or gender-equal in her appearance, marriage, or career but instead adhered to what Americans might cite as the same traditional gender norms of their own country.

Soviet Women Participating in Capitalism

When discussing the female dancers offstage, reporters often emphasized how much they liked to shop, what they bought, and what aspects of American commercial culture they favored. Images of Soviet women being seduced by the wonders of capitalism fit Cold War narratives that depicted a harsh, impoverished life for those living under communism. A telling episode occurred when reporters invited several female company members on a shopping expedition. The Moiseyev granted five dancers permission to go on the shopping trip, and Mrs. Moiseyev came along as well as soon as she "heard the word 'shopping'" to which Igor Moiseyev sighed, "Everywhere we go, my wife goes shopping."[52]

The dancers and reporters exchanged cigarettes, shopped for dresses and shoes, and discussed Hollywood stars. Articles describing the shopping expedition lavished attention on all the minor details. For example, relaying one such shopping trip a reporter noted how they sang "You Are My Sunshine" for the dancers, and they replied with "Moscow Is Smiling at Me," "a snappy ditty with lots of hand-waving." One dancer "practically swooned" over a Tyrone Power poster and inquired whether or not he was dead. Another added that she thought Robert Taylor almost as handsome as Tyrone Power and asked how he was too.[53]

Local reporters were eager to show Soviet desire for American goods and celebrate America's superiority. But at the same time, they emphasized Soviet and American female solidarity—at least as far as shopping was concerned: "Turn a flock of Russian women loose on a New York shopping spree and you can't tell the communists from the capitalists." Similarly, the *New York Journal American*'s article recounting the shopping trip was entitled: "Communist or Capitalist . . . Girls will be Girls Russian Dancers See, Sigh and Buy in N.Y. Shops." Journalists noted that Soviet women were "just as bargain-minded as any American housewife" and "they tried to buy everything but [Tyrone] Power, who isn't on sale."[54]

Coverage of this kind of shopping event usually utilized images of the dancers smiling and buying items or trying on clothing, such as a photograph of dancer Lydia Skriabina wearing a "fancy, pink flowered balloon dress in Gibels [*sic*]."[55] Reporters seemed to think that American readers would be interested in what the Soviet women shopped for and that the readers would be able to relate to them better in this bourgeois, capitalistic context. Underlining the dancers' delight in acquiring American products certainly speaks to the American need to compete with the Soviet Union on all levels during the Cold War. In this instance, Americans clearly felt they came out on top.

Depiction of Male–Female Relationships

The Moiseyev's repertoire included dances specifically for male dancers, others female dancers and still others for mixed casts of men and women. The mixed dances typically depicted heteronormative relationships, and American reporters and critics were quick to analyze these depictions. For instance, the "City Quadrille" dance featured "four very proper couples from the country dancing in the open air."[56] The dances fit a certain stereotype of male-female relations in the countryside, exuding "wholesomeness in the attitude of boy to girl,"[57] and the movement was gendered: "Men and women move differently. The men are spectacular, the women lyric."[58] Overall, the men came across as "swaggering, show-off rustics. The women for the most part, are of the fairly coy outdoor-girl variety."[59] The men were depicted as virile, especially in the *Yurochka* dance in which the male lead dancer romped and flirted with each girl onstage.[60] This "Don Juan," after chasing after each girl in the village was then rejected "en masse" by them all.[61] While amusing, this dance also implied that only traditional monogamous relationships are acceptable and successful. The lighthearted and uncomplicated depiction of heteronormative relationships, it is argued here, supported American positive reception as a comforting message in this time period.

The only time this male–female relationship changed was in the dance "Partisans." Here instead, "The sexes are equal even to wearing the same garments and doing the same neck-breaking steps."[62] "Partisans" served as the only exception to the heteronormative relationships the Moiseyev depicted. This dance celebrated the role of the Russian people in the World War II resistance; it demonstrated how average men and women took up the call to defend their homeland. In this moment of Soviet history, gender lines were blurred, and the goal of victory over the Nazis took precedence. This was emphasized by the costumes, which were dark and amorphous rather than

FIGURE 7. A female fighter in "Partisans." Source: M. Chudnovsky, *The Folk Dance Company of the USSR: Igor Moiseyev, Art Director* (Moscow: Foreign Languages Publishing House, 1959), 84.

colorful and folkloric. The more gender-neutral attire and narrative of the dance did not deter the American audience nor lead to a change in positive reception, simply proving to be another example of how amazing and fascinating the troupe could be.

Critic Alfred Frankenstein of the *San Francisco Chronicle* argued that gender-designated steps and dances indicated a certain kind of universality: "one gathers that regardless of period, place, or politics, both life and art derive a vast amount of their dynamism from the fact that human beings are of two kinds—male and female." Although the Moiseyev portrayed peoples from different regions and cultures, gender, as the company depicted it, cut across borders. "Whether the boys be Ukrainians of [sic] Byelorussians or Tatars, they would not leap that way in the villages if there were no girls on hand to see them, nor would the girls dance with such poetry and zest if they had only their sisters for audience."[63] He, like the other reporters, noted the differences in what male versus female dancers could do on stage. For him, the men were always depicted as athletes. While the women could "be equally vigorous," for the most part their grace and lyricism were meant to be a contrast to the men's athleticism. These transparent differences between men and women in the dances reinforced the message of traditional heteronormative values.

Indeed, the female dancers often appeared to need the male dancers. In coverage of a European performance of the Moiseyev in 1956, *Dance Magazine* described the "Ukrainian Suite" dance which involved two young people in love who must part. With this parting, at first the dance "is an expression of sorrow by the girls of the village. They step slowly across the stage, in simple but continually changing groups and formations, conveying by the inclination of their heads and bodies as well as by facial expression, a mood of gentle melancholy." The girls are forlorn without the men and do not dance with the same pep and zip as they do when the men are onstage. Once the young lovers reunite, however, the dance moves into a series of joyful and ecstatic steps.[64] It is only with the return of the male dancers that the women are again inspired to demonstrate the true extent of their skills and enthusiasm and fulfill their role as romantic partner to the men.

Reporters also noted how men and women interacted offstage. While above instances of men acting more how Americans might expect men to interact with women, like giving up their seat for them, could be found there were also instances aligning more with the narrative of Soviet gender equality. During the Disneyland trip, a report claimed "It was easier to pick the Russian men dancers of out the large crowd. Because of their haircuts, for one thing, and another, their attitude toward women. Equality of the sexes was the order of the day. No concession was made to the women in the way of handing them in and out of conveyances, or carrying their packages, or allowing them to precede the men into an amusement center." This conduct confirmed the American perception of gender relations in the Soviet Union, where the genders were equal and the social niceties of deference to women had been eliminated.[65] While the dances depicted a certain stereotypical heteronormative relationship, in reality—and in contrast to American contemporary society—the dancers did not always conform to traditional gender roles. The American press made note of these differences but did not describe the Soviet women as dejected or ill-treated. The expression of gender equality is noted, but not emphasized or exaggerated to fit in to the Cold War narrative in which the Soviet ideal of gender equality would be viewed as negative and the antithesis of American deference and condescension towards women.

In viewing the Moiseyev dancers onstage and in press and television coverage, Americans sought to learn how individuals functioned within Soviet society. Various reactions indicated that Americans' preconceived notions of the Soviet gender roles were often dispelled by the performances or, on occasion, reinforced by the male dancers' lack of deference to women offstage. Perhaps most importantly, however, was the observation that these Soviet men and women were quite similar to American men and women. Rather than seeing, as the American Cold War narrative encouraged, two entirely different cultures reflecting differing political and economic ideas, Americans saw people they could relate to, who shared everything from shopping habits and Hollywood gossip to hopes, dreams, and life goals. At the same time, it is important to note that this reception functioned within a larger discourse of Cold War fears of inferiority, both in terms of American culture and masculinity, leading to a questioning of Americans' ability to compete with the likes of the Moiseyev dancers. Moiseyev's particular brand of folk dance, in which heteronormative relationships dominated and were not complicated by any form of eroticism. This depiction of relationships held the potential to calm American concern about gender roles and homosexuality prevalent in this time period. Moiseyev carefully crafted his message to make the dances appealing and accessible; the dances did not require a high degree of thought or understanding. If a dance or dance suite had a plot, it was simple and easy to follow. The use of the short dance scenes as opposed to larger narrative ballet meant focus and a lengthy attention span were not necessary as the different dances progressed throughout the performance. Moiseyev presented American (and international) audiences with a simplified worldview which Americans took comfort in during the upheaval and uncertainty of the Cold War period.

CHAPTER 7

American Notions of Race

One of the key acts is to help folklorists who want to transplant their materials to the theater to recognize what it unimportant, eliminate it, and to exploit those ingredients that already possess certain aspect of theater. In Egypt, for example, I suggested ways to elevate the "danse du ventre" from its almost prostituted state in some of the cheaper clubs to a genuine artistic level. After all, it is a dance traditional to the Egyptians and it should be used. There is no reason why it cannot be used artistically.

—Igor Moiseyev, qtd. in *New York Herald Tribune*, April 30, 1961

As with gender, in viewing the Moiseyev, Americans drew comparisons between their own notions of American identity and the Soviet identity the Moiseyev dancers displayed. Americans saw similarities between themselves and their Soviet counterparts in the multiplicity of dances and cultures that made up the Moiseyev's vision of the Soviet Union. Indeed, Americans saw a Soviet multicultural identity that corresponded to a similar American notion that people from varying ethnic and cultural backgrounds could lay claim to being American. This Soviet-presented vision of a multicultural identity allowing for the free expression of various cultural and ethnic backgrounds corresponded to the Cold War narrative that positioned America as the epitome of democracy and freedom. The contrast between this ideal of American multiculturalism and the reality of Americans of different ethnic and racial backgrounds living together underscores how the Moiseyev dance company assuaged American anxieties and fear around national and racial identity.

The dancers and dances presented a carefree, happy-go-lucky vision of cultural difference as viewed and embodied by members of the privileged caste. This of course was a fabrication of how national groups lived in the

Soviet Union; the Moiseyev also presented an escapist view of life in the Soviet Union, which had recently witnessed the upheavals of World War II with the death of over 20 million citizens, economic and urban devastation (about one fourth of Soviet capital resources were destroyed and industrial and agricultural output dropped to below prewar levels), and the forced displacements of 1.5 million people by the Stalin regime.

Additionally, as will be emphasized below, while Americans realized there were diverse groups on display, there was also a complete absence of Black dancers or peoples. This absence and corresponding presentation of a multicultural identity without Black people was easy to take in and contributed to the sense of comfort and escapism the dances afforded, especially in light of racial violence in the United States in this time period.[1] While certainly racial issues and anxieties in the United States cannot be conflated with the Soviet Union's own challenges around national and ethnic identities, we can explore the parallels and how the Soviets viewed American racial issues, as this had an impact on the Cold War and on cultural and traditional diplomacy.

When viewing the dances, Americans felt the onstage depictions represented authentic Soviet national and ethnic identities. Consequently, they claimed to understand Soviet people through both these performed dances as well as offstage interactions and reporting. It's clear from critical and personal responses that Americans' alleged understanding of Soviet identity included the diversity of peoples on stage and this came up repeatedly in the 1958 and later tours.

In response to the 1958 tour, for instance, critics emphasized the many different kinds of dances the Moiseyev repertoire contained and how these dances came from a variety of places. Articles and reviews of the Moiseyev noted that there were dances from Kazan, Moldavia, and the Ukraine, among others.[2] Indeed, the number of peoples that made up the Soviet Union whose dances the Moiseyev drew from varied somewhat, though usually topping out at 180 different groups,[3] with a dance repertory based on three thousand dances from the peoples of the Soviet Union.[4] Circulating these numbers fed the sense of the Soviet Union as a vast territory with differing locales and peoples. One critic felt that the Moiseyev was evidence that Russia "possesses more varieties of indigenous culture than any other nation on earth." The Moiseyev dances sprang from a variety of locations, including Central Asia and the Artic and Europe. They also represented a broad spectrum of social constructs, from Western to non-Western and traditional folkways to modern lifestyles.[5]

It should be noted, however, that those going to see the Moiseyev perform did not necessarily know much about these places whose dances were represented or any details about each group's culture. In describing the dances, critics could employ such terms as "faraway people with strange sounding names as Adzharians, Tatars of Kazan, Moldavians, Byelorussians, etc."[6] For many Americans, the dancers on stage were their only point of reference for that culture or nation. Accordingly, once more, visible differences played a major role in American perception of the peoples living in the Soviet Union through the Moiseyev dances and Americans felt they could trust the image and characterization of the cultures on stage as depicted by the dancers and Igor Moiseyev's choreography.

Even the costumes reflected the variety present in the Moiseyev. A *Boston Globe* article noted that when traveling, the company took with it three thousand costumes and two thousand shoes. Such numbers, however, were necessary because of the many different ethnic groups being represented by the company. Consequently, each dance needed a completely different costume to properly depict the different dances and peoples on stage. In contrast to classical ballet, in which dancing shoes would be used a few times and then disposed of, the Moiseyev Dance Company could not part with their shoes so easily since "shoes are an essential part of a national costume." As a result, the company, unlike other dance companies, brought a shoemaker with them to repair the essential shoes for performances.[7] Once more, the number of shoes the Moiseyev brought with them served to reinforce the multiple cultures the dancers depicted on stage. Americans took in the multicultural message the Moiseyev Dance Company performed and its appeal stemmed from Americans' own notions of race and ethnicity as well as American national identity and who could become a member of the American citizenry.

American Views of Race, Ethnicity, and Nationalism

American citizenship being defined by race was not new; the Nationality Act of 1790 allowed for citizenship only for white people, and race would remain part of who could or could not be an American citizen until the

McCarran-Walter Act in 1952. Early twentieth century immigration restric-
tions underpin American views of national identity and, as Mae Ngai
argues, influenced not only ideas but "practices about citizenship, race,
and the nation-state." The Johnson-Reed Act of 1924 inaugurated numeri-
cal limits and reinforced a sense of hierarchy among different ethnic and
racial identities. While the creation and reinforcement of racial and ethnic
hierarchies is not new in American history, in the twentieth century the
immigration restriction legislation emanating from the 1920s added further
structure and concreteness to these hierarchies.[8]

Though immigration law frequently drew on national or ethnic labels
in its regulations, race inherently took part; Europeans came under the
white racial grouping, which not only put them at the top of the racial hierarchy, but also had the added connotation of the ability to be assimilated
into American culture and society. Indeed, the Johnson-Reed Act excluded
Asian groups such as Japanese and Indian peoples because of their race. As
Nagai argues, while those in the "white" category with European ethnic origins could become full-fledged American citizens and contributing members to society, those with certain ethnic identities had that ethnic label
inextricably tied to a racial category and "cast them as permanently foreign
and unassimilable."[9]

With the Cold War came a strong emphasis on nationalism and a global
audience for American nationalism. This new emphasis garnered reactions
on both ends of the spectrum when it came to thinking about immigration
in the United States; for some, it meant a desire for greater scrutiny of non-
Americans and immigrants as potentially subversive or unpatriotic and
on the other, a liberal pluralism to combat a negative view abroad of the
United States as racist.[10]

Leading up to the Cold War, progressive thinkers critiqued nativism
and racism and supported pluralism and cultural relativism in considering
who belonged in the United States. The 1930s saw this more pluralistic view
gather some more emphasis and momentum and the rise of fascism amplified it, with more discourse on racism and fascism emphasizing the United
States as a "nation of nations" that celebrated diversity based on a need for
national unity in the face of the fascism in Europe. The needs of World
War II also pushed these notions forward, including, for instance, Congress
repealing the Chinese Exclusion Act in response to Japanese propaganda
highlighting the inherent racism.[11]

During the Cold War, the Senate created a subcommittee to review immigration policy and, like many political endeavors in this period, the conflict influenced the subcommittee's actions. Subcommittee Chair Pat McCarran felt concern about the spread of communism and the subsequent McCarran-Walter Act of 1952 put the goal of maintaining America as bastion of democracy at its heart. Though the new law did remove racial requirements for US citizenship, it did also solidify the racial hierarchy. For instance, the law limited immigration from newly formed countries resulting from decolonization and whose people were Black. The act, which President Truman vetoed to no avail over concerns for its racist emphases, did elicit responses from liberal reformers. They pointed to the law's issues and endeavored to emphasize the American origin story as a nation of immigrants. Indeed, they recognized not just the racist nature of the law but that the anxiety over communism had no doubt contributed to its virulence. These thinkers often still functioned within the framing of nationalism of the Cold War period, noting how having limitations on immigration did not align with their sense of American nationalism and damaged America's reputation of the bastion of democracy in the Cold War world. Instead, they sought legislation that did not privilege one group over another.[12]

For both sides of the immigration law question (both those who wanted to continue limiting and those who wanted to remove them), there was concern around defining who belongs as an American citizen, which could not be separated from understandings of ethnicity and race. This kind of discourse about American identity were not limited to the political arena. For instance, the contemporary writings of American sociologist Nathan Glazer influenced American perception of ethnicity, race, and these concepts' role in American society. Glazer analyzed the various peoples of the United States in order to explain political and social phenomena and would similarly create categories and corresponding interests and actions for peoples in those categories. While studying membership in the American Communist Party, Glazer separated the groups according to ethnic and racial background, as well as class and education level, asserting that certain groups were more attracted to communism. Though the Communist Party reasoned that it would gain the greatest support of those who were the most oppressed, specifically industrial workers and Black Americans, Glazer's study found greater membership among professionals and middle-class people, especially those with a Jewish background, and intellectual and cultural figures.[13]

Glazer further developed his conception of the makeup of American society in *Beyond the Melting Pot: The Negroes, Puerto Ricans, Jews, Italians, and Irish of New York City* (1970). Here he explored the how race and ethnicity influenced New York City's society. Glazer noted that the notion of America as a melting pot (and especially New York with its extremely heterogeneous population) was important to America and its values but was both outdated and inaccurate with regard to contemporary American society.[14]

Glazer's works broke down the makeup of American society and American identity during the Cold War. As America strove to define itself in opposition to the Soviet Union during the Cold War period and to assemble a coherent sense of American identity, Glazer looked closely at the influence of race, ethnicity, and gender roles on American society. Throughout these writings, there is a recurrence of the theme of anxiety on the part of Americans and these concepts. Glazer broke down the idealized view of a multicultural melting pot to demonstrate continued expressions of difference and concern about how one's race or ethnicity influenced the way they functioned in society and the political arena.

American Perception of Race and Ethnicity as Displayed by the Moiseyev

It is clear that the Soviet Union's goals for the Moiseyev included showing off the different races, ethnicities, and nationalities within its borders in a positive manner as part of contributing to the larger Cold War discourse around which form of government truly supported diverse peoples. The Soviet government endeavored to paint a picture of peaceful, respectful existence within the Soviet Union, and the Moiseyev helped to embellish this picture. At the same time, as evidenced by thinkers like Nathan Glazer, Americans expressed concern over American identity and the role of multiple ethnicities and races within the body politic. In viewing the Moiseyev and its depiction of multiple nationalities and ethnicities, Americans responded positively to this message of multiculturalism—they "bought" what the Moiseyev "sold." Still, it is difficult to determine just how nuanced American understanding was of the different groups on stage. Americans did have a sense that the dances came from a variety of peoples and places but the question remains, what did they think of these identities and what it meant for Soviet identity overall?

One of the programs for the 1958 tour can provide a more detailed idea of what Americans may have known about the dances' corresponding nations and ethnicities and their place within Soviet identity. The program alludes to how there are more than "180 different national groups" in the USSR and that the goal of the troupe was to take the dances of all these different peoples and, through "painstaking research and study," give them "polish, and a professional expression" before in turn bringing them to global audiences. The program claimed even the makeup of the dancers themselves as diverse, coming from all backgrounds, from amateur to professional with experience in different kinds of dance. Moiseyev's molding of the dance company itself is presented a perfect melding of varied peoples: "From this mixed group, representing various styles of dancing, there had to be created a company with a single style of its own. The exuberance and spontaneity of the amateur was to be blended with the training and sense of tradition of the professional." Moiseyev achieved the perfectly balanced blend, to the point where "The breathtaking leaps of the Ukrainian Hopak and the graceful beauty of the dances of Central Asia became as much a part of the skill of the company as the dances of Lithuania, Moldavia or Karalia."[15] The depiction here is the dance troupe as a multicultural group which melted the different identities of the dancers into a singular identity and one in which they can all understand and celebrate the multiple ethnicities and nationalities in the Soviet Union and its neighbors.

At the same time, Americans remarked on the visible differences in terms of the dances' styles and presentation, such as the "fierce dance of the Tartars, the stalking dance to the thin beat of the Caucasian drum[,] the Amazonian fury of 'Partisans' with its beautifully lighted effects of cloaked riders."[16] Americans took note of the diversity in kinds and styles of dance moves, costumes, and the style of the dances.[17] Critics particularly noted the variety of the dances and how the different peoples came to be represented as a result. For instance, the Estonian polka song showed a traditional gender relationship with "a young man [who] is harassed into an unflagging performance by his inexhaustible girl-friend," contrasting with the "Russian reel that wound itself into a fantastic climax (two gyrating circles of linked dancers spinning like mad dervishes)."[18]

Views of ethnicity, race, and who belongs informed Americans' sense of their own national identity and how they interpreted the various identities put on display by the Moiseyev dancers. The Moiseyev put forth a multicultural message, which Americans found comforting as it reflected an idealized multicultural melting pot, which formed one part of America's Cold War narrative but which contrasted with the reality of ethnic and racial tensions. Indeed, the notion of an American citizenry made up of diverse peoples from across the globe has been enshrined in American culture and contributed to the mythologization of American inclusivity and exceptionalism.[19]

That being said, even as they ate up the multicultural vision onstage, Americans felt viewing the dancers enabled them to better understand the specifics of "Russian" identity and expanded their knowledge of Russian culture. Many felt that the Moiseyev contradicted the stereotypical American perception of Russian ethnicity and character. Critic W. G. Rogers noted how "wonderfully gay" the dances were, and this contrasted with his impression that the "Russian character had a darker side."[20] The Moiseyev contradicted the American opinion that "Russians have no sense of humor" in their dances, like the "Football" dance.[21] In particular, Americans were surprised by the fact that the Russians appeared to have a sense of humor. The "Football" dance was one example which taught Americans to ignore their traditional stereotype of Russians as a sober, stern people.[22] Americans, though perhaps not the biggest soccer fans, still understood the humor of the dance on stage, and took part in it with their Soviet counterparts.

While some comparisons to other groups, ethnicities and artists took place when the Moiseyev performed, perhaps the most important aspect of audience reaction was the recognition that the peoples living in the Soviet Union were real people who expressed emotions (especially positive emotions) and that American audiences could understand them, even without knowing their languages. This aspect of reception could be labeled a "strong non-dance element," more specifically, the "indisputable excitement that comes of seeing Russians—real people—laughing, dancing, waving. For forty years the door has been shut. We have known Soviet citizens only by hearsay. The impact of having these dancers immediately before us, charming and spirited, evokes an emotion like that of meeting a member of the family who has been away for a very long time."[23]

FIGURE 8. "Football" Dance. Source: Anna Ilupina and Yelena Lutskaya, *Moiseyev's Dance Company*, trans. Olga Shartse (Moscow: Progress Publishers, 1966), 127.

Igor Moiseyev as Intrepid Anthropologist

Beyond the dancers and dances themselves, another contributing factor enabling Americans to see the Moiseyev Dance Company as presenting a fair, multicultural picture of peoples living together was the depiction of Igor Moiseyev and his choreographic method. Often the discussion of the different ethnicities and nationalities depicted by the Moiseyev went hand-in-hand with the story of the group's founding and Moiseyev's ability to "discover" and preserve dances from a wide variety of Soviet territories. The *Boston Globe* wrote the company's founding story involving Moiseyev's search for the perfect folk material and perfect dancers:

> Thirty-three years ago, dancer Igor Moiseyev switched careers. Glumly aware that he would soon be a little long in the tooth for his energetic lead roles in the Bolshoi Ballet, he began combing the backwater villages of the Soviet Union—sometimes on foot, oftener on donkey back—for remnants of the fast-disappearing art of the folk dance. The result of those travels, with or without a donkey, is being seen by Americans in 20 cities this season as the Moiseyev Dancers make their fourth tour of the country and their first since 1965. [24]

Like Soviet publications, American coverage portrayed Igor Moiseyev as a kind of anthropologist—a Johnny Appleseed studying other cultures and bringing their dances to light. It is interesting that his rationale for pursuing folk dance source material for choreographic purposes is described as due to his concern about getting lead roles as he aged, but nonetheless, his pursuit allowed Americans to see and engage with the multiple Soviet cultures. Moiseyev's methods are seen as both adept and appropriate; he can translate the dances into forms anyone can understand and show how different groups live happily in the Soviet Union.

Another retelling of the company's origins noted that Moiseyev had a special interest in folk dance and accordingly "traveled extensively throughout the Soviet Union studying local customs and dances." As a result of his study, Moiseyev devised new ways to train and coordinate folk dancers, a task entirely without precedent (according to American newspapers). Igor Moiseyev put together the dances but also founded a special school that "would train a dancer in recreating diversified national images and styles, beginning with ancient and primitive dances and ending with modern works in which present day features, characters and emotion are reflected."[25] Moiseyev is lauded as preserving and passing on knowledge of these folk dances in a positive manner that represents the different ethnicities and nationalities fairly.

Moiseyev himself continuously emphasized how much diversity the Soviet Union had as well as how his approach to capturing that diversity was both authentic and elevating for the nations in question. He used vocabulary such as "huge variety of national folk-dances" and "so diversified in their character and style." Once again, his travels and the descriptions of who he learned from underscore diversity: Moiseyev "learned from hunter

and the mountain dweller; from the peasant and the Dijguit horseman."
Moiseyev insisted that in the end, he was representing not just the dance of
a people, but the way of life and spirit.[26]

The American press celebrated Moiseyev as a brilliant societal observer,
cataloger, and artist. He is portrayed as a Soviet citizen with a superior ability to study and choreograph dances across differing time periods and cultures. While his actions in putting together the dances for his troupe are
not directly linked to the Soviet government's orders, the government's
encouragement and approval are implied. Moiseyev, as the Soviet government's representative, acted as mediator between cultures and brought
their dances to a wider audience. The Soviet government through Moiseyev
revealed a cultural sensitivity and positive intent—the government desired
to celebrate the cultures living within its borders.

In specialty publications devoted to dancing, the writers were savvy
enough to realize that the Moiseyev did not present entirely authentic
dances. They noted that these dances were highly stylized and geared toward
their audiences so they could be easily understood. While acknowledging
the amazing skills and the entertaining nature of the Moiseyev, these writers also emphasized that the dances made "no great artistic demands on
the audience. The performers reach out graciously to give you easy-to-take
pleasure." The Moiseyev dances were neither intellectually nor artistically
challenging for the audience; they were middlebrow, mainstream entertainment (as discussed above) which presented an idealized, stylized view of
the Soviet Union. The stylized nature of the dances did not, however, take
away from the overall folk "feel" of the performances, as the Moiseyev "still
retains its warm-hearted folk quality. The Russian folk music—melodious,
melancholy, gay, and mischievous—is irresistible."[27] Even those reviewers who were more critical of Moiseyev's source material and questioned
his notion of authenticity could not deny the dances' appeal and their ability to represent folk cultures, if only in a distilled version.

Some critics recognized an even larger multicultural message beyond
the territories of the Soviet Union. Walter Terry described other countries
that Igor Moiseyev visited and studied:

> The Moiseyev repertory not only contains folk elements representing the
> republics, regions, villages and the many nationalities which comprise
> the Soviet Union but also many dances from countries (China, Hungary,
> Czechoslovakia) which Mr. Moiseyev classified as being "in our bloc."

His dance duties and interests, however, take him beyond the "bloc" but in the role of consultant, rather than choreographer. . . . His services as a dance adviser have taken him to many lands, among them Lebanon (where he remained for two months in 1956) and Egypt.[28]

Terry recognized that the Moiseyev hoped to represent the many peoples of the USSR and also other places under Soviet influence or with whom the Soviet Union had friendly relations. Igor Moiseyev stated that he used his techniques to help other countries recognize the value of their folk material while allegedly being respectful of the country's beliefs and traditions.[29] Terry saw the potential in the Moiseyev to reach other peoples with its multicultural message. This potential had wider political implications in the context of the Cold War as the United States and Soviet Union vied for influence in territories across the globe.

Audrey Kearns also recognized this powerful message: "The heart of a nation speaks to other peoples most eloquently through its folksongs and dances." According to Kearns, the Moiseyev fully communicated this message with dances that came from over 180 different cultures from within the Soviet Union.[30] While most felt that these dances celebrated the variety and differences among the cultures of the Soviet Union, a few critics felt that the Moiseyev demonstrated how "basically homogenized the world's people are."[31] This homogenization view did not dominate the response to the multicultural nature of the Moiseyev, but it does support another theme that surfaces again and again when Americans viewed the Moiseyev generally— that Soviets are people too.

Recent American Experience with Folk Dance

Americans saw a multicultural vision in the Moiseyev Dance Company which comforted them. While multiple factors played into this ability to comfort, such as heteronormative love stories and the absence of Black people or dances, another factor may have been specifically the gender and racial connotations Americans may have associated with folk dance. It is worth briefly discussing Americans' recent history and experience with folk dance, which reflects familiarity with how folk dance, like that of the Moiseyev Dance Company, could impart comforting gender and racial messages. Domestic folk dance performed a similar function to the Moiseyev in the late nineteenth and at least into the first part of the twentieth century. Daniel Walkowitz examines how folk dance, primarily in the form of English Country Dance (ECD) became more popular socially and in American physical education in response to urbanization and its corresponding social changes. The traditional, heteronormative values ECD entailed as well as its more demure dance movements compared to early 1900s dance hall dances cemented a growing view of ECD as a way to properly educate young people in the United States. Social reformers thought wholesome and traditional values could be imparted through dance and correspondingly, individuals like Elizabeth Burchenal ensured folk dance became part of female education in New York Public schools along with similar movements in other American cities.[32]

Given the very structured approach to ECD, including positions for certain social classes and who went first, it could feel comforting in presenting a structured view of society; views and concerns over race and class formed part of the reason behind ECD popularity in this time period.[33] Megan Pugh expands on the notions undergirding the rising interest in folk dance and highlights the continued evolution as Square Dance became more prominent, as can be seen in examples like "The Country Dance Society" which aired Sunday evenings starting in 1941 on *CBS*. Pugh unpacks how praise of folk dance could go hand-in-hand with notions of white supremacy and nostalgia for an allegedly "simpler" time. Henry Ford took up the cause of folk dance, specifically in the form of Square Dancing, with these notions in mind and campaigned to have Detroit and Dearborn schools include square dancing in their physical education curricula. Dearborn and Detroit schools agreed to this and other American school also adopted square dancing into their curricula and by 1942, at least 378 cities had square dancing classes. As argued here with regard to the Moiseyev Dance Company, Pugh argues that Square Dancing popularity and success of campaigns like Ford's stemmed from Square Dancing's ability to assuage anxiety and played into contemporary nostalgia for early rural America.[34]

Certainly, American racial and ethnic issues cannot be directly compared with those of the Soviet Union. However, in this exploration of how Americans viewed Soviet identity as portrayed by the dancers, it is beneficial to further flesh out Soviet views of the American racial environment, how the Soviet Union used American racism to support its cultural diplomacy efforts, and to highlight where specific discussions of Soviet versus American treatment of Black peoples came into play.

Soviet Views of Race and Nationalism
in the United States

When the Soviet Union looked to recruit American workers who had expertise in industrialization and modern agriculture in the 1930s, many African Americans answered their call. Scholar Kimberly St. Julian-Varnon works to better understand the lived experience of African Americans in the Soviet Union and their reason for emigrating to the USSR. One such experience is that of Margaret Glasgow, an unsuccessful hair dresser due to clients not wishing to work with a Black woman, who moved to the Soviet Union in 1934. Glasgow felt welcomed in her new homeland and that her blackness was no longer the main marker of her identity to others.[35] In addition to actively recruiting African Americans to move to the Soviet Union, Soviet cultural efforts highlighted American racism and Soviet inclusivity. For instance, St. Julian-Varnon points to the 1936 Soviet film *Tsirk* (*Circus*) featuring as its heroine an American actress who has fled to the Soviet Union to hide her secret, which is eventually revealed to be that she has a Black son and the movie ends happily with her Soviet community welcoming the baby with open arms, intended as a stark contrast to what American treatment of the baby would have been like.[36] Clearly, in the Soviet Union there was awareness of American racial issues and intolerance.

Indeed, information about African Americans was publicly available in the Soviet Union; the 1920s and 1930s saw publication of works addressing African Americans, either those written by Americans and translated into Russian or by Soviets who visited the United States. Some of these works were by Black Americans themselves expressing views of the racial oppression of early twentieth century America. The Comintern similarly portrayed Black Americans as without equal rights and freedoms; it in fact lumped African Americans into the category for the "East," as with other colonial countries struggling against oppression. The Soviets guided African Americans to "see racial oppression as aligned to class oppression." Lenin and other communists emphasized the ways racial oppression through imperialism could be linked with working class oppression through capitalism. In 1928, the Comintern put forth a "Resolution on the Negro Question in the United States" which specifically proclaimed that the plight of African Americans must be viewed with the plight of Africans internationally. This view of the similarity of these struggles influenced cultural products in the Soviet Union in the 1920s and 1930s, including films and travelogues.

For instance, in Soviet author's Boris Pilniak's work after his visit to the United States in 1931, he emphasized the disastrous situation the Depression rendered and spoke about the mistreatment of African Americans, including the Scottsboro Boys, lynchings, and the huge difference in the standard of living between white and Black Americans. The Comintern would take this a step further by tying oppression of Black Americans in the American South as particularly harrowing and as inextricably tied to American capitalism to the point where the area could be considered a colony of the American capitalistic and inherently imperialistic project. Another travelogue in 1936, this time by writers Ilya Ilf and Evgeny Petrov, continued to highlight the terrible living and working conditions of Black Americans. The work notes how white Americans thought themselves superior to Black Americans and reinforced this idea through cultural products such as Black characters in film appearing simple-minded. Indeed, white Americans who hired Black Americans demonstrated a "slave-owning mentality." Ilf and Petrov's depiction critiqued America's claim to be a democracy, meant to contrast with the Soviet welcoming and inclusive treatment of its people and desire to support those oppressed elsewhere.[37]

Black Americans Engaging with the Soviet Union

Leftist Black Americans drew a direct connection between Russians and Black Americans and claimed a certain kinship; for instance, musical artist and actor Paul Robeson proclaimed how the grandfather of the Russian poet Alexander Pushkin was African.[38] Some Black American artists visited or even directly collaborated on cultural products or performances with the Soviet Union. For example, writer Langston Hughes went to the Soviet Union in 1932 to help make a film about Black American workers, though this fell through.[39]

Robeson visited the Soviet Union in 1935 with much press coverage involved. A *Daily Worker* article points out how Robeson is the son of a slave and is being received by sons of serfs. When interviewed specifically about whether he saw a "race question" during his Soviet visit, Robeson highlighted how he understood that "the Soviet theory is that all races are equal—really equal, socially equal, too, as well as economically and politically." Robeson underscored again "the enthusiastic joy of Russian workers and artists, they or their fathers also once slaves of capitalist and landlord, who now welcome in addition a man they feel is a brother artist from abroad." He expressed surprise about his "feeling of safety and abundance and freedom," including when he realized he had some issue with his passport but this presented no obstacle to the border authorities, no doubt a radical departure from what he would have experienced in the United States in similar circumstances. Even when questioned about recent counterrevolutionary executions, Robeson brushed this aside, noting it as justified and that "all the masses of every race are contented and support their government."[40]

Robeson continued his engagement with the Soviet Union event after World War II and the start of the Cold War. As chairman of the Council for African Affairs (listed as a subversive organization by the Department of Justice), Robeson stated in 1948 that he would continue working with communists "because Communists are against many of the injustices which he himself has long opposed." While noting he did not feel he was being unpatriotic, he did note that being critical of the racial situation in America was necessary and that the Cold War impacted not only the domestic but the international situation for Black peoples. He pointed out that the European Recovery Plan would continue the exploitation of African colonies and peoples and that the United States was acting in this way as part of its efforts to ensure global influence.[41]

In 1956, Robeson had to testify before HUAC and they highlighted a statement Robeson made in which he again emphasized a lack of racism in the Soviet Union: "Why should the Negroes ever fight against the only nations of the world where racial discrimination is prohibited, and where the people can live freely? Never! I can assure you, they will never fight against either the Soviet Union or the peoples' democracies." In his testimony, he stated again "In Russia I felt for the first time like a full human being. No color prejudice like in Mississippi, no color prejudice like in Washington. It was the first time I felt like a human being. Where I did not feel the pressure of color as I feel in this Committee today."[42] Robeson again and again made a direct connection between how difference was handled by the American democratic system versus the Soviet communist one. The Moiseyev Dance Company's propaganda message mirrored the view Robeson and others put forth; that in the Soviet Union, difference was both accepted and celebrated and that the opposite was true in the United States.

The Impact of Contemporary Racial Events

The American Cold War narrative emphasized multiculturalism and freedom as two major aspects of American identity, even though the reality of American life in this time period entailed anxiety, tension, oppression of peoples of color, and racial violence. Recent events related to race in the United States would influence the ways Americans viewed the Moiseyev Dance Company, especially given how the Soviet Union took pains to amplify every instance of American racial oppression and persecution. These events influenced the American audience for cultural exchange and also influenced the American government's domestic and political actions.

For instance, the recent *Brown vs. Board of Education* (May 1954) decision which declared segregated public schools unconstitutional had domestic and international repercussions. Thomas Borstelmann demonstrates how both the court's decision and how the Eisenhower administration acted on it were influenced by the international situations of the Cold War and newly forming countries in Africa and Asia. If the judges had decided against declaring segregation unconstitutional, there would have been dire consequences for the United States internationally as it combated Soviet accusations of racism and as it endeavored to engender friendly relations with newly formed countries. The Eisenhower administration immediately took note of how the decision could be used internationally and focused more on what it would mean for the image of America abroad than anything else. The State Department and the USIA immediately took up the decision to use it as propaganda demonstrating Black Americans' position in American society progressing, feeding into the American Cold War narrative of the United States as an equitable place to live for all.[43]

The September 1957 Little Rock crisis would be another racial event fresh in American audiences' minds during the 1958 Moiseyev Dance Company tour. Arkansas Governor Orval Faubus resisted the *Brown vs. Board of Education* decision being carried out at Central High School in Little Rock by utilizing the Arkansas National Guard and encouraging white mobs to keep nine Black students from attending school. Press coverage again would have been of great concern to the American government in the Cold War, especially the contrast between children trying to attend school and the harassment they endured from adults. Little Rock became well known internationally and once more, the Eisenhower administration strove to use it as positive propaganda for America, though this contradicted the actual views of the Eisenhower administration, which concerned itself far more with what the event meant for international relations rather than with what the event meant in terms of larger domestic racial issues in America.[44]

Additionally, Americans would have been aware of the way the Eisenhower administration identified jazz, a music form directly associated with Black Americans, as part of its own Cold War cultural exchange efforts. The administration hoped that jazz could repair international views of the United States as racist and anti-democratic. Some Americans questioned the use of jazz, feeling it was not a worthy cultural representation of America. However, the American government proceeded despite any concerns and strove to make the message of racial tolerance as explicitly as they could; for instance, using a historical narrative of the progression of jazz as being performed in increasingly sophisticated ways and contexts as a purported parallel for racial progress in the United States.[45] In the context of the racial issues of 1950s America, the Moiseyev's utopia of a variety of peoples living together harmoniously had widespread appeal. As the US government proclaimed itself a democratic, freedom-loving nation in jarring contrast to the reality of American domestic turmoil, the Moiseyev functioned as an escape for the American audience. In the Moiseyev performances, Americans found a highly entertaining version of their own multicultural ideal without the nitty-gritty, violent details of the actual contemporary American racial situation.

Lack of Race in American Reception

The Moiseyev claimed to represent a variety of peoples in terms of dance, style, and appearance and offered the opportunity for Americans to evaluate them. Americans noted the visible differences present between the different dances and correspondingly pulled certain characteristics as representing the Soviet national and ethnic groups. For the most part, there is an absence of commentary on race or any allusion to non-white Soviet or American peoples in the American audience's reactions, again speaking to the escapist opportunity the Moiseyev represented. However, racial commentary can be found in one critic's discussion of a Caucasian dance (Adzharian Hero) with drums: "Although these virile Soviet dancers were well-clad, one felt much the same trial ceremony could be performed by naked Negro primitives."[46]

FIGURE 9. Caucasian war dance "Khorumi." Source: Anna Ilupina and Yelena Lutskaya, *Moiseyev's Dance Company*, trans. Olga Shartse (Moscow: Progress Publishers, 1966), 110.

This critic took a particular dance and classified it as representing a lower rung on the civilizational hierarchy in the Soviet Union. He then linked this ethnic group with a racial group that he considered to be at a similarly low level in the American hierarchy.

In terms of ethnicity and race, the Moiseyev's rhetoric and the variety of dances it displayed supported an alleged Soviet multicultural identity. This identity conformed with American Cold War rhetoric lauding American ideals of freedom and tolerance (in opposition to Soviet repression). While it is debatable how nuanced American perception of the different races and ethnicities the Moiseyev displayed was, Americans still understood the multicultural message on at least a general level and embraced it. The appeal of the message stemmed from a simplified view of different peoples living together, a view which did not include any Black dances or dancers. Igor Moiseyev presented a vision of heteronormative and multicultural utopia in the form of middlebrow entertainment which Americans found soothing.

CONCLUSION

The Moiseyev Dance Company enjoyed and continues to enjoy domestic and international success. In its rhetoric and performances, the troupe made certain assertions. It claimed to represent a vibrant multiculturalism in the Soviet Union. By choosing to represent the multiple nationalities of the Soviet Union and celebrating the differences on stage for Soviet and international audiences, the Moiseyev claimed a corresponding Soviet respect and tolerance for national and cultural differences. Contemporary Soviet writers and Moiseyev himself underscored this cultural inspiration in the dance creation process; a Moiseyev dance was the result of careful study of a particular culture and its people in order to draw out the national character. Igor Moiseyev claimed after the creative process, his version of the dance represented an authentic folk dance. Moiseyev defended his changes he made to the original material; he claimed that, for instance, the Byelorussians recognized the Moiseyev's *Bulba* dance as an authentic Belarusian dance that existed long before Moiseyev modified it.

Finally, as its success grew, Soviet writers and Moiseyev depicted the dance troupe as a specifically Soviet art form. The dance troupe was created when socialist realism was the rule of the day and artists struggled to conform to these new strictures after the 1920s era of avant-garde experimentation in Soviet art. Socialist realism exhorted Soviet artists to create pieces that represented proletarian culture, that, according to Stalin, Gorky, and other influential figures, meant art accessible to the masses and realist in style. In contrast, "formalism," experimentation, and modernism were viewed by the regime as decadent and bourgeois; Western and formalist influence had to be avoided at all costs; creating a piece that could be labeled as such would mean public censure, at the very least, if not arrest and possible prison time or execution. In this atmosphere, ballet choreographers grappled with identifying and creating specifically "Soviet" ballets that conformed to socialist realist guidelines. Igor Moiseyev claimed folk dance, specifically his vision of folk dance, represented the direction Soviet ballet should take. Folk dance, because of its origins, better represented the makeup of Soviet society and successfully overrode the bourgeois, Western origins of classical ballet.

However, these claims did not represent the reality of life in the Soviet Union. Though the Moiseyev formed under the policy of korenizatsiia, which celebrated and supported the flourishing of nationalism and nationalistic artistic expression, at the same time, Stalin soon revoked the policy (and even as early as 1935, claimed Russian nationalism as foremost among nationalism in the Soviet Union and as the nationalism responsible for the 1917 Revolution). The shift in policy involved not only an emphasis on the superiority of Russian nationalism but also prejudice against and the persecution of national groups. Communist officials representing local national elites became victims of the Great Terror (1937–1939). Thus, even as the Moiseyev claimed to celebrate the Tatars by dancing the *Dance of the Tatars of Kazan*, the NKVD carried out the forced relocation of the Tatars. In reality, the allegedly "authentic" dances Igor Moiseyev created involved drastic changes with the company's audience and artistic success always in mind. Igor Moiseyev (and the other artists like costume designers and musicians who also took part in the dances' creations) endeavored to make the dances as entertaining as possible, which meant dances with dramatic leaps, precisely synchronized moves by part or all of the company's cast, and flashy costumes that looked superb in motion and were modernized so that they were not too outdated and showed off the dancers' fit bodies. In addition, Soviet writers and Moiseyev claimed he was an appropriate judge of which dances represented a particular nationality, what should be changed while maintaining "authenticity," and what characteristics embodied a nationality. The result was a multicultural message with a Russian bent; Moiseyev as the "discoverer" or "preserver" of a nation's folk dance came across as superior to the nationalities he studied and the dancers themselves, and, for the most part, reflected a Russian ethnicity and only "acted" in the roles representing other nationalities. The Moiseyev dances, furthermore, still drew on Russian classical ballet within some of its dance steps and in the Moiseyev dancers' training. While Igor Moiseyev and contemporary writers asserted that he created true "Soviet" ballet, Moiseyev used Russia's rich dance traditions in his own work and continued an established tradition of using folk/national/character dance established in the previous century and used more recently by choreographers like Fokine.

Though the Moiseyev were hypocritical in many aspects of its rhetoric, it was able to survive the changes in leadership and policy during the Soviet period through today. The troupe survived the changes due to multiple reasons, but prominent among them was the personal and official patronage of the Soviet regime. Stalin admired Moiseyev's parade work and continued his support with the State Academic Ensemble of Folk Dance in the USSR. The Soviet regime felt the Moiseyev dances reflected socialist realism and could be labeled as Soviet ballet. After Stalin's death, the company thrived because the Soviet regime recognized the benefits of using the Moiseyev as a diplomatic tool. The troupe toured extensively in the Soviet Union from its early years, and after World War II, helped welcome Soviet Eastern European Bloc countries into the communist fold. As the troupe traveled outside of the Soviet Union and Eastern Europe, it presented an extremely positive picture of the Soviet Union to the Cold War world. This image demonstrated the vibrancy of Soviet culture and, as noted above, supposed support of multiculturalism in Soviet society. The Soviet regime's continued support of the Moiseyev until 1991 was also tied to Igor Moiseyev's ability to maneuver the troupe so that it conformed to contemporary cultural policy under Stalin and then became an irreplaceable cultural tool. Moiseyev's personal and political charisma ensured domestic and international recognition of the company throughout the Soviet and post-Soviet period. Moiseyev used this savvy particularly when the Soviet regime selected the company to function as the first large-scale cultural representation sent to the United States in the Cold War. The company toured the United States in a time of anxiety; the American government and Americans in general struggled to identify a specifically "American" identity after World War II. With the international spotlight highlighting any domestic issues and constantly comparing the two Cold War superpowers, Americans experienced a fear of cultural inferiority in comparison to their Soviet counterparts. The Soviets, with their wealth of cultural tradition and famous artists to draw on, appeared to have cornered the high culture market in the Cold War conflict.

In this period of the Cold War and the contemporary discussion of proper masculinity, femininity, and the place of different races and ethnicities in the American identity, the Moiseyev tour served as a way to compare

American and Soviet identity side by side. Americans noted the high level of masculinity the male dancers displayed and assessed this masculinity using Cold War terms associated with the Soviet Union, like "sputniks" and "steel." However, though contemporary and more recent scholars discussed the concern with regard to American masculinity and sexuality, Americans did not shrink away from their appreciation of the Moiseyev due to the male dancers' incredibly muscular bodies and astounding abilities. The American audience similarly looked for markers of the Soviet ideal of gender equality in evaluating the female dancers of the Moiseyev and while offstage they found some evidence of this, Americans took to heart the more feminine aspects of the dancers and chose to emphasize their similarities to American women in appearance, habits, and desires (in both material goods and men). Accordingly, the American reaction to notions of gender and sexuality the Moiseyev displayed onstage and offstage did not further stereotypes of how the Soviet genders differed from American genders, but instead drew out the two peoples' similarities and ability to relate to one another.

In a similar vein, Americans found comfort in the dance company's depiction of national identity and its relationship to ethnicity and race. The dances presented a kaleidoscope of colors, dance moves, and tones to demonstrate the multiple nationalities and ethnicities in the Soviet Union coming together with precision and clear unity. There was a notable absence of Black bodies as part of this multicultural vision; in a time of racial upheaval (and global coverage of it) in the United States, this simplified view of different peoples living together functioned as an escape and salve. Even as both the Soviet Union and Black Americans strove to point to the horrors of American racism, Americans themselves enjoyed this unproblematic portrayal of different peoples living together harmoniously.

For its time period, the 1958 Moiseyev tour also marked a performance and event that a large number of Americans witnessed. Between the performances and the *Ed Sullivan Show* appearance, the Moiseyev reached an audience of over forty million. The Soviet and American governments privileged culture and its ability to change minds, and, after seeing the Moiseyev, Americans heartily concurred. They believed the Moiseyev could bolster political relations and were more effective than traditional diplomats. American reception complicates our view of the Cold War experience and the more recent scholarly discussion of the Cold War narrative.

FIGURE 10. A group of Moiseyev dancers with Igor Moiseyev (center). Source: M. Chudnovsky, *The Folk Dance Company of the USSR: Igor Moiseyev, Art Director* (Moscow: Foreign Languages Publishing House, 1959), 96.

Americans became fascinated by the Moiseyev, but not simply for its enter-tainment value. After learning all the details of how the Moiseyev dancers lived in the Soviet Union, what they looked like, what they ate, and their goals in life, Americans felt Soviet people thought, acted, and lived just like them. Soviet people did not represent an enemy with whom the United States would never be able to cooperate, as espoused by the Cold War narra-tive. Rather, Americans could see something of themselves in their counter-parts behind the Iron Curtain.

EPILOGUE

No doubt, we are now in a period of decline, of decadence [of] all art forms. Unfortunately, this is not surprising. Art is not divorced from life, but, on the contrary, expresses it in the form of images. Art reflects our morals. [There has been a] recent extraordinary decline of morals. Culturally, our society is heading into a deep abyss. Look at your TV, [the way] all singing is in English, [even while] not knowing the English language. . . . [Young people] are completely forgetting that they are Russian, that there is a great Russian culture and Russian music. . . . Unfortunately, imitation and fascination with everything American captured not only our country. . . . This art is very much dilettantism. . . . What's going on stage? Solid amateurism, coarsening tastes. Shake your hips, sing a few words . . . strum the guitar and— [this is] a huge success. . . . In these conditions maintain staff becomes more difficult.

—Igor Moiseyev, *IA vcponmnimaiu . . . (I Recall)*

In 1985, Mikhail Gorbachev became General Secretary of the Communist Party and set a new tone for the Soviet Union. Gorbachev instituted a series of reforms, guided by *perestroika* (restructuring) and *glasnost* (openness). Gorbachev's reforms, which introduced a semi-free market economy, increased participation in government and greater freedom of expression, led to a variety of opinions of what the future of the Soviet Union should entail. A few short years later, citizens in the Soviet Union and Eastern Bloc countries moved toward independence in largely nonviolent revolutions, and the Soviet Union fell on Christmas Day, 1991. Throughout this period of upheaval and beyond the Soviet Union's end, the Moiseyev continued to tour internationally and continued to achieve a great deal of success on its tours. After the fall of the Soviet Union, with a mild name change (from State Academic Folk Dance Ensemble of the USSR to State Academic Folk Dance Ensemble), the Moiseyev sustained an international reputation and an enthusiastic international audience. However, the simple fact of the

Moiseyev's continued existence does not address how American reception of the Moiseyev has changed during this time period.

Though glasnost allowed for greater experimentation in choreography in the Soviet Union, *New York Times* critic Anna Kiselgoff noted that Soviet choreographers and artists still felt beholden to American audiences, who wanted the same kinds of dances when attending a Soviet troupe's performance. Thus, even though Igor Moiseyev declared an interest in jazz and creating a jazz-inspired dance for the troupe in 1988, Americans were not interested.[1] In the opening excerpt above, Moiseyev bemoaned the domination of American culture and its attraction worldwide. He felt Russian culture was now being neglected; the international audience and artists from Russia and elsewhere ignored rich Russian cultural history. However, this criticism of the dominance of American culture did not stop Moiseyev from continuing to utilize the more popular, if repetitive, dances American audiences knew and loved.

For cultural exchange, glasnost entailed more secondary artistic troupes being able to travel to the United States.[2] The Moiseyev enjoyed continued popularity in the 1980s but now it was much easier to sign Soviet artists to visit the United States—the Soviet regime was no longer in charge of all aspects of exchange and groups could enter into their own agreements.[3] However, at the same time, a few individual Americans felt the need and ability, in the period of glasnost, to decry the Moiseyev's representation of Soviet life. In a letter to the editor published in the *New York Times* on February 5, 1989, one Vera Toman of Port Jefferson, NY, accused Moiseyev of holding too narrow a view of multiculturalism. She believed Moiseyev only supported a specifically Russian view of the Soviet Union: "Even though much of the folk dance material he has theatricalized came from many ethnic groups within the Soviet Union, he does not acknowledge them as non-Russian. At age 83, he cannot be expected to change the imperialistic views he learned in the czarist and Communist empires."[4]

Additionally, Toman pointed out that the above *New York Times* article from November 13, 1988 utilized a photograph of the Ukrainian Hopak to erroneously illustrate Russian folklore.[5] Almost two years later, in another letter to the *New York Times* editor, Seymour Yusem of New York claimed that the *New York Times* "failed to mention the outright propagand[ist] nature" of Soviet cultural exchange.[6] Yusem asserted that the Moiseyev was the worst example of this, "for three decades [it] has been promoting the picture of happy Soviet ethnics busy doing their native dances."[7] He disparaged the depiction of giggling peasant girls and athletic peasant boys all living and working together in perfect harmony. Additionally, Yusem found the militant nature of some of the dances disturbing, especially the dance of Cossacks, a group that had murdered thousands of Jews, and which enjoyed a positive depiction in the Moiseyev dance. In conclusion, Yusem declared: "It is time to deliver a glasnost message to the Moiseyev troupe, with its militaristic idealization and phony ethnic paradise."[8] With Gorbachev's reforms in the 1980s and the movement toward independence of Eastern European Bloc countries and Soviet republics, harsh criticisms of the Moiseyev and its message made their way into the American press. While reviews of the Moiseyev's performances continued to be positive, they went hand-in-hand with criticism of the Moiseyev's political message.

Seventy-seven years later, how the Moiseyev Dance Company is viewed and remembered is complex. In Moiseyev's obituary, the *New York Times* described him as the creator of "a new form of theatrical folk dance . . . and whose troupe was one of the most popular dance companies of the 20th century." In the same obituary, controversy over the "ideological content" is cited because of how the Moiseyev conformed to the ideas of socialist realism. At the same time, Moiseyev himself refused to join the Communist Party and "did more than parrot officially sanctioned views" and admired American culture.[9] Dealing with its propagandistic past as an official tool of cultural diplomacy still haunts the Moiseyev. Despite some criticism, like in the examples above, of the Moiseyev's utopian vision of life in the Soviet Union, on its website today the Moiseyev still proudly states that "In 1989, immediately following the ensemble's Israeli tour, Russia and Israel established diplomatic relations."[10] The legacy of the Moiseyev is also present in the folk-dance ensembles of the republics of the former Soviet Union and the Eastern Bloc. The Moiseyev was the "model for most professional folk companies," but as such, similar issues of "ideological content" were present in these companies.[11] The Moiseyev Dance Company's legacy is complex; both the company's and Soviet regime's goals are a vital part of evaluating the troupe's impact and the Cold War context in America and abroad. However, despite the propagandistic nature of the troupe it has survived beyond the Soviet Union and demonstrates the huge impact it had on American–Soviet relations and on international cultural exchange, making it still popular today.

Text of the Lacy-Zaroubin Agreement, January 27, 1958

Agreement between the United States of America and the Union of Soviet Socialist Republics on exchanges in the cultural, technical, and educational fields.[1] By agreement between the governments of the United States of America and the Union of Soviet Socialist Republics, delegations headed on the United States side by Ambassador William S. B. Lacy and on the Soviet side by Ambassador G. N. Zaroubin conducted negotiations in Washington from October 28, 1957 to January 27, 1958, with regard to cultural, technical, and educational exchanges between the United States of America and the Union of Soviet Socialist Republics. As a result of these negotiations, which have been carried on in a spirit of mutual understanding, the United States and the Soviet Union have agreed to provide for the specific exchanges which are set forth in the following Sections during 1958 and 1959 in the belief that these exchanges will contribute significantly to the betterment of relations between the two countries, thereby contributing to a lessening of international tensions.[2]

SECTION 1: General

(1) The visits and exchanges enumerated in the following sections are not intended to be exclusive of others which may be arranged by the two countries or undertaken by their citizens.

(2) The exchanges provided for in the following sections shall be subject to the Constitution and applicable laws and regulations in force in the respective countries. It is understood that both parties will use their best efforts to have these exchanges effected in accordance with the following sections.

SECTION II: Exchanges of Radio and Television Broadcasts

(1) Both parties will provide for an exchange of radio and television broadcasts on the subjects of science, technology, industry, agriculture, education, public health, and sports.

(2) Both parties will provide for regular exchanges of radio and television programs, which will include the exchange of transcribed classical, folk, and contemporary musical production on magnetic tape and records; and the exchange of filmed musical, literary, theatrical, and similar television productions.

(3) For the purpose of strengthening mutual understanding and developing friendly relations between the United States and the Union of Soviet Socialist Republics, both parties agree to organize from time to time an exchange of broadcasts devoted to discussion of such international political problems as may be agreed upon between the two parties. The details of the exchanges shall be agreed upon at the working level.

(4) Both parties will provide for an exchange of samples of equipment for sound recording and telecasting and their technical specifications.

(5) Both parties will provide for an exchange of delegations of specialists in 1958 to study the production of radio and television programs; the techniques of sound recording; the equipment of radio and television studios; and the manufacture of films, recording tape, tape recorders, and records.

SECTION III: Exchange of Groups of Specialists in Industry, Agriculture, and Medicine

(1) Both parties agree to provide for an exchange of delegations in 1958 in the fields of iron and steel, mining (iron ore), and plastics. Both parties agree as to the desirability of arranging additional exchanges in industry during 1958–1959.

(2) Both sides will provide for the exchange of delegations of specialists in agriculture, the American side receiving during 1958–1959 nine delegations of Soviet specialists in the following fields: mechanization

of agriculture, animal husbandry, veterinary science, mixed feeds, cotton growing, agricultural construction and electrification, horticulture (including vegetable growing), hydroengineering (irrigation) and reclamation, forestry, lumber, and millwork. In 1958–1959 the Soviet side will receive nine American delegations of specialists in the following fields: the study of agricultural crops, veterinary science, soil use and the use of water resources (irrigation and drainage), mechanization of agriculture, agricultural economics (excluding distribution of agricultural products), cotton growing and plant physiology, sheep raising, biological control of agricultural pests, forestry, lumber, and millwork.

Details of the exchanges will be agreed upon by representatives of the Department of State of the United States of America and of the Embassy of the Union Soviet Socialist Republics in the United States America.

(3) Both parties agree to provide for the exchange 1958–1959 of eight medical delegations of five to six specialists for periods of two to six weeks to become familiar with research and achievement in the following field: new antibiotics, microbiology, physiology and pharmacology of the nervous system, radiobiology, biochemistry, metabolic diseases, endocrinology, community, and industrial hygiene.

Both parties recognize the desirability of providing exchange of delegations in the field of the manufacture of medical apparatuses and instruments.

(4) Both parties agree in principle to provide for an exchange in 1958 of delegations of specialists in fisheries.

SECTION IV: Visits by Representatives of Cultural, Civic, Youth and Student Groups

(1) For the purpose of establishing contacts, exchanging experiences, and becoming more familiar with the public and cultural life of both countries, the Soviet side will arrange to invite to the Union of Soviet Socialist Republics during 1958 groups of American writers (five to six persons), composers (five to six persons), painters, and sculptors (three to four persons). In 1958, the United States side

reciprocally will arrange to invite similar Soviet groups to visit the United States.

(2) Both parties will provide for the exchange in 1958–1959 of delegations of representatives of youth and delegations of women in various professions.

(3) Both parties agree to provide for an exchange of delegations of student and youth newspaper editors 1958–1959.

(4) Both parties will promote the development and strengthening of friendly contacts between Soviet American cities.

SECTION V: Exchange of Visits of Delegations of Members of the United States Congress and Deputies of the Supreme Soviet of the USSR

The proposal to exchange delegations of members of the United States Congress and deputies of the Supreme Soviet of the Union of Soviet Socialist Republics will be subject to further discussion between the two parties.

SECTION VI: Joint Conferences of USA and USSR Organizations

The desirability of agreement to hold joint conferences of interparliamentary groups in 1958 and 1959 or meetings of representatives of the United States and Soviet associations for the United Nations and UNESCO is a matter for the organizations concerned.

SECTION VII: Cooperation in the Field of Cinematography

Recognizing the importance of developing mutual cooperation between the United States of America and the Union of Soviet Socialist Republics in the field of motion pictures, both parties have agreed to the following:

(1) To make provisions for the sale and purchase of motion pictures by the film industries of both countries under the principles of equality and on mutually acceptable financial terms. Toward this end, not later than January 1958, Sovexportfilm will enter into contact with

representatives of the motion picture industry in the United States, to be approved by the Department of State of the United States, for the purpose of the sale and purchase of films in 1958.

(2) To arrange for the holding simultaneously in the United States of America and the Union of Soviet Socialist Republics of film premieres (American films in the Union of Soviet Socialist Republics and Soviet films in the United States of America, respectively), inviting to . . . premieres leading personalities of the film industries of both countries.

(3) To produce and exchange of twelve to fifteen documentary films in 1958 in accordance with a list to be mutually agreed upon by the two parties. On the Soviet side, the exchange of documentary films will be carried out by Sovexportfilm, with such films to be recorded in the English language, and for the United States of America by the United States Information Agency, with such films to recorded in the Russian language.

(4) In the second half of 1958 to provide for carrying . . . for a period of up to one month an interchange of delegations of leading motion picture personalities, scenario writers, and technical personnel to be approved by each side for the purpose of becoming acquainted with experiences in the production of motion pictures in the respective countries.

(5) To recognize the desirability and usefulness of organizing the joint production of artistic, popular science, and documentary films and of the conducting, not later than May 1958, of concrete negotiations between Soviet Union organizations and United States film companies on this subject, with such United States companies to be approved by the Department of State of the United States. The subject matter of the films will be mutually agreed upon the two parties.

(6) To recommend to the appropriate United States organizations the making of arrangements for the holding of a Soviet Film Week in the United States in 1958; to recommend to the appropriate motion picture organizations of the Soviet Union the making of arrangements for the holding of a United States Film Week in the Soviet Union in 1958; and to envision the participation in these film weeks of delegations from each side numbering three or four motion picture personalities for a period of two weeks.

(7) To recognize the desirability of producing feature films, documentary films, and concert films for television or non-theatrical showing in the United States by Soviet motion picture organizations and the producing of similar films by appropriate United States organizations for television or non-theatrical showing in the Soviet Union. Additional concrete negotiations on this question will be carried on between the Department of State of the United States and the Soviet Embassy in the United States of America.

(8) To designate a standing committee of four members, two from the United States and two from the Soviet Union, the powers of which will be for a period of one year and which will meet once in Moscow and once in Washington during that year to examine problems which may arise in connection with the implementation of the provisions of this section. The authority of this committee may be extended by mutual agreement.

SECTION VIII: Exchange of Theatrical, Choral, and Choreographic

Groups, Symphony Orchestras, and Artistic Performers

(1) The Ministry of Culture of the Union of Soviet Socialist Republics will invite the Philadelphia Symphony Orchestra to visit the Soviet Union in May or June 1958 and will send the ballet troupe of the Bolshoi Theatre of the Soviet Union, numbering 110–120 persons, to the United States in 1959 for a period of one month.

(2) The Ministry of Culture of the Union of Soviet Socialist Republics, on the basis of an existing agreement with Hurok Attractions, Inc., and the Academy of the National Theatre and Drama, will send two Soviet performers—E. Gilels, pianist, and L. Kogan, violinist—to the United States in January–April, 1958, and will invite two American soloists—B. Thebom, vocalist, and L. Warren, vocalist—to visit the Soviet Union.

(3) The Ministry of Culture of the Union of Soviet Socialist Republics will send Soviet vocalists I. Petrov, P. Lisitsian, and Z. Dolukhanova, as well as I. Bezrodni, violinist, and V. Ashkenazi, pianist, to the United States; and will invite R. Peters, vocalist, L. Stokowski, conductor, and others to visit the Soviet Union.

(4) The Ministry of Culture of the Union of Soviet Socialist Republics, in accordance with an agreement with Hurok Attractions, Inc., will send the State Folk Dance Ensemble of the Union of Soviet Socialist Republics to the United States in April–May, 1958 and will consider inviting a leading American theatrical or choreographic group to the Soviet Union in 1959.

(5) The Soviet side will send the Red Banner Song and Dance Ensemble of the Soviet Army or the Choreographic Ensemble "Beriozka" to the United States in the fourth quarter of 1958 and invite one of the leading American choreographic groups to visit the Soviet Union.

SECTION IX: Visits by Scientists

(1) The Academy of Sciences of the Union of Soviet Socialist Republics and the National Academy of Sciences of the United States will, on a reciprocal basis, provide for the exchange of groups or individual scientists and specialists for delivering lectures and holding seminars on various problems of science and technology.

(2) The Academy of Sciences of the Union of Soviet Socialist Republics and the National Academy of Sciences of the United States will, on a reciprocal basis, provide for the exchange of scientific personnel and specialists for the purpose of conducting joint studies and for specialization for a period of up to one year.

(3) The details of exchanges mentioned in paragraphs (1) and (2) will be agreed upon directly between the presidents of the Academy of Sciences of the Union of Soviet Socialist Republics and the National Academy of Sciences of the United States in Moscow in the early part of 1958.

(4) The Ministry of Health of the Union of Soviet Socialist Republics will send in 1958 to the United States a group of Soviet medical scientists (three to four persons) for a period of two to three weeks to deliver lectures and exchange experiences; and will receive a similar group of United States medical scientists to deliver lectures and exchange experiences at the Institutes of the Academy of Medical Sciences of the Union of Soviet Socialist Republics and at medical institutes in Moscow, Leningrad, and Kiev.

(5) In 1958 the Ministry of Agriculture of the Union of Soviet Socialist Republics will, on a reciprocal basis, invite United States scientists to visit the Union of Soviet Socialist Republics for the purpose of delivering lectures and exchanging experiences in the fields of biology, selection, pedigreed stockbreeding, agrotechny, mechanization of agriculture, stockbreeding, and others.

SECTION X: Exchange of University Delegations

(1) Both parties will provide for the exchange in 1958 of four delegations of university professors and instructors for a period of two to three weeks in the fields of natural sciences, engineering education, and liberal arts, and the study of the systems of higher education in the United States and the Soviet Union, each delegation to consist of from five to eight persons.

(2) Both parties will provide for an exchange of delegations of professors and instructors between Moscow and Columbia Universities and Leningrad and Harvard Universities. Further exchanges of delegations of professors and instructors of other universities of the United States of America and the Union of Soviet Socialist Republics, shall be decided upon as appropriate by both parties.

(3) Both parties will provide for an exchange of students between Moscow and Leningrad Universities, on the one hand, and United States universities, on the other, amounting to twenty persons on each side for the period of the academic year 1958–1959. For the academic year 1959–1960, the number will be thirty. The composition of the student groups shall be determined by each side.

(4) Both parties will provide for an exchange of delegations of educators (eight to ten persons) for a period of days in the latter part of 1958.

SECTION XI: Exchange of Individual Athletes and Athletic Teams

Both parties will provide for an exchange of individual athletes and athletic teams and in 1958–1959 will provide for the holding of the following contests in the United States and in the Union of Soviet Socialist Republics.

(1) Basketball games between representative men's and women's teams to be held in the Soviet Union in April 1958.

(2) Basketball games between representative men's and women's teams to be held in the United States in 1959.

(3) Wrestling matches between representative teams to be held in the United States in February 1958.

(4) Wrestling matches between representative teams to be held in the Soviet Union in 1959.

(5) Track and field contests between representative teams to be held in the Soviet Union in July 1958.

(6) Track and field contests between representative teams to be held in the United States in 1959.

(7) Weight lifting contests between representative teams to be held in the United States in May 1958.

(8) Canadian hockey games between representative teams to be held in the Soviet Union in March–April 1958.

(9) Chess tournaments between representative teams be held in the United States in 1958.

The details of these exchanges of athletes and athletic teams as well as financial arrangements for these exchanges shall be discussed between appropriate America and Soviet sports organizations.

SECTION XII: Development of Tourism

Both parties will promote the development of tourism.

SECTION XIII: Exchange of Exhibits and Publications

(1) Both sides agree in principle on the usefulness exhibits as an effective means of developing mutual understanding between the peoples of the United States and the Soviet Union. Toward this end both sides will provide for an exchange of exhibits on the peaceful uses of atomic energy in 1958.

(2) Both parties will promote the further development of the exchange of publications and various works in the field of science and technology between scientific institutions and societies and between individual scientists and specialists.

(3) Provisions will be made for the Central Scientific Medical Library of the Ministry of Health of the Union of Soviet Socialist Republics and corresponding medical libraries in the United States to exchange medical journals.

(4) Both parties will promote the exchange of curricula, textbooks, and scientific pedagogical literature through the appropriate agencies of higher and secondary education and directly between educational institutions.

(5) The Ministry of Health of the Union of Soviet Socialist Republics will arrange to make available in 1958 from eight to ten medical films for presentation in the United States. On a reciprocal basis, the United States will arrange to make available the same number of American medical films for presentation in the Soviet Union.

(6) The Ministry of Agriculture of the Union of Soviet Socialist Republics and the Department of Agriculture the United States are prepared to exchange in 1958 on such agricultural subjects as stockbreeding, mechanization of agriculture, construction and utilization of irrigation and drainage systems, protection of plants from pests and blights, and the fight against erosion.

(7) The representatives of the American and Soviet having exchanged their views on the problems of distributing the magazines *Amerika* in the Soviet Union and *USSR* in the United States, have agreed on the desirability and necessity of promoting the distribution of magazines on the basis of reciprocity. Examination of measures taken by both parties to achieve this end continue at the ambassadorial level.

SECTION XIV: Establishment of Direct Air Flights

Both parties agree in principle to establish on the basis of reciprocity direct air flights between the United States and the Soviet Union. Negotiations on terms and conditions satisfactory to both parties will be conducted by appropriate representatives of each government at a mutually convenient date to be determined later.

SECTION XV: Entry into Force

The present agreement shall enter into force on January 27, 1958.

[IN WITNESS WHEREOF, the undersigned, duly authorized, have signed the present agreement and have affixed their seals thereto.

DONE, in duplicate, in the English and Russian languages, both equally authentic, at Washington this twenty-seventh day of January, one thousand nine hundred fifty-eight.

FOR THE UNITED STATES OF AMERICA:
WILLIAM S. B. LACY
FOR THE UNION OF SOVIET SOCIALIST REPUBLICS:
ZAROUBIN]

Transcribed Table of 1958 Ticket Sales in Full

Table 2. Transcribed RGALI Chart of Attendance during 1958 Tour

DATE	CITY	VENUE	ATTENDEES
4.14	New York	Metropolitan Opera House	3,287
4.15	New York	Metropolitan Opera House	3,304
4.16	New York	Metropolitan Opera House	3,305
4.17	New York	Metropolitan Opera House	3,541
4.18 matinee	New York	Metropolitan Opera House	3,808
4.19 matinee	New York	Metropolitan Opera House	3,741
4.19 evening	New York	Metropolitan Opera House	3,816
4.21	New York	Metropolitan Opera House	3,816
4.22	New York	Metropolitan Opera House	3,846
4.23	New York	Metropolitan Opera House	3,816
4.24	New York	Metropolitan Opera House	3,816
4.25	New York	Metropolitan Opera House	3,816
4.26 matinee	New York	Metropolitan Opera House	3,816
4.26 evening	New York	Metropolitan Opera House	3,816
4.28	New York	Metropolitan Opera House	3,816
4.29	New York	Metropolitan Opera House	3,816
4.30	New York	Metropolitan Opera House	3,816
5.1	New York	Metropolitan Opera House	3,816
5.2	New York	Metropolitan Opera House	3,816
5.3 matinee	New York	Metropolitan Opera House	3,816
5.3 evening	New York	Metropolitan Opera House	3,816
5.5	Montreal	Forum	5,740
5.6	Montreal	Forum	6,963
5.7	Montreal	Forum	7,822
5.8	Montreal	Forum	8,063
5.9	Toronto	Leaf Garden	7,653
5.10 matinee	Toronto	Leaf Garden	6,003
5.10 evening	Toronto	Leaf Garden	8,901

(*continued*)

Table 2 (*continued*)

DATE	CITY	VENUE	ATTENDEES
5.12	Detroit	Masonic Auditorium	4,522
5.13	Detroit	Masonic Auditorium	4,734
5.14	Detroit	Masonic Auditorium	4,799
5.15	Chicago	Opera House	3,507
5.17	Chicago	Opera House	3,553
5.18 matinee	Chicago	Opera House	3,549
5.19	Chicago	Opera House	3,541
5.20	Chicago	Opera House	3,534
5.21 matinee	Chicago	Opera House	3,564
5.21 evening	Chicago	Opera House	3,535
5.24	Los Angeles	Shrine Auditorium	6,385
5.25 matinee	Los Angeles	Shrine Auditorium	6,390
5.27	Los Angeles	Shrine Auditorium	6,419
5.28	Los Angeles	Shrine Auditorium	6,413
5.29 matinee	Los Angeles	Shrine Auditorium	6,480
5.29 evening	Los Angeles	Shrine Auditorium	6,444
5.30	Los Angeles	Shrine Auditorium	6,444?
5.31	San Francisco	Opera House	3,175
6.1 matinee	San Francisco	Opera House	3,216
6.2	San Francisco	Opera House	3,182
6.3	San Francisco	Opera House	3,186
6.4	San Francisco	Opera House	3,188
6.5 matinee	San Francisco	Opera House	3,222
6.5 evening	San Francisco	Opera House	3,218
6.8	St. Louis	Keel Auditorium	8,919
6.10	Cleveland	Cleveland Opera	9,522
6.11	Philadelphia	Convention Hall	9,714
6.12	Philadelphia	Convention Hall	9,918
6.13	Boston	Boston Garden	10,894
6.14	Boston	Boston Garden	11,512
6.16	Washington, DC	Capitol Theatre	3,267
6.17	Washington, DC	Capitol Theatre	3,400
6.18	Washington, DC	Capitol Theatre	3,395
6.20	New York	Madison Square Garden	12,326
6.21	New York	Madison Square Garden	12,482

Table 2 (*continued*)

DATE	CITY	VENUE	ATTENDEES
6.22 matinee	New York	Madison Square Garden	12,095
6.22 evening	New York	Madison Square Garden	12,380
6.24	New York	Madison Square Garden	12,731
6.25	New York	Madison Square Garden	12,815
6.28 matinee	New York	Madison Square Garden	12,815
6.28 evening	New York	Madison Square Garden	12,815
Television program	New York	*Ed Sullivan Show*	More than 40 million viewers

Source: Chart of Moiseyev Performances during 1958 American Tour, RGALI, f 2483 o 1 d 267, 71, p. 1.

Early American Tour Repertoires

1958 Tour

Igor Moiseyev—Artistic Director
Samson Galperin—Conductor

Dancers:

Tamara Zeifert	Lev Golovanov	Sergei Tsvetkov
Tamara Golovanova	Irina Konyeva	Nina Kuznetsova
Lydia Skryabina	Lilya Shaldina	Mikhail Alexandrov
Ivan Voronkov	Nikolai Danilov	Nikolai Kosogorov
Boris Berezin	Vassili Savin	Anatoli Fyodorov
Galina Korolkova	Viacheslav Larionov	Gorgony Shliapnikov
Boris Petrov	Ljudmilla Butenina	Igor Fylatov
Stanislav Kulikov		

Dances:

I. Suite of Old Russian Dances
    First episode—Maiden's Entrance
    Second episode—The Round Dance *Khorovod*
    Third episode—A Peddler's Box *Korobochka*
    Fourth episode—The Grass *Travushka*
    Fifth episode—Male Dances and Finale
II. The Dance of the Tatars from Kazan
III. *Yurochka*
IV. *Khorumi*
V. *Polyanka* (The Meadow)
VI. *Zhok*: A Moldavian Suite
    Hora—a female round dance
    Chiokyrlie (The Lark)
    Zhok—mass dance

VII. Mongolian Figurine
VIII. City Quadrille
IX. *Bulba* (Potatoes)
X. Partisans
XI. Football
XII. Two Boys in a Fight
XIII. Ukrainian Suite—*Vesnyanki* (Spring Tide Ritual Songs)

1965 Tour

Igor Moiseyev—Artistic Director
Nikolai Nekrassov—Musical Director and Conductor

Dances:

I. Exercises on a Russian Theme
II. Partisans
III. Sunday
IV. *Zhok*: A Moldavian Suite
    Hora—a female round dance
    Chiokyrlie (The Lark)
    Zhok—mass dance
V. *Pontozoo* (Hungarian)
VI. *Lyavonikha* (Hungarian)
VII. Bulgarian Dances
VIII. Two Studies in Mood (Polish Krakowiak and Russian Trepak)
IX. Caucasian Dances (Georgia)
X. *Sanchakou* (China)
XI. Gypsies
XII. Old City Quadrille
XIII. Two Boys in a Fight
XIV. *Gopak*

1970 Tour

Igor Moiseyev—Artistic Director
Nikolai Nekrassov—Musical Director and Conductor
Sergei Kolobkov—Conductor

Soloists of the Dance Company:

Mikhail Alexandrov	Yuri Alexandrov	Boris Berezin
Nelly Bondarenko	Anatoli Fyodorov	Lev Golanov
Rhudi Khodzhoyan	Nikolai Kosogorov	Stanislav Kulikov
Olga Moiseyeva	Boris Petrov	Ninel Samsonova
Boris Sankin	Vassily Savin	Galina Yeliseyeva
Alfat Yenikeyev		

Dances:

I. Suite of Old Russian Dances
      First episode—Maiden's Entrance
      Second episode—The Round Dance *Khorovod*
      Third episode—A Peddler's Box *Korobochka*
      Fourth episode—The Grass *Travushka*
      Fifth episode—Male Dances and Finale
II. Yurochka
III. *Khorumi*
IV. *Polyanka* (The Meadow)
V. *Zhok*: A Moldavian Suite
      Hora—a female round dance
      Chiokyrlie (The Lark)
      Zhok—mass dance
VI. Old City Quadrille
VII. Partisans
VIII. Sicilian Tarantella
IX. *Gaucho*
X. Sunday
XI. Dance of the Buffoons
XII. Gypsies
XIII. Two Boys in a Fight
XIV. *Gopak*

A Selection of Moiseyev Dances

Name: Suite of Old Russian Dances
First episode—Maiden's Entrance
Second episode—The Round Dance *Khorovod*
Third episode—A Peddler's Box *Korobochka*
Fourth episode—The Grass *Travushka*
Fifth episode—Male Dances and Finale
Origin: Russian
Characteristics: *Travushka* is a play dance and utilizes humor and the
   Russian popular song "Vosem' devok odin ya" (Eight girls and a
   single boy)

Name: The Dance of the Tatars from Kazan
Origin: Tatar (from the Tatar Republic)
Characteristics: Use of humor and spectacular acrobatics for the men.
   The plot involves two young women playing a trick on two young
   men.

Name: *Yurochka* (Georgie)
Origin: Byelorussian
Characteristics: Depicts a peasant Don Juan who chases all the local
   girls but they in turn spurn him.

Name: *Khorumi* (an odd number)
Origin: Adzharian (Western Soviet Union, ethnically related to the
   Georgians)
Characteristics: Use of ancient warrior costumes—depicts warriors
   out scouting for their enemy and then the battle. Utilizes Caucasian
   drum for sharp, staccato rhythms.

Name: Partisans (from dance cycle Soviet Pictures)
Origin: Various nationalities
Characteristics: Depicts soldiers of different nationalities forming
    partisan groups to fight the Germans in the Northern Caucasus.
    Use of dark cloaks to imitate the movement of riding horseback.

Name: *Zhok*: A Moldavian Suite
Hora—a female round dance
Chiokyrlie (The Lark)
Zhok—mass dance
Origin: Moldavian
Characteristics: The *Chiokyrlie* dance uses individual and group dances
    and finishing with a large round dance. The *Zhok* is a mass dance
    with precisely executed patterns.

Name: Seven Girls
Origin: Bashkirian (Bashkir Republic located in southeast)
Characteristics: A female folk dance depicting a legend of seven beauti-
    ful girls.

Name: Old City Quadrille from cycle Pictures of the Past
Origin: Russian
Characteristics: Shows customs of pre-revolutionary Russia in the form
    of young men showing off for young women.

Name: Two Boys in a Fight
Origin: Nanaian (Siberia)
Characteristics: Utilizing a single dancer, it depicts a wrestling match
    between two people.

Name: *Polyanka* (Meadow)
Origin: Russian
Characteristics: Characterized by increasing tempo and speed of dance
    steps ending in a round dance with tambourines and balalaikas as
    accompaniment.

Name: Ukrainian Suite—*Vesnyanki* (Spring Tide Ritual Songs)
Origin: Ukrainian
Characteristics: Depicts two young lovers who part. The women dance
    slowly across the stage to impart the sadness of the lovers' parting

but then try to cheer her up with more active dancing. Once the male lover and other men return, the dancers move in a celebratory manner and finish with the *Hopak* (or *Gopak*) utilizing *prisyadkas* (the squat step) and leaps.

Name: Football from cycle Soviet Pictures
Origin: Modern/Soviet
Characteristics: Depicts a soccer match using fantastic acrobatics.

Name: *Bulba* (Potatoes)
Origin: Byelorussian
Characteristics: Depicts the planting and harvesting of potatoes.

Name: Mongolian Figurine
Origin: Mongolian
Characteristics: A female solo dance utilizing Mongolian religious figures and ornaments.

Name: Venzelya
Origin: Russian
Characteristics: Use of Russian popular Russian melodies and use of interweaving patterns formed by the dancers.

Name: Summer from The Seasons
Origin: Russian
Characteristics: Depicts love and marriages.

Name: Bulgarian Dances
Origin: Bulgarian
Characteristics: Complex rhythm and rapid movements

Name: Exercises on a Russian Theme
Origin: Russian
Characteristics: Depicts a ballet exercise class including warm up and practice exercises performed at the bar demonstrating basic steps of Russian folk dance.

Name: *Trepak*
Origin: Russian
Characteristics: Depicts family life in pre-revolutionary Russian village.

Name: *Lyavonikha*
Origin: Byelorussian
Characteristics: The "classic" Byelorussian folk dance using light, airy movements.

Name: *Pontozoo*
Origin: Hungarian
Characteristics: A male dance with syncopated rhythm enunciated by the dancers slapping their hand on their boottops.

Name: Sunday from cycle Pictures of the Past
Origin: Russian
Characteristics: Life and customs of pre-revolutionary Russia

Name: Gypsies or Gypsy Dance
Origin: Bessarabia near the Romanian border
Characteristics: Depicts a campfire scene of gypsies and the female gypsies dancing in a seductive manner.

Name: *Sanchakou*
Origin: Chinese
Characteristics: Tells the story of General Tsiao-Tsian in China a thousand years ago and mistaken identity.

Name: Dance of Buffoons
Origin: Russian
Characteristics: A dance of folk jesters from pre-revolutionary Russia

Name: Sicilian Tarantella
Origin: Sicilian
Characteristics: Based off of Moiseyev's travels to Italy depicting chariots.

Name: *Gaucho*
Origin: Argentinean
Characteristics: Combination of Spanish *zapateado* with dancing on the side of the soles to depict the gait of Argentinean cowboys.

Notes

Abbreviations

NYPL–PAD: New York Public Library Performing Arts Division
JRDD-NYPL: Jerome Robbins Dance Division, New York Public Library
NARA: National Archives and Records Administration
RGALI: Russian State Archive of Literature and Art

Introduction

1 Established by President Eisenhower in 1954, the President's Fund supported international cultural exchange.
2 A cultural exchange agreement signed between the United States and the Soviet Union calling for exchange in the "Cultural, Technical and Education Fields" which solidified government sponsored exchanges that would continue throughout the remainder of the Cold War. For the full text of the agreement, see appendix A. "Russian Ballet Arrives Here," *New York Journal-American*, April 10, 1958, NYPL–PAD.
3 Among those most often reporting (and most often used in this project) are: *Dance News, Dance Magazine, Dance Observer, Dancing Times, New York Times, New York Herald Tribune, New York Journal-American, Boston Globe, L.A. Times, Chicago Tribune, Toronto Star, Chicago Sun-Times, San Francisco Examiner, Detroit Free Press, The Detroit News, The Washington Post, Milwaukee Journal Sentinel*, and *Los Angeles Examiner*.
4 Dorsey Callaghan, "Soviet Ballet Dazzles Audience: Dancers Set Stage Ablaze," *Detroit Free Press*, May 13, 1958, 12.
5 See David K. Johnson's *The Lavender Scare* (2004), Christina Ezrahi's *Swans of the Kremlin: Ballet and Power in Soviet Russia* (2012), and Catherine Gunther Kodat's *Don't Act, Just Dance: The Metapolitics of Cold War Culture* (2015).
6 Simo Mikkonen and Pekka Suutari, "Introduction to the Logic of East-West Artistic Interactions," *Music, Art and Diplomacy: East-West Cultural Interactions and the Cold War* (Burlington, VT: Ashgate, 2016), 2.
7 Natalia Sheremetyevskaya, *Rediscovery of the Dance: Folk Dance Ensemble of the USSR under the Direction of Moiseyev*, trans. J. Guralsky (Moscow: Novosti Press Agency Publishing House, 1960), 30.
8 Igor Moiseyev, "Folk Art: A Living, Moving Process," *Boston Globe*, May 30, 1965, Moiseyev Scrapbooks, 14, JRDD-NYPL.

9   Winston Churchill, "The Iron Curtain Speech (March 5, 1946), *The Origins of the Cold War, 1941–1947: A Historical Problem with Interpretations and Documents*, ed. Walter LaFeber (New York: Wiley, 1971), 137–38.

10 George F. Kennan, "George F. Kennan's 'Long Telegram,'" in *Debating the Origins of the Cold War: American and Russian Perspectives*, ed. Ralph B. Levering, Vladimir O. Pechatnov, Verena Botzenhart-Viehe, and C. Earl Edmondson (Lanham, MD: Rowman & Littlefield, 2002), 69–71.

11 Harry Truman, "President Harry S. Truman's Speech to Congress, March 12, 1947," in Levering, Pechatnov, Botzenhart-Viehe, and Edmondson, *Debating the Origins of the Cold War*, 82.

12 Levering, Pechatnov, Botzenhart-Viehe, and Edmondson, *Debating the Origins of the Cold War*, 82.

13 In 1958, American pianist Van Cliburn competed in and won the Tchaikovsky Piano Competition. Peter Edson, "Russian Salad Is 'Tough Meal,'" *Sarasota Journal*, July 11, 1958, 4.

14 Drew Pearson, "Ike's Russian Visit More Needful Than K's," *Gadsden Times*, September 10, 1959.

15 Clare Croft, *Dancers as Diplomats: American Choreography in Cultural Exchange* (New York: Oxford University Press, 2015), 16.

16 Kiril Tomoff, *Virtuosi Abroad: Soviet Music and Imperial Competition during the Early Cold War, 1945–1958*, (Ithaca, NY: Cornell University Press, 2015), 9.

17 Tomoff, *Virtuosi Abroad*, 7.

18 Simo Mikkonen, "Interference or Friendly Gestures? Soviet Cultural Diplomacy and Finnish Elections, 1945–56," *Cold War History* 20, no. 3 (2020): 364.

19 Meri Elisabet Heerala, "Pianist Sviatoslav Richter: The Soviet Union Launches a 'Cultural Sputnik' to the United States in 1960," in Mikkonen and Suutari, *Music, Art and Diplomacy*, 103.

20 Heerala, "Pianist Sviatoslav Richter," 88.

21 Tomoff, *Virtuosi Abroad*, 11 and 116.

22 On its 1958 tour, the Moiseyev included over one hundred performers.

23 Yale Richmond, *U.S.-Soviet Cultural Exchanges, 1958–1986* (Boulder, CO: Westview Press, 1987), 3–4.

24 Helen B. Shaffer, "Cultural Exchanges," *The Spokesman-Review*, July 6, 1959, 4.

25 Yale Richmond, *Cultural Exchange & The Cold War: Raising the Iron Curtain* (University Park: Penn State University Press, 2003), 20.

CHAPTER 1
Creation of the State Academic Folk Dance Ensemble of the USSR

1   Anna Ilupina and Yelena Lutskaya, *Moiseyev's Dance Company*, trans. Olga Shartse (Moscow: Progress Publishers, 1966), 3.

2   As quoted by M. Chudnovsky, *The Folk Dance Company of the USSR: Igor Moiseyev, Art Director* (Moscow: Foreign Languages Publishing House, 1959), 93.

3   Terry Martin, *The Affirmative Action Empire: Nations and Nationalism in the Soviet Union, 1923–1939* (Ithaca, NY: Cornell University Press, 2001), 2–3.

4 Michael Rouland, "A Nation on Stage: Music and the 1936 Festival of Kazakh Arts," in *Soviet Music and Society under Lenin and Stalin: The Baton and Sickle*, ed. Neil Edmunds (New York: Routledge, 2004), 183.

5 Martin, *Affirmative Action Empire*, 19.

6 Martin, *Affirmative Action Empire*, 88, 300–3.

7 Jeffrey Burds, "The Soviet War against 'Fifth Columnists': The Case of Chechnya, 1942–4," *Journal of Contemporary History* 42, no. 2 (2007): 269–70.

8 Stalin's secret police.

9 Martin, *Affirmative Action Empire*, 432, 439, and 452; Burds, "The Soviet War," 289 and 307.

10 "Resolution of the State Defense Committee, September 22, 1941, On Removal of Germans from Certain Areas of Ukraine," in *Revelations from the Russian Archives*, ed. Diane P. Koenker and Ronald D. Bachman (Washington, DC: Library of Congress, 1997), 203–4.

11 "Decree of the State Defense Committee, May 11, 1944, Signed by Stalin, On Deportation of Crimean Tatars to Uzbekistan," *Revelations from the Russian Archives*, ed. Diane P. Koenker and Ronald D. Bachman (Washington, DC: Library of Congress, 1997), 205.

12 "State Defense Committee Resolution, June 2, 1944, to Evict from the Crimean Autonomous Republic 37,000 Bulgarians, Greeks, and Armenians, Cited as German Collaborators," in Koenker and Bachman, *Revelations from the Russian Archives*, 209; "Report from Beria to Stalin, July 4, 1944, Stating that Resettlement of Tatars, Bulgarians, Greeks, Armenians, and Others from the Crimean Has Been Completed," in Koenker and Bachman, *Revelations from the Russian Archives*, 211.

13 "Report from Beria to Stalin," 319–23.

14 Andy Nercessian, "National Identity, Cultural Policy and the Soviet Folk Ensemble in Armenia," in Edmunds, *Soviet Music and Society under Lenin and Stalin*, 152–55.

15 Michael Rouland, "A Nation on Stage: Music and the 1936 Festival of Kazakh Arts," in Edmunds, *Soviet Music and Society under Lenin and Stalin*, 181–86.

16 P. Kerzhents, "The Folk Dance," *Pravda*, November 2, 1936, 4.

17 Victorina Krieger, "Against the Falsification of Folk Dance Festival Results," *Izvestiia*, [date illegible] 1936, 4, caption of image, and 4.

18 Chudnovsky, *Folk Dance Company*, 16.

19 Chudnovsky, *Folk Dance Company*, 16.

20 Igor Moiseyev, *IA vcponmnimaiu . . . (I Recall)* (Moscow: Agreement, 1996), 177.

21 Chudnovsky, *Folk Dance Company*, 14.

22 Chudnovsky, *Folk Dance Company*, 14.

23 Chudnovsky, *Folk Dance Company*, 14–15.

24 Chudnovsky, *Folk Dance Company*, 15.

25 Anthony Shay, *The Igor Moiseyev Dance Company: Dancing Diplomats* (Chicago, IL: University of Chicago Press, 2019), 115 and 119.

26 Natalia Sheremetyevskaya, *Rediscovery of the Dance: Folk Dance Ensemble of the USSR Under the Direction of Moiseyev*, trans. J. Guralsky (Moscow: Novosti Press Agency Publishing House, 1960), 30–31.

27 Chudnovsky, *Folk Dance Company*, 15.
28 Sheremetyevskaya, *Rediscovery of the Dance*, 30–31.
29 Moiseyev, *I Recall*, 181.
30 Moiseyev, *I Recall*, 172.
31 Ilupina and Lutskaya, *Moiseyev's Dance Company*, 10.
32 Chudnovsky, *Folk Dance Company*, 17; Ilupina and Lutskaya, *Moiseyev's Dance Company*, 4.
33 Sheremetyevskaya, *Rediscovery of the Dance*, 29–30.
34 Chudnovsky, *Folk Dance Company*, 17–18.
35 Chudnovsky, *Folk Dance Company*, 18; Ilupina and Lutskaya, *Moiseyev's Dance Company*, 4; Chudnovsky, *Folk Dance Company*, 19.
36 Chudnovsky, *Folk Dance Company*, 19–20.
37 Chudnovsky, *Folk Dance Company*, 19, 76.
38 Letter, July 30, 1938, RGALI, f. 3162 op 2 d 8, 5, 1.
39 Letter, July 30, 1938, RGALI, f. 3162 op 2 d 8, 5, 1–3.
40 Moiseyev, *I Recall*, 172, 176.
41 Moiseyev, *I Recall*, 177.
42 Chudnovsky, *Folk Dance Company*, 18–19
43 Chudnovsky, *Folk Dance Company*, 18.
44 Sheremetyevskaya, *Rediscovery of the Dance*, 31.
45 Sheremetyevskaya, *Rediscovery of the Dance*, 48.
46 Sheremetyevskaya, *Rediscovery of the Dance*, 32; Igor Moiseyev, "The Ballet and Reality," *Ulanova Moiseyev & Zakharov on Soviet Ballet*, ed. Peter Brinson, trans. E. Fox and D. Fry, (London: SCR, 1954), originally published *Literaturnaya Gazeta*, April 24, 1952, 18.
47 Ilupina and Lutskaya, *Moiseyev's Dance Company*, 4.
48 Ilupina and Lutskaya, *Moiseyev's Dance Company*, 69–70.
49 Ilupina and Lutskaya, *Moiseyev's Dance Company*, 69.
50 Moiseyev, *I Recall*, 178–79.
51 M. Chudnovsky, *Dancing to Fame: Folk Dance Company of the U.S.S.R.* (Moscow: Foreign Languages Publishing House, 1959), 40, 50.
52 Vladimir Potapov, "National Dances in the U.S.S.R.," in *The Soviet Ballet*, ed. Juri Slonimsky (New York: The Philosophical Library, 1947), 153.
53 Sheremetyevskaya, *Rediscovery of the Dance*, 11.
54 Moiseyev, "Folk Dances of the Peoples of the USSR," in Slonimsky *The Soviet Ballet*, 134–35.

CHAPTER 2
Internal and External Propaganda Tool

1 Igor Moiseyev, *IA vcponmnimaiu . . . (I Recall)* (Moscow: Agreement, 1996), 35–6.
2 Youth division of the Soviet Union's Communist Party.
3 Moiseyev, *I Recall*, 36–37.
4 Moiseyev, *I Recall*, 38–39.
5 Moiseyev, *I Recall*, 41.

6 Moiseyev, *I Recall*, 42–45.
7 Moiseyev, *I Recall*, 45–48.
8 Moiseyev, *I Recall*, 48.
9 Moiseyev, *I Recall*, 50.
10 Alison L. Hilton, "Remaking Folk Art: from Russian Revival to Proletcult," in *New Perspectives on Russian and Soviet Artistic Culture: Selected Papers from the Fourth World Congress for Soviet and East European Studies*, ed. John O. Norman (New York: St. Martin's, 1990), 80, 87.
11 Hilton, "Remaking Folk Art," 80, 87.
12 Marina Frolova-Walker, *Stalin's Music Prize: Soviet Culture and Politics* (New Haven, CT: Yale Scholarship Online, 2016), 290, online edition.
13 Solomon Volkov, *Shostakovich and Stalin: The Extraordinary Relationship between the Great Composer and the Brutal Dictator* (New York: Alfred A. Knopf, 2004), 16, 92.
14 Frolova-Walker, *Stalin's Music Prize*, 62–63, and 287–88.
15 Kiril Tomoff, *Virtuosi Abroad: Soviet Music and Imperial Competition during the Early Cold War, 1945–1958* (Ithaca, NY: Cornell University Press, 2015), 8.
16 Katerina Clark, "Shostakovich's Turn to the String Quartet and the Debates about Socialist Realism in Music," *Slavic Review* 72, no. 3 (2013): 573–74.
17 Clark, "Shostakovich's Turn," 574–75.
18 Elizabeth Souritz, *Soviet Choreographers in the 1920s*, trans. Lynn Visson, ed. Sally Banes (Durham, NC: Duke University Press, 1990), 316–20.
19 Elizabeth Souritz, "Moscow's Island of Dance, 1934–1941," *Dance Chronicle* 17, no. 1 (1994): 3, 6, 14, 21, 63.
20 Moiseyev, *I Recall*, 187; Natalia Sheremetyevskaya, *Rediscovery of the Dance: Folk Dance Ensemble of the USSR Under the Direction of Moiseyev*, trans. J. Guralsky (Moscow: Novosti Press Agency Publishing House, 1960), 30.
21 Régine Robin, "Stalinism and Popular Culture," in *The Culture of the Stalin Period*, ed. Hans Gunther (New York: St. Martin's Press, 1990), 28.
22 Vladimir Potapov, "National Dances in the U.S.S.R.," in *The Soviet Ballet*, ed. Juri Slonimsky (New York: The Philosophical Library, 1947), 147.
23 Slonimsky, *The Soviet Ballet*, 5.
24 M. Chudnovsky, *The Folk Dance Company of the USSR: Igor Moiseyev, Art Director* (Moscow: Foreign Languages Publishing House, 1959), 33–34; Potapov, "National Dances," 152.
25 Potapov, "National Dances," 152–53.
26 Slonimsky, *The Soviet Ballet*, 5.
27 Slonimsky, *The Soviet Ballet*, 136; Igor Moiseyev, "The Ballet and Reality," in *Ulanova Moiseyev & Zakharov on Soviet Ballet*, ed. Peter Brinson, trans. E. Fox and D. Fry (London: SCR, 1954), originally published in *Literaturnaya Gazeta*, April 24, 1952, 18.
28 Marian Smith and Lisa Arkin, "National Dance in the Romantic Ballet," in *Rethinking the Sylph: New Perspectives on the Romantic Ballet*, ed. Lynn Garafola (Hanover, NH: Wesleyan University Press/University Press of New England, 1997), 14–26.

29 Smith and Arkin, "National Dance," 31–32.

30 Smith and Arkin, "National Dance," 34–35.

31 Smith and Arkin, "National Dance," 9, 11.

32 Lynn Garafola, "Diaghilev, Serge," in *International Encyclopedia of Dance*, vol. 2, ed. Selma Jeanne Cohen et al. (New York: Oxford University Press, 1998), 407.

33 Suzanne Carbonneau, "Fokine, Michel" in *International Encyclopedia of Dance*, vol. 3, ed. Selma Jeanne Cohen et al. (New York: Oxford University Press, 1998), 14.

34 Chudnovsky, *Folk Dance Company*, 21.

35 Chudnovsky, *Folk Dance Company*, 74–77.

36 Chudnovsky, *Folk Dance Company*, 76–78.

37 Moiseyev, *I Recall*, 50; Chudnovsky, *Folk Dance Company*, 78.

38 Anna Ilupina and Yelena Lutskaya, *Moiseyev's Dance Company*, trans. Olga Shartse (Moscow: Progress Publishers, 1966), 16.

39 Ilupina and Lutskaya, *Moiseyev's Dance Company*, 16.

40 Chudnovsky, *Folk Dance Company*, 78.

41 Sheremetyevskaya, *Rediscovery of the Dance*, 66.

42 Anne Searcy, *Ballet in the Cold War: A Soviet-American Exchange* (New York: Oxford University Press, 2020), 3.

43 Tomoff, *Virtuosi Abroad*, 11.

44 Chudnovsky, *Folk Dance Company*, 81–84.

45 Chudnovsky, *Folk Dance Company*, 81–83.

46 Chudnovsky, *Folk Dance Company*, 79–81.

47 John Martin, "Dance: From the Ukraine: Some Bravos for the State Company," *New York Times*, May 6, 1962, 156.

48 Anna Kisselgoff, "Dance: Ukrainian State Company," *New York Times*, January 13, 1988.

49 John Martin, "Dance: Calendar: Stravinsky Birthday Honors," *New York Times*, April 29, 1962, 131, 156.

50 Kisselgoff, "Dance: Ukrainian State Company."

51 "B.U. Celebrity Series Corners World's Top Talent," *Boston Globe*, April 17, 1966, A62.

52 George McKinnon, "Dancers Capture Wild, Zestful Life," *Boston Globe*, January 13, 1967, 21.

53 Martin, "Dance: From the Ukraine," 156.

54 Anthony Shay, "Parallel Traditions: State Folk Dance Ensembles and Folk Dance in 'The Field,'" *Dance Research Journal* 31, no. 1 (1999): 29 and 37.

55 Shay, "Parallel Traditions, 29–30, 47.

56 Shay, "Parallel Traditions, 35.

57 Shay, "Parallel Traditions, 36.

58 Tomoff, *Virtuosi Abroad*, 10–11.

59 Tomoff, *Virtuosi Abroad*, 116.

60 Simo Mikkonen, "Interference or Friendly Gestures? Soviet Cultural Diplomacy and Finnish Elections, 1945–56," *Cold War History* 20, no. 3 (2020): 349–64.

61 Mikkonen, "Interference or Friendly Gestures," 349–64.

62 Tomoff, *Virtuosi Abroad*, 2.

63 Meri Elisabet Heerala, "Pianist Sviatoslav Richter: The Soviet Union Launches a 'Cultural Sputnik' to the United States in 1960," in *Music, Art and Diplomacy: East-west Cultural Interactions and the Cold War*, ed. Simo Mikkonen and Pekka Suutari (Burlington, VT: Ashgate, 2016), 103.

64 Tomoff, *Virtuosi Abroad*, 6–7.

65 Stéphanie Goncalves, "Ballet as a Tool for Cultural Diplomacy in the Cold War: Soviet Ballets in Paris and London, 1954–68," in Mikkonen and Suutari, *Music, Art and Diplomacy: East-west Cultural Interactions and the Cold War*, 146–47.

66 Tomoff, *Virtuosi Abroad*, 12–13.

67 Simo Mikkonen, Jari Parkkinen, and Giles Scott-Smith, "Exploring Culture in and of the Cold War," in *Entangled East and West: Cultural Diplomacy and Artistic Interaction During the Cold War* (Boston: De Gruyter, 2019), 8.

68 Tomoff, *Virtuosi Abroad*, 9.

69 Chudnovsky, *Folk Dance Company*, 5.

70 Sheremetyevskaya, *Rediscovery of the Dance*, 92.

71 Ilupina and Lutskaya, *Moiseyev's Dance Company*, 5–6.

72 Chudnovsky, *Folk Dance Company*, 84.

73 Chudnovsky, *Folk Dance Company*, 85–86.

74 Chudnovsky, *Folk Dance Company*, 93–94.

75 Sheremetyevskaya, *Rediscovery of the Dance*, 115.

76 Sheremetyevskaya, *Rediscovery of the Dance*, 92, 50.

77 Sheremetyevskaya, *Rediscovery of the Dance*, 98; Chudnovsky, *Folk Dance Company*, 86.

78 Chudnovsky, *Folk Dance Company*, 86–88.

79 Chudnovsky, *Folk Dance Company*, 89–90.

CHAPTER 3
Paving the Way for the 1958 Tour

1 In this respect, this case study echoes other more recent works that complicate the Cold War experience, such as Andrew Faulk's *Upstaging the Cold War: American Dissent and Cultural Diplomacy, 1940–1960* (2010) which argues that dissenting cultural products actually had a greater positive impact on the international opinion of America rather than the more black-and-white cultural productions of the State Department.

2 Jacqueline Martin and Willmar Sauter, *Understanding Theatre: Performance Analysis in Theory and Practice* (Stockholm: Almqvist & Wiksell International, 1995), 26–31.

3 Susan Bennett, *Theatre Audiences: A Theory of Production and Reception* (New York: Routledge, 1990), 8, 94–95.

4 Melissa R. Klapper, *Ballet Class: An American History* (New York: Oxford Academic, 2020).

5 Natalie Rouland, "How the Nutcracker Gave Birth to American Ballet," *Wilson Center*, December 11, 2020, https://www.wilsoncenter.org/blog-post/how-nutcracker-gave-birth-american-ballet.

6 Klapper, *Ballet Class*; Rouland, "How the Nutcracker."

7 Nicholas Cull, *The Cold War and the United States Information Agency: America Propaganda and Public Diplomacy, 1945–1989* (New York: Cambridge University Press, 2008), xiii, 22–24.

8 Laura Belmonte, *Selling the American Way* (Philadelphia: University of Pennsylvania Press, 2008), 4, 24.

9 Cull, *The Cold War*, 22.

10 Cull, *The Cold War*, xii, 73, 115, and 163.

11 Victor Rosenberg, *Soviet-American Relations, 1953–1960: Diplomacy and Cultural Exchange during the Eisenhower Presidency* (Jefferson, NC: McFarland, 2005), 1.

12 Nikita Khrushchev, "Secret Speech to the Twentieth Party Congress (February 25, 1956)," in *The World Transformed: 1945 to the Present: A Documentary Reader*, ed. Michael H. Hunt (New York: Bedford/St. Martins, 2004), 135–41.

13 Kristin Roth-Ey, *Moscow Primetime: How the Soviet Union Built the Media Empire That Lost the Cultural Cold War* (Ithaca, NY: Cornell University Press, 2011), 1–9.

14 Victoria Phillips, *Martha Graham's Cold War: The Dance of American Diplomacy* (New York: Oxford University Press, 2020), 2.

15 Graham Carr, "Diplomatic Notes: American Musicians and Cold War Politics in the Near and Middle East, 1954–60," *Popular Music History* 1, no. 1 (2004): 38–39.

16 Clare Croft, *Dancers as Diplomats: American Choreography in Cultural Exchange* (New York: Oxford University Press, 2015), 12.

17 Carr, "Diplomatic Notes," 38–39.

18 "Sol Hurok Dead at 85," *Boston Globe*, March 6, 1974, 15.

19 Harlow Robinson, *The Last Impresario: The Life, Times and Legacy of Sol Hurok* (New York: Viking Press, 1994), 325.

20 "Department of State Memo," March 15, 1956, NARA 032/3–1556.

21 "Department of State Memo," April 30, 1956, NARA 032/413056.

22 Robinson, *The Last Impresario*, 347–54.

23 "NSC 5607, 'East-West Exchanges,'" from Yale Richmond, *U.S.-Soviet Cultural Exchanges, 1958–1986* (Boulder, CO: Westview Press, 1987), 133.

24 "NSC 5607," 244–45.

25 "NSC 5607," 244–45.

26 "Telegram from the Department of State to the Embassy in the Soviet Union," November 13, 1956, in *Foreign Relations of the United States, 1955–1957, Volume XXIV*, ed. John P. Glennon, Ronald D. Landa, Aaron D. Miller, and Charles S. Sampson (Washington, DC: United States Government Printing Office, 1989), 253.

27 "United States and U.S.S.R. Sign Agreement on East-West Exchanges," *State Department Bulletin* 38, no. 973, (February 17, 1958): 243. http://archive.org/stream /departmentofstat381958unit#page/n3/mode/2up. For full text of agreement, see appendix A.

28 "United States and U.S.S.R. Sign Agreement," 244–46.

29 Yale Richmond, *Cultural Exchange and the Cold War: Raising the Iron Curtain* (University Park: Penn State University Press, 2003), 16.

30 Richmond, *Cultural Exchange and the Cold War*, 15–16.

31 Cull, *The Cold War*, 161–62.

32 "Moscow Hails U.S. Pianist," *Chicago Daily Tribune*, April 12, 1958, 19.

33 "Tall at the Keyboard: Van Cliburn," Special to the *New York Times*, *New York Times*, April 14, 1958, 18.

34 Rosenberg, *Soviet-American Relations*, 124.

35 "Guidelines for the tour in the United States and Canada," RGALI, f 2483 0 1 d 267, 16, p 1.

36 "Communication from Moiseyev to Ministry of Culture Comrade Mikhailov regarding preparation for the American tour," RGALI, f 2483 0 1 d 267, 1.

37 Peter Edson, "Cultural Exchange Booming," *The Pittsburgh Press*, May 14, 1958.

38 Walter Terry, "Russian Dancers to Perform Here," *New York Herald Tribune*, April 14, 1958, 4. "Prisyadkas" are the dance step where, from a squatting position, the dancer alternates extending each leg forward.

39 "Tickets in Great Demand for First Moiseyev N.Y. Season," *Dance News*, April 1958, 1.

40 Terry, "Russian Dancers to Perform Here," 4.

41 Mary Clarke, "Moiseyev Dancers from Moscow," *Dance Magazine*, February 1956, 20.

42 Walter Terry, Untitled Article, *New York Herald Tribune*, April 20, 1958.

43 Miles Kastendieck, "Soviet Group Very Special," *New York Journal American*, April 15, 1958, 11.

44 Hugh Thomson, "3,600 Stand, Cheer Red Ballet in N.Y.," *Toronto Daily Star*, April 15, 1958, 21.

45 Alice Hughes, "A Woman's New York," *Reading Eagle*, April 21, 1958, 11.

46 "Still More Moiseyev Perfs," *Dance Magazine*, June 1958, 3.

47 Anatole Chujoy, "Moiseyev Garden Encore Sold Out in Advance," *Dance News*, June 1958, 1.

48 "Still More Moiseyev Perfs," 3.

49 "Moiseyev Tickets," *Boston Globe*, May 14, 1958, 41.

50 Joe Harrington, "Big Milk Order . . . But Only Chin High," *Boston Globe*, July 4, 1958, 9.

51 "Still More Moiseyev Perfs," 3.

52 Elizabeth W. Driscoll, "Moiseyev Dancers A $200,000 Bargain," *Boston Globe*, June 30, 1958.

53 Elizabeth W. Driscoll, "Ed Sullivan Brings Rare Talent Show," *Boston Globe*, June 23, 1958, 17.

54 Chujoy, "Moiseyev Garden Encore Sold Out in Advance," 1.

55 Claudia Cassidy, "On the Aisle: Something New in Russian Virtuosi: The Combustible Moiseyevs," *Chicago Daily Tribune*, May 17, 1958.

56 Rose MacDonald, "Moiseyev Dancers Were Brilliant and Beautiful," *The Telegram Toronto*, May 18, 1958.

57 Excerpt from Show World on *WXYZ Radio*, May 13, 1958, page 8A, NYPL–PAD.

58 Glenna Syse, "Soviet Dance Troupe a Fast-Moving Hit," *Chicago Sun-Times*, May 17, 1958.
59 Alexander Fried, "Moiseyev Dancers, a 'Popular Show,' Put on an Exciting Opera House First Night," *San Francisco Examiner*, June 22, 1958, 3.
60 "Red Dancers Shade Diplomat in Chicago," *Milwaukee Journal*, May 17, 1958, 5.

CHAPTER 4
Reception and the Cold War Narrative

1 Lydia Joel, "The Moiseyev Dance Company: What is it? What is its Appeal? What is its Lesson?" *Dance Magazine*, June 1958, 30; *Daily News*, April 16, 1958.
2 Ernest B. Vaccaro, "Nagy Execution Gets Varied U.S. Reactions," *Eugene Register-Guard*, June 17, 1958.
3 "Mr. Dulles Calls Off Cold War for Three Hours," *Sydney Morning Herald*, June 17, 1958, 3.
4 "Foreign Service Dispatch from American Legation in Budapest to Department of State," July 3, 1958, NARA 032/7–358.
5 Joel, "The Moiseyev Dance Company," 30.
6 Walter Terry, Untitled Article, *New York Herald Tribune*, April 20, 1958.
7 Rabbi Mordecai Levy, "Bridging the Chasm: Letter to the Editor," *Boston Globe*, June 17, 1965, 16.
8 Alice Hughes, "A Woman's New York," *Reading Eagle*, April 21, 1958, 11.
9 Joesf Mossman, "Standing Ovation Won by Russian Dancers," 3.
10 Letter from Jeanette McCoy to Moiseyev, May 21, 1958, RGALI, f 2483 0 1 d 267, 115, 1.
11 Undated, anonymous letter, RGALI, f 2483 0 1 d 267, 96, 2–3.
12 "Glamour Dancers," *Los Angeles Times*, May 26, 1958, 7.
13 Bob Thomas, "Hollywood 'Conquered' by Russian Dance Company," *Schenectady Gazette*, May 26, 1958, 6.
14 "Glamour Dancers."
15 "Anti-American Russian Agitator Stirs Flurry in Garden," *Boston Globe*, June 14, 1958, 1.
16 "Directors Fired for Refusing to Discuss Alleged Red Ties," *Owosso Argus-Press*, June 20, 1958.
17 Lloyd Shearer, "Must Reading: The Spy War Who's Winning—We or the Russians?" *Boston Globe*, May 6, 1962.
18 John Crosby, "Moiseyev Ballet Show Proves Art IS Popular," *Boston Globe*, July 2, 1958, 44.
19 Peggy Boyle, "Moiseyev 'Incident' Flops," *Boston Evening American*, June 14, 1958.
20 Photograph caption, *Montreal Gazette*, May 13, 1965, 1.
21 "Soviet Dancers Picketed to Protest Jews' Plight," *Boston Globe*, October 5, 1970, 3.
22 "Gas Stops Soviet Debut in Chicago," *Milwaukee Journal*, August 27, 1970, 1 and 3.
23 "Tear Gas Stops the Show," *Sydney Morning Herald*, August 28, 1970, 3.
24 "Gas Stops Soviet Debut in Chicago," 1.

25 "Tear Gas Stops the Show," 3.

26 "Gas Stops Soviet Debut in Chicago," 3.

27 "US Apologizes for Ballet Bomb," *Milwaukee Journal*, August 28, 1970, 13.

28 "Russia Raps Zionists, Cancels Bolshoi Tour," *Boston Globe*, December 12, 1970, 2.

29 "World-National: Chile vows end of US dependence," *Boston Globe*, September 7, 1970, 2. The most prominent ballet defections to the West included Rudolph Nureyev in 1961, Natalia Makarova in 1970 and Mikhail Baryshnikov in 1974. See David Caute's *The Dancer Defects: The Struggle for Cultural Supremacy during the Cold War* (New York: Oxford University Press, 2005) for an overview of the importance allotted to Soviet defections.

30 "Russian Defector Join Ballet," *The Pittsburgh Press*, October 13, 1970, 15.

31 Walter Terry, *New York Herald Tribune*, April 20, 1958.

32 Terry, *New York Herald Tribune*, April 20, 1958.

33 Terry, *New York Herald Tribune*, April 20, 1958.

34 Catherine Gunther Kodat, *Don't Act, Just Dance: The Metapolitics of Cold War Culture* (New Brunswick, NJ: Rutgers University Press, 2015), 20.

35 Clare Croft, *Dancers as Diplomats: American Choreography in Cultural Exchange* (New York: Oxford University Press, 2015), 12, 22.

36 Victoria Phillips, *Martha Graham's Cold War: The Dance of American Diplomacy* (New York: Oxford University Press, 2020), 1–2, 38, 63, 57–58.

37 Anne Searcy, *Ballet in the Cold War: A Soviet-American Exchange* (New York: Oxford University Press, 2020), 4.

38 Phillips, *Martha Graham's Cold War*, 70.

39 Croft, *Dancers as Diplomats*, 38. For further discussion of America's usage of dance in its cultural exchange endeavors, including reception of American dance company tours abroad, see Victoria Phillips' *Martha Graham's Cold War* and Clare Croft's *Dancers as Diplomats*.

40 Glenna Syse, "Soviet Dance Troupe a Fast-Moving Hit," *Chicago Sun-Times*, May 17, 1958.

41 "Universal Language," *Sarasota Herald-Tribune*, April 30, 1958, 4.

42 Thomas Mallon and Pankaj Mishra, "Highbrow, Lowbrow, Middlebrow—Do These Kinds of Cultural Categories Mean Anything Anymore?" *New York Times*, July 29, 2014.

43 Tad Friend, "The Case for Middlebrow," *New Republic* 206, no. 9 (March 2, 1992): 24.

44 Virginia Woolf, "Middlebrow: A Letter Written but Not Sent," *The Atlantic*, July 1942.

45 As qtd. in Franklin Foer, "The Browbeater," *New Republic*, November 23, 2011.

46 Foer, "The Browbeater."

47 Joan Shelley Rubin, *The Making of Middlebrow Culture* (Chapel Hill: University of North Carolina Press, 1992), xi.

48 Trysh Travis, "Middlebrow Culture in the Cold War: Books USA Advertisements, 1967," *PMLA* 128, no. 2 (March 2013): 468.

49 Steven Mintz, "Whatever Happened to Middlebrow Culture?" *Higher Ed Gamma* on *Inside Higher Ed*, September 2022, 26.

50 Pauline Fairclough, "Was Soviet Music Middlebrow? Shostakovich's Fifth Symphony, Socialist Realism, and the Mass Listener in the 1930s," *Journal of Musicology* 35, no. 3 (Summer 2018): 344, 367.

51 1958 Tour Program, Carl Van Vechten Papers, Yale Collection of American Literature, Beinecke Rare Book and Manuscript Library.

52 Lauren Erin Brown, "'Cultural Czars': American Nationalism, Dance, and Cold War Arts Funding, 1945–1989" (Phd diss., Harvard University, 2008), 12 and 211.

53 1958 Tour Program, Carl Van Vechten Papers.

54 Margo Miller, "Weekend: Russian Ballet at Music Hall," *Boston Globe*, October 2, 1970, 15.

55 "First Soviet Troupe Arrives Under Exchange Agreement," *Dance News*, May 1958, 4.

56 Anatole Chujoy, "Moiseyev Garden Encore Sold Out in Advance," *Dance News*, June 1958, 1–2.

57 Igor Moiseyev, "We Meet America," *Dance Magazine*, October 1958, 26.

58 Moiseyev, "We Meet America,"26.

59 Moiseyev, "We Meet America,"26.

60 Undated letter by Igor Moiseyev, RGALI, f 2483 o 1 d 267, 40, 1–2.

61 Igor Moiseyev, *IA vcponmnimaiu . . . (I Recall)* (Moscow: Agreement, 1996), 140.

62 "Moiseyev Short Report about the Tour of the State Academic Folk Dance Ensemble of the USSR to the United States and Canada from 9 April to 1 July," to RGALI, f 2483 o 1 d 267, 58, 1.

63 "Moiseyev Short Report about the Tour," 1.

64 RGALI, f 2483 o 1 d 267, 68, 11.

65 RGALI, f 2483 o 1 d 267, 59, 2.

66 RGALI, f 2483 o 1 d 267, 59, 2.

67 "Moiseyev Short Report about the Tour of the State Academic Folk Dance Ensemble of the USSR to the United States and Canada from 9 April to 1 July," to RGALI, f 2483 o 1 d 267, 64, 7.

68 Moiseyev, *I Recall*, 141.

69 Moiseyev, *I Recall*, 136.

70 RGALI, f 2483 o 1 d 267, 66, 9.

71 Moiseyev, *I Recall*, 135.

72 Moiseyev, *I Recall*, 135.

73 "Uncle Dudley, As People to People," *Boston Globe*, April 18, 1959, 4.

74 Letter from Pavel Romanov, December 25, 1958, Departmental records of the Soviet Department of Culture from the holdings of the Russian State Archive of Contemporary History (RGANI) fond 5 opis 36 delo 57, Microfilm (Woodbridge, CT: Research Publications, 2003), reel 296.

75 Letters from Igor Moiseyev, February 19 and 26, 1959, Departmental records of the Soviet Department of Culture from the holdings of the Russian State Archive of Contemporary History (RGANI), fond 5 opis 36 delo 57, Microfilm (Woodbridge, CT: Research Publications, 2003), reel 296.

76 Letter from Dmitri Polikarpov and B. Yarustovsky, March 13, 1959, Departmental records of the Soviet Department of Culture from the holdings of the

Russian State Archive of Contemporary History (RGANI) fond 5 opis 36 delo 57, Microfilm (Woodbridge, CT: Research Publications, 2003), reel 296.

77 Moiseyev, *I Recall*, 141–43.

78 "Report by the Ministry of Culture about the results of the tour of the State Academic Folk Dance Ensemble of the USSR in the United States and Canada," RGALI, f 2483 o 1 d 267, 73, 1.

79 RGALI, f 2483 o 1 d 267, 74, 2.

80 M. Chudnovsky, *The Folk Dance Company of the USSR: Igor Moiseyev, Art Director* (Moscow: Foreign Languages Publishing House, 1959), 97.

81 Chudnovsky, *Folk Dance Company*, 94, 95.

82 Chudnovsky, *Folk Dance Company*, 95–97, 95.

83 "Dance Magazine's Awards Presentation: Dance Builds Friendship among Nations," *Dance Magazine*, June 1961, 30–35.

84 Natalia Sheremetyevskaya, *Rediscovery of the Dance: Folk Dance Ensemble of the USSR under the Direction of Moiseyev*, trans. J. Guralsky (Moscow: Novosti Press Agency Publishing House, 1960), 106.

85 Chudnovsky, *Folk Dance Company*, 95.

86 Sheremetyevskaya, *Rediscovery of the Dance*, 93.

87 Chudnovsky, *Folk Dance Company*, 96–97.

CHAPTER 5
Fascinating Human Beings

1 Danielle Fosler-Lussier, *Music in America's Cold War Diplomacy* (Oakland: University of California Press, 2015), 205–11.

2 W. G. Rogers, "Moiseyev Dancers Believe in Travel," *Evening Sun*, May 16, 1958.

3 "A Summit Session on the Upper West Side," *New York Post*, April 27, 1958, 14.

4 "A Summit Session," 14.

5 Untitled Article, *Milwaukee Sentinel*, April 21, 1965, 3.

6 "Soviet Dancers All A-Go-Go," *St. Petersburg Times*, April 21, 1965.

7 Bob Thomas, "Hollywood 'Conquered' by Russian Dance Company," *Schenectady Gazette*, May 26, 1958, 6.

8 Alma Gowdy, "After-Theater Party Fetes Russian Dance Troupe," *Los Angeles World & Express*, n.d.

9 "Tough Guy Tierney Fails Trying to Crash Liz's Party," *Boston Globe*, June 30, 1961, 17.

10 Cordell Hicks, "Russ Dancers Take in Disneyland's Wonders," *Los Angeles Times*, May 27, 1958, 1.

11 Scripps-Howard, "'Shopping' Routine is Worn Out," *San Francisco News*, June 2, 1958, 3.

12 Letter from Ona Storkins Mamaroneck to Igor Moiseyev, May 11, 1958, RGALI, f 2483 o 1 d 267, 105.

13 Letter from Mrs. Seymour M. Hallbron to Igor Moiseyev May 22, 1958, RGALI, f 2483 o 1 d 267, 106, 1–3.

14 Letter from Sherley Ashton to Moiseyev, RGALI, f 2483 o 1 d 267, 84, 1.

15 Letter from Donald Ludgin to Moiseyev, May 17, 1958, RGALI, f 2483 0 1 d 267, 90, 1.
16 Greeting card from Roger J. Dumont to Moiseyev, June 2, 1958, RGALI, f 2483 0 1 d 267, 32.
17 Letter from Peter Gawura, August 11, 1958, RGALI, f 2483 0 1 d 267, 123, 1.
18 Telegram from Folk Dance Federation of California to Moiseyev, Mary 17, 1958, RGALI, f 2483 0 1 d 267, 114, 1.
19 Letter from W. B. Hirschmann to Moiseyev, May 27, 1958, RGALI, RGALI, f 2483 0 1 d 267, 111, 1.
20 Letter from Karoun Tootikian to Moiseyev, May 28, 1958, RGALI, f 2483 0 1 d 267, 87, 1.
21 Ted Ashby, "It's 'OK' . . . With the Russian Ballet," *Boston Globe*, June 20, 1958, 18.
22 Letter from Elizabeth Palmer to Igor Moiseyev, dated May 17, 1958, RGALI, f 2483 0 1 d 267,101, 1.
23 Dawn Watson Francis and Robert Boyd, "Russians Typical Tourists—Love to Snap Pictures," *Detroit Free Press*, May 14, 1958, 17. This song is often identified as Russian.
24 Josef Mossman, "Visiting Russians See Fords, but Not a Ford," *Detroit News*, May 14, 1958, 3.
25 "The Sightseers," *New York Post*, May 14, 1958, M3.
26 Harlow Robinson, *The Last Impresario: The Life, Times and Legacy of Sol Hurok* (New York: Viking Press, 1994), 363.
27 "Russian Dancers Act Like Typical Tourists," *Ocala Star-Banner*, May 2, 1958, 14.
28 Harlow Robinson, "Superstar Hits All the Right Notes," *Boston Globe*, February 20, 2011, N4.
29 "American Hoedown," *The Norwalk Hour*, May 5, 1958, 4
30 John Martin, "Moiseyev Troupe Ends Run Here with 'Virginia Reel' as Encore," *New York Times*, May 4, 1948, 86.
31 Lillian Moore, "Class with Igor Moiseyev," *Dance Magazine*, August 1958, 19–20.
32 Bob Thomas, "Hollywood 'Conquered' by Russian Dance Company," *Schenectady Gazette*, May 26, 1958, 9.
33 Thomas, "Hollywood 'Conquered,'" 9.
34 "Moscow Is Preparing," *Lakeland Ledger*, April 5, 1961, 4.
35 Harry Bernstein, "Review: Moiseyev Dance Company: Metropolitan Opera House April 18–May 6, 1961," *Dance Observer*, June–July 1961, 89, NYPL–PAD.
36 John Martin, *New York Times*, April 9, 1961.
37 "Presstime News," *Dance Magazine*, June 1961, 3.
38 "A 3-Decker City Feast: Ballet, Modern, Ethnic," *New York Herald Tribune*, April 16, 1961.
39 Doris Herring, "Reviews: Moiseyev Dance Co.," *New York Times*, 20–21.
40 Kevin Kelly, "Moiseyev Dance Company Captures Boston Garden," *Boston Globe*, May 15, 1961.
41 Marjorie Sherman, "Society: Moiseyev Dance Opening to Benefit Foreign Students," *Boston Globe*, 39.

42 Invitation to reception, MSS 154, Fredric R. Mann Papers in the Irving S. Gilmore Music Library of Yale University.

43 Jacqueline Maskey, "Review: Moiseyev Dance Company Metropolitan Opera House May 18–29, 1965," *Dance Magazine*, July 1965, 61–62.

44 Margo Miller, "Incredible Russian Dance Again Here," *Boston Globe*, June 11, 1965, 26.

45 Interview with Igor Moiseyev and Sol Hurok, Helen Gillespie as translator, hosted by Marian Horosko. Recorded in 1966 in Hurok's New York office and broadcast by radio, NYPL- PAD.

46 Maskey, "Review: Moiseyev Dance Company," 165.

47 Letter from George A. Perper to Ministry of Culture, RGALI, f 3162 o 1 d 226, 24.

CHAPTER 6
American Notions of Gender

1 K. A. Cuordileone, *Manhood and American Political Culture in the Cold War* (New York: Routledge, 2005).

2 Cuordileone, *Manhood and American*, 120.

3 Robert D. Dean, *Imperial Brotherhood: Gender and the Making of Cold War Foreign Policy* (Amherst: University of Massachusetts Press, 2001), 37.

4 David K. Johnson, *The Lavender Scare: The Cold War Persecution of Gays and Lesbians in the Federal Government* (Chicago: The University of Chicago Press, 2004), 1.

5 Johnson, *The Lavender Scare*, 111.

6 Johnson, *The Lavender Scare*, 119–20.

7 Ian Nicholson, "'Shocking' Masculinity: Stanley Milgram, 'Obedience to Authority,' and the 'Crisis of Manhood' in Cold War America," *The History of Science Society* 102, no. 2 (June 2011): 243.

8 Nicholson, "'Shocking' Masculinity," 239–41.

9 Nicholson, "'Shocking' Masculinity," 245–6.

10 Ann Douglas, "War Envy and Amnesia: American Cold War Rewrites of Russia's War," in *Uncertain Empire: American History and the Idea of the Cold War*, ed. Joes Isaac and Duncan Bell (New York: Oxford University Press, 2012), 117.

11 Douglas, "War Envy and Amnesia," 124–25.

12 Jacqueline Foertsch, "'A Battle of Silence': Women's Magazines and the Polio Crisis in Post-war UK and USA," in *American Cold War Culture*, ed. Douglas Field (Edinburgh: Edinburgh University Press, 2005), 17.

13 Robert J. Corber, *Cold War Femme: Lesbianism, National Identity, and Hollywood Cinema* (Durham, NC: Duke University Press, 2011), 1–13.

14 Wendy Z. Goldman, *Women at the Gates: Gender and Industry in Stalin's Russia* (New York: Cambridge University Press, 2002), 3.

15 David Caute, *The Dancer Defects: The Struggle for Cultural Supremacy During the Cold War* (New York: Oxford University Press, 2005), 42.

16 Harlow Robinson, *Russians in Hollywood, Hollywood's Russians: Biography of an Image* (Boston: Northeastern University Press, 2007), 103, 111, 172.

17 Robinson, *Russians in Hollywood*, 107.
18 Robinson, *Russians in Hollywood*, 105–6.
19 Louis Horst, "Reviews of the Month: Moiseyev Dance Company," *Dance Observer*, June–July 1958, 87.
20 Josef Mossman, "Visiting Russians See Fords, but Not a Ford," *Detroit News*, May 14, 1958, 3.
21 Walter Terry, Untitled Article, *New York Herald Tribune*, April 20, 1958.
22 "First Soviet Troupe Arrives under Exchange Agreement," *Dance News*, May 1958, 4.
23 *Dance News*, May 1958, 8.
24 Kevin Kelly, "Moiseyev Dance Company Captures Boston Garden," *Boston Globe*, May 15, 1961.
25 Frank Quinn, "Soviet Dance Troupe is Breath-Taking," *New York Mirror*, April 15, 1958.
26 Francis Herridge, "Russian Dance Troupe Cheered at Metropolitan," *New York Post*, April 15, 1958, 45.
27 Claudia Cassidy, "On the Aisle: Something New in Russian Virtuosi: The Combustible Moiseyevs," *Chicago Daily Tribune*, May 17, 1958.
28 Paul R. Allerup, "Russian Dancers Surprise New York," *Los Angeles Examiner*, April 16, 1958, 4.
29 W. G. Rogers, "Moiseyev Dancers Believe in Travel," *The Evening Sun* (Hanover, PA), May 16, 1958.
30 Kelly, "Moiseyev Dance Company."
31 *Boston Traveler*, June 13, 1958.
32 Ted Ashby, "It's 'O.K.' ... with Russian Ballet," *Boston Globe*, June 20, 1958, 18.
33 "Red Girls Cool on Red-Hot Music in US," *Boston Globe*, April 27, 1958, 5.
34 Charles Manos, "A Moscow Girl in Detroit: Dancing, Kissing, Pie," *Detroit Times*, May 14, 1958.
35 Frank Quinn, "Soviet Dance Troupe Is Breath-Taking," *New York Mirror*, April 15, 1958.
36 Dorris Herring, "Reviews: Moiseyev Dance Company Metropolitan Opera House April 14-May 3, 1958," *Dance Magazine*, June 1958, 35.
37 J. Dorsey Callaghan, "Soviet Ballet Dazzles Audience: Dancers Set Stage Ablaze," *Detroit Free Press*, May 13, 1958, 12. For a description of the Bulba, see appendix D.
38 Cassidy, "On the Aisle."
39 Arthur Bloom [illegible], "Ovation for Russians," *San Francisco Call-Bulletin*, June 2, 1958.
40 *Dance News*, May 1958.
41 Cordell Hicks, "Russ Dancers Take in Disneyland's Wonders," *Los Angeles Times*, May 27, 1958, 1.
42 Hicks, "Russ Dancers," 1.
43 Program for *WXYZ Radio* "Local" Detroit, May 15, 1958.
44 Will Stev [illegible], "Famous Russ Moiseyev Troupe Here."
45 Will Stev [illegible], "Famous Russ."

46 Lucile Preuss, "Little Sightseeing Time for Russian Dancers," *Milwaukee Journal*, May 20, 1958.

47 Manos, "A Moscow Girl."

48 Manos, "A Moscow Girl."

49 *Dance News*, May 1958.

50 "At Home With . . . Mrs. Igor Moiseyev," *New York Post*, June 22, 1958.

51 "At Home With . . . Mrs. Igor Moiseyev." It should also be noted that the discussion of the fruit may involve a mistranslation of *klyuvka* (cranberry).

52 "Soviet Women Shop Our Stores—And Love It" and Olga Curtis, "Communist or Capitalist: Ah, Women! Soviet Dancers See, Sigh and Buy!" *New York Journal American: An American Paper for The American People*, April 25, 1958, 1.

53 "Russian Women on American Shopping Spree: Dancers Have Gay Time in New York Stores—And You Can't Tell Them from Capitalists," *St. Louis Post-Dispatch*, April 29, 1958, 2D.

54 Curtis, "Communist or Capitalist," 1, 17.

55 Curtis, "Communist or Capitalist," 1, 17.

56 *Dance News*, May 1958, 8. For a description of the City Quadrille, see appendix D.

57 Ann Barzel, "Russ Dancers Awe Inspiring," *Chicago American*, May 17, 1958.

58 Barzel, "Russ Dancers Awe Inspiring."

59 Hugh Thomson, "3,600 Stand, Cheer Red Ballet in N.Y.," *Toronto Daily Star*, April 15, 1958, 21.

60 Horst, "Reviews of the Month," 87. For a description of the Yurochka, see appendix D.

61 Abigail Kuflik, "He Hunted on Donkeys to Find Russian Dances," *Boston Globe*, 1 August 1, 1970, 1.

62 Barzel, "Russ Dancers Awe Inspiring."

63 Alfred Frankenstein, "Moiseyev Dancers Open—Power, Poetry, Art," *San Francisco Chronicle*, June 2, 1958.

64 Mary Clarke, "Moiseyev Dancers from Moscow," *Dance Magazine*, February 1956, 20–23.

65 Hicks, "Russ Dancers," 1.

CHAPTER 7
American Notions of Race

1 In terms of the dance company's depiction of other races, there were dances from Asian nations or groups, such as Mongolia.

2 Peggy Boyle, "Moiseyev 'Incident' Flops," *Boston Evening American*, June 14, 1958.

3 Walter Terry, "Russian Dancers to Perform Here," *New York Herald Tribune*, April 13, 1958, 1.

4 "Its 106 Dancers Will Draw from a Repertory Based on 3,000 Dances of the U.S.S.R.," *Parents' Magazine*, undated.

5 Alfred Frankenstein, "Moiseyev Dancers Open—Power, Poetry, Art," *San Francisco Chronicle*, June 2, 1958.

6 Harry MacArthur, "Russia Sends Us Some Exciting Folk Dancers," *Evening Star* (Washington, DC), June 17, 1958.

7 "Cultural Carload: 100 Dancers, 3000 Costumes and 2000 Shoes," *Boston Globe*, May 7, 1961, A9.

8 Mae M. Ngai, *Impossible Subjects: Illegal Aliens and the Making of Modern America—Updated Edition* (Princeton, NJ: Princeton University Press, 2014), 37–38, 3, and 7.

9 Ngai, *Impossible Subjects*, 7–8.

10 Ngai, *Impossible Subjects*, 230–31.

11 Ngai, *Impossible Subjects*, 230–33.

12 Ngai, *Impossible Subjects*, 236–45.

13 Nathan Glazer, *The Social Basis of American Communism* (New York: Harcourt, 1961), 6 and 8.

14 Nathan Glazer and Daniel Patrick Moynihan, *Beyond the Melting Pot: The Negroes, Puerto Ricans, Jews, Italians, and Irish of New York City*, 2nd ed.(Cambridge, MA: MIT Press, 1970), xcvii, 288.

15 1958 Tour Program, Carl Van Vechten Papers, Yale Collection of American Literature, Beinecke Rare Book and Manuscript Library.

16 Claudia Cassidy, "On the Aisle: Something New in Russian Virtuosi: The Combustible Moiseyevs," *Chicago Daily Tribune*, May 17, 1958.

17 Ann Barzel, "Russ Dancers Awe Inspiring," *Chicago American*, May 17, 1958.

18 Kevin Kelly, "Moiseyev Dance Company Captures Boston Garden," *Boston Globe*, May 15, 1961.

19 Ngai, *Impossible Subjects*, 5.

20 W. G. Rogers, "Moiseyev Dancers Believe in Travel," *Evening Sun* (Hanover, PA), May 16, 1958.

21 Arthur Bloom [illegible], "Ovation for Russians," *San Francisco Call-Bulletin*, June 2, 1958.

22 Bloom [illegible].

23 Lydia Joel, "The Moiseyev Dance Company: What is it? What is its Appeal? What is its Lesson?" *Dance Magazine*, June 1958, 30.

24 Abigail Kuflik, "He Hunted on Donkeys to Find Russian Dances," *Boston Globe*, August 1, 1970, 1.

25 "180 Soviet Groups Made Repertory for Moiseyev," *Boston Globe*, April 23, 1961, 64.

26 1958 Tour Program, Carl Van Vechten Papers, Yale Collection of American Literature, Beinecke Rare Book and Manuscript Library.

27 Joel, "The Moiseyev Dance Company," 30.

28 Walter Terry, "A Magician of Folklore," *New York Herald Tribune*, April 30, 1961.

29 Terry, "A Magician of Folklore."

30 Audrey Kearns, "Troupe Big Hit at Shrine," *Citizen News*, May 26, 1958, 12.

31 "Moiseyev's Dances Aim to Synthesize National Character," A13.

32 Daniel Walkowitz, "Gender and the Dancing Body in English Country Dance," in *Perspectives on American Dance: The Twentieth Century*, ed. Jennifer Atkins, Sally R. Sommer, and Tricia Henry Young (Gainesville: University Press of Florida, 2018), 260–68.

33 Walkowitz, "Gender and the Dancing Body," 264–65.
34 Megan Pugh, *America Dancing: From the Cakewalk to the Moonwalk* (New Haven, CT: Yale University Press, 2015), 157–61.
35 Kimberly St. Julian-Varnon, "Black Skin in the Red Land: African Americans and the Soviet Experiment," *The Russia File, blog of the Kennan Institute* (blog), February 28, 2020. https://www.wilsoncenter.org/blog-post/black-skin-red-land-african-americans-and-soviet-experiment
36 Kristen de Groot, "African American in the 'Raceless' Soviet Union," *Penn Today*, August 9, 2021.
37 The Comintern was an international communist organization founded by Lenin to support communism internationally. Katerina Clark, "The Representation of the African American as Colonial Oppressed in Texts of the Soviet Interwar Years," *The Russian Review* 75, no. 3 (July 2016): 368–80.
38 Clark, "The Representation of the African American," 376.
39 Martin Summers, "Langston Hughes (1902–1967): Playwright, Librettist and Civil Rights Advocate," *Social Welfare History Project*, https://socialwelfare.library.vcu.edu/eras/hughes-langston/.
40 "'I Am at Home,' Says Robeson at Reception in Soviet Union," *Daily Worker*, January 15, 1935, https://revolutionarydemocracy.org/rdv4n2/ussrpr.htm.
41 "Robeson Says He'll Continue Work with Reds," *New York Herald Tribune*, April 7, 1948, 17.
42 Congress, House, Committee on Un-American Activities, *Investigation of the Unauthorized Use of U.S. Passports*, 84th Congress, Part 3, June 12, 1956; in *Thirty Years of Treason: Excerpts from Hearings Before the House Committee on Un-American Activities, 1938–1968*, ed. Eric Bentley (New York: Viking Press, 1971), 770, https://historymatters.gmu.edu/d/6440.
43 Thomas Borstelmann, *The Cold War and the Color Line: American Race Relations in the Global Arena* (Cambridge, MA: Harvard University Press, 2001), 57–58, 94.
44 Borstelmann, *The Cold War and the Color Line*, 103–4.
45 Danielle Fosler-Lussier, *Music in America's Cold War Diplomacy* (Oakland: University of California Press, 2015), 77–84.
46 Hugh Thomson, "3,600 Stand, Cheer Red Ballet in N.Y.," *Toronto Daily Star*, April 15, 1958, 21.

Epilogue

1 Anna Kisselgoff, "For Moiseyev, Change is Afoot," *New York Times*, January 15, 1989, H1.
2 Anna Kisellgoff, "Secondary Troupes Bring Soviet Ballet into Sharper Focus: Dance View," *New York Times*, November 13, 1988, H8.
3 Harlow Robinson, "Booking Soviet Musicians is Not Yet a Bowl of Borscht," *New York Times*, May 21, 1989, H23.
4 Vera Toman, "Drink Deep, We'll Dance: Hardly Russian," *New York Times*, February 5, 1989, H3.
5 Toman, "Drink Deep," H3.

6 Seymour Yusem, "Shy Maidens, Cossack Thugs: Moiseyev Messages," *New York Times*, January 27, 1991, H4

7 Yusem, "Shy Maidens," H4.

8 Yusem, "Shy Maidens," H4, 26.

9 Jack Anderson, "Igor Moiseyev, 101, Choreographer, Dies," *New York Times*, November 3, 2007, B7.

10 "Igor Moiseyev Ballet History," http://www.moiseyev.ru/.

11 Anna Kisselgoff, "Dance View: Folk Dancing in Eastern Europe: What Lies Ahead?," *New York Times*, April 8, 1990.

APPENDIX A
Text of the Lacy-Zarubin Agreement, January 27, 1958

1 Please note: the text has been taken mostly verbatim with small edits to improve legibility.

2 "United States and U.S.S.R. Sign Agreement on East-West Exchanges," *State Department Bulletin*, 38, no. 973 (February 17, 1958): 243–46.

Index